WULF THE SAXON
A Story of the Norman Conquest

By
G. A. HENTY

Wulf The Saxon
A Story of the Norman Conquest

by **G. A. Henty**

Copyright © 2024

All Rights reserved.
No part of this publication may be reproduced, stored in a retrieval system, or transmitted in any form or by any means, electronic, mechanical, photocopying or Otherwise, without the written permission of the publisher.

The author/editor asserts the moral right to be identified as the author/editor of this work.

ISBN: 978-93-57272-67-4

Published by

DOUBLE 9 BOOKS

2/13-B, Ansari Road, Daryaganj
New Delhi - 110002
info@double9books.com
www.double9books.com
Tel. 011-40042856

This book is under public domain

ABOUT THE AUTHOR

English author and war correspondent George Alfred Henty lived from 8 December 1832 to 16 November 1902. He is most well-known for his historical fiction and adventure books, including The Dragon ... The Raven (1886), For The Temple (1888), Under Drake's Flag (1883), and In Freedom's Cause (1883). (1885). He was a British journalist who served as G. A. Henty's war correspondent. He was raised in Cambridge and finished his education there at Gonville and Caius College. He continued to cover important wars that followed, such as the Italian and Austro-Italian Wars. He wrote 122 books, most of which were geared toward young readers. He also wrote non-fiction, adult fiction, and short tales. In Henty's stories, the main character is a boy or young man who is going through a challenging situation. His characters are consistently low-key, astute, courageous, truthful, and resourceful with a lot of "pluck." The date was put at the bottom of the title page of each of Henty's 122 historical fiction works in their first printings. All his books were published in the UK before those in the United States. The only Henty novel to be published in America prior to the UK book was In the Hands of the Cave-Dwellers from 1900.

CONTENTS

PREFACE. 7
CHAPTER I. – A QUARREL. 8
CHAPTER II. – COUNTRY LIFE. 23
CHAPTER III. – AT COURT. 37
CHAPTER IV. – A STORM. 53
CHAPTER V. – ROUEN. 67
CHAPTER VI. – RELEASE OF THE EARL 81
CHAPTER VII. – THE OATH. 95
CHAPTER VIII. – TROUBLE WITH WALES. 110
CHAPTER IX. – IN THE WELSH VALLEYS. 125
CHAPTER X. – PORTHWYN. 139
CHAPTER XI. – THE SECRET PASSAGE. 153
CHAPTER XII. – EDITH. 167
CHAPTER XIII. – HAROLD, THE KING. 181
CHAPTER XIV. – WULF'S SUSPICIONS. 195
CHAPTER XV. – A MEETING BY THE RIVER. 210
CHAPTER XVI. – A VOYAGE NORTH. 222
CHAPTER XVII. – AN ATTEMPT AT ASSASSINATION. 236
CHAPTER XVIII. – THE NORTHERN INVASION 250
CHAPTER XIX. – STAMFORD BRIDGE. 263
CHAPTER XX. – THE LANDING OF THE FOE. 276
CHAPTER XXI. – HASTINGS. 289
CHAPTER XXII. – THE LORD OF BRAMBER. 303

PREFACE.

Although the immediate results of the Battle of Hastings may have been of less importance to the world than were those of some other great battles, the struggle has, in the long run, had a greater influence upon the destiny of mankind than any other similar event that has ever taken place. That admixture of Saxon, Danish, and British races which had come to be known under the general name of English, was in most respects far behind the rest of Europe. The island was, as it had always been, — except during the rule of two or three exceptionally strong kings, — distracted by internal dissensions. Broad lines of division still separated the North from the South, and under weak Kings the powerful Earls became almost independent. The enterprise that had distinguished their Saxon and Danish ancestors seems to have died out. There was a general indisposition to change, and except in her ecclesiastical buildings, England made but little progress in civilization from the time of Alfred to that of Harold. Its insular position cut it off from taking part in that rapid advance which, beginning in Italy, was extending throughout Europe. The arrival, however, of the impetuous Norman race, securing as it did a close connection with the Continent, quickened the intellect of the people, raised their intelligence, was of inestimable benefit to the English, and played a most important part in raising England among the nations. Moreover, it has helped to produce the race that has peopled Northern America, Australia, and the south of Africa, holds possession of India, and stands forth as the greatest civilizer in the world. The Conquest of England by the Normans was achieved without even a shadow of right or justice. It was at the time an unmixed curse to England; but now we can recognize the enormous benefits that accrued when in his turn the Englishman conquered the Norman, and the foreign invaders became an integral portion of the people they had overcome. For the historical details of the story, I have only had to go to Freeman's magnificent *History of the Norman Conquest of England*, which I hope will be perused by all of my readers who are able to obtain it.

G. A. HENTY

CHAPTER I. — A QUARREL.

The great Abbey of Westminster was approaching its completion; an army of masons and labourers swarmed like bees upon and around it, and although differing widely in its massive architecture, with round Saxon windows and arches, from the edifice that was two or three generations later to be reared in its place, — to serve as a still more fitting tomb for the ashes of its pious founder, — it was a stately abbey, rivalling the most famous of the English fanes of the period.

From his palace hard by King Edward had watched with the deepest interest the erection of the minster that was the dearest object of his life. The King was surrounded by Normans, the people among whom he had lived until called from his retirement to ascend the throne of England, and whom he loved far better than those over whom he reigned. He himself still lived almost the life of a recluse. He was sincerely anxious for the good of his people, but took small pains to ensure it, his life being largely passed in religious devotions, and in watching over the rise of the abbey he had founded.

A town had risen around minster and palace, and here the workmen employed found their lodgings, while craftsmen of all descriptions administered to the wants both of these and of the nobles of Edward's court.

From one of the side doors of the palace a page, some fifteen or sixteen years of age, ran down the steps in haste. He was evidently a Saxon by his fair hair and fresh complexion, and any observer of the time would have seen that he must, therefore, be in the employment of Earl Harold, the great minister, who had for many years virtually ruled England in the name of its king.

The young page was strongly and sturdily built. His garb was an English one, but with some admixture of Norman fashions. He wore tightly-fitting leg coverings, a garment somewhat resembling a blouse of blue cloth girded in by a belt at the waist, and falling in folds to the knee. Over his shoulders hung a short mantle of orange colour with a hood. On his head was a cap with a wide brim that was turned up closely behind, and projected in a pointed shovel shape in front. In his belt was a small dagger. He wore shoes of light yellow leather fastened by bands over the insteps. As he ran down the steps of the palace he came into sharp contact with another page who had just turned the corner of the street.

"I crave your pardon, Walter Fitz-Urse," he said hurriedly, "but I was in haste and saw you not."

The other lad was as clearly Norman as the speaker was Saxon. He was perhaps a year the senior in point of age, and taller by half a head, but was of slighter build. The expression of his face differed as widely from that of the Saxon as did his swarthy complexion and dark hair, for while the latter face wore a frank and pleasant expression, that of the Norman was haughty and arrogant.

"You did it on purpose," he said angrily, "and were we not under the shadow of the palace I would chastise you as you deserve."

The smile died suddenly out from the Saxon's face. "Chastise me!" he repeated. "You would find it somewhat difficult, Master Fitz-Urse. Do you think you are talking to a Norman serf? You will please to remember you are in England; but if you are not satisfied with my apology, I will ride with you a few miles into the country, and we will then try with equal arms where the chastisement is to fall."

The Norman put his hand to his dagger, but there was an ominous growl from some men who had paused to listen to the quarrel.

"You are an insolent boor, Wulf of Steyning, and some day I will punish you as you deserve."

"Some day," the Saxon laughed, "we shall, I hope, see you and all your tribe sent across the Channel. There are few of us here who would not see your backs with pleasure."

"What is this?" an imperious voice demanded; and turning round, Wulf saw William, the Norman Bishop of London, who, followed by several monks and pages, had pushed his way through the crowd. "Walter Fitz-Urse, what means this altercation?"

"The Saxon ran against me of set purpose, my lord," Walter Fitz-Urse said, in tones of deep humility, "and because I complained he challenged me to ride with him into the country to fight, and then he said he hoped that some day all the Normans would be sent across the Channel."

"Is this so?" the prelate said sternly to Wulf; "did you thus insult not only my page, but all of us, his countrymen?"

"I ran against him by accident," Wulf said, looking up fearlessly in the prelate's face. "I apologized, though I know not that I was more in fault than he; but instead of taking my apology as one of gentle blood should do, he spoke like a churl, and threatened me with chastisement, and then I did say that I hoped he and all other Normans in the land would some day be packed across the Channel."

"Your ears ought to be slit as an insolent varlet."

"I meant no insolence, my Lord Bishop; and as to the slitting of my ears, I fancy Earl Harold, my master, would have something to say on that score."

The prelate was about to reply, but glancing at the angry faces of the growing crowd, he said coldly:

"I shall lay the matter before him. Come, Walter, enough of this. You are also somewhat to blame for not having received more courteously the apologies of this saucy page."

The crowd fell back with angry mutterings as he turned, and, followed by Walter Fitz-Urse and the ecclesiastics, made his way along the street to the principal entrance of the palace. Without waiting to watch his departure, Wulf, the Saxon page, pushed his way through the crowd, and went off at full speed to carry the message with which he had been charged.

"Our king is a good king," a squarely-built man, — whose bare arms with the knotted muscles showing through the skin, and hands begrimed with charcoal, indicated that he was a smith, — remarked to a gossip as the little crowd broke up, "but it is a grievous pity that he was brought up a Norman, still more that he was not left in peace to pass his life as a monk as he desired. He fills the land with his Normans; soon as an English bishop dies, straightway a Norman is clapped into his place. All the offices at court are filled with them, and it is seldom a word of honest English is spoken in the palace. The Norman castles are rising over the land, and his favourites divide among them the territory of every English earl or thane who incurs the king's displeasure. Were it not for Earl Harold, one might as well be under Norman sway altogether."

"Nay, nay, neighbour Ulred, matters are not so bad as that. I dare say they would have been as you say had it not been for Earl Godwin and his sons. But it was a great check that Godwin gave them when he returned after his banishment, and the Norman bishops and nobles hurried across the seas in a panic. For years now the king has left all matters in the hands of Harold, and is well content if only he can fast and pray like any monk, and give all his thoughts and treasure to the building of yonder abbey."

"We want neither a monk nor a Norman over us," the smith said roughly, "still less one who is both Norman and monk I would rather have a Dane, like Canute, who was a strong man and a firm one, than this king, who, I doubt not, is full of good intentions, and is a holy and pious monarch, but who is not strong enough for a ruler. He leaves it to another to preserve England in peace, to keep in order the great Earls of Mercia and the North, to hold the land against Harold of Norway, Sweyn, and others, and, above all, to watch the Normans across the water. A monk is well enough in a convent, but truly 'tis bad for a country to have a monk as its king."

"There have been some war-loving prelates, Ulred; men as ambitious as any of the great earls, and more dangerous, because they have learning."

"Ay, there have been great prelates," the smith agreed. "Look at Lyfing of Worcester, to whom next only to Godwin the king owed his throne. He was an Englishman first and a bishop afterwards, and was a proof, if needed, that a man can be a great churchman and a great patriot and statesman too. It was he rather than Godwin who overcame the opposition of the Danish party, and got the Witan at last to acquiesce in the choice of London and Wessex, and to give their vote to Edward.

"Well was it he did so. For had he failed we should have had as great a struggle in England as when Alfred battled against the Danes. We of London and the men of Wessex under the great Earl were bent upon being ruled by a prince of our own blood. The last two Danish kings had shown us that anything is better than being governed by the Northmen. It was Lyfing who persuaded the Earl of Mercia to side with Wessex rather than with Northumbria, but since Lyfing, what great Englishman have we had in the church? Every bishopric was granted by Edward to Norman priests, until Godwin and his sons got the upper hand after their exile. Since then most of them have been given to Germans. It would seem that the king was so set against Englishmen that only by bringing in foreigners can Harold prevent all preferment going to Normans. But what is the consequence? They say now that our church is governed from Rome, whereas before Edward's time we Englishmen did not think of taking our orders from Italy.

"There will trouble come of it all, neighbour. Perhaps not so long as Edward reigns, but at his death. There is but one of the royal race surviving, and he, like Edward, has lived all his life abroad. There can be no doubt what the choice of Englishmen will be. Harold has been our real ruler for years. He is wise and politic as well as brave, and a great general. He is our own earl, and will assuredly be chosen. Then we shall have trouble with the Normans. Already they bear themselves as if they were our masters, and they will not give up their hold without a struggle. Men say that William, their duke, makes no secret of his hope to become master of England, in which case God help us all. But that won't come as long as Harold lives and Englishmen can wield sword and battle-axe. As for myself, I have patched many a Norman suit of armour, but, by St. Swithin, I shall have far more pleasure in marring than I have ever had in mending them."

"Know you who were the boys who had that contention just now?"

"The Norman is a page of William, our Norman bishop; I know no more of him than that the other is Wulf, who is a ward and page of Earl Harold. His father was thane of Steyning in South Sussex, one of Godwin's men, and at his death two years ago Harold took the lad into his household, for he bore great affection for Gyrth, who had accompanied him in his pilgrimage to Rome, and fought by his side when he conquered the Welsh. It was there Gyrth got the wound that at last brought about his death. Wulf has been to my smithy many times, sometimes about matters of repairs to arms, but more often, I think, to see my son Osgod. He had seen him once or twice in calling at the shop, when one day Osgod, who is somewhat given to mischief, was playing at ball, and drove it into the face of a son of one of the Norman lords at court. The boy drew his dagger, and there would have been blood shed, but Wulf, who was passing at the time, and saw that the thing was a pure mishap and not the result of set intention, threw himself between them.

"There was a great fuss over it, for the boy took his tale to his father, who demanded that Osgod should be punished, and would doubtless have gained his end had not Wulf spoken to Earl Harold, who intervened in the matter and persuaded the Norman to let it drop. Since then the boys have been great friends in their way. Osgod is a year older than the young thane, and has already made up his mind to be his man when he grows up, and he has got me to agree to it, though I would rather that he had stuck to my handicraft. Still, the prospect is not a bad one. Harold will be King of England, Wulf will be a powerful thane, and will doubtless some day hold high place at court, and as he seems to have taken a real liking to Osgod, the boy may have good chances.

"Wulf will make a good fighting man one of these days. Harold sees that all his pages are well instructed in arms, and the two boys often have a bout with blunted swords when Wulf comes to my smithy; and, by my faith, though I have taught Osgod myself, and he already uses his arms well, the young thane is fully a match for him. You would hardly believe that the boy can read as well as a monk, but it is so. Earl Harold, you know, thinks a good deal of education, and has founded a college at Waltham. He persuaded Wulf's father to send him there, and, indeed, will take none as his pages unless they can read. I see not what good reading can do to most men, but doubtless for one who is at court and may hold some day a high post there, it is useful to be able to read deeds and grants of estates, instead of having to trust others' interpretation."

"I wondered to see you press forward so suddenly into the crowd, neighbour, seeing that you are a busy man, but I understand now that you had an interest in the affair."

"That had I. I was holding myself in readiness, if that Norman boy drew his dagger, to give him such a blow across the wrist with my cudgel that it would be long before he handled a weapon again. I fear Wulf has got himself into trouble. The bishop will doubtless complain to the king of the language used by one of Harold's pages, and though the earl is well able to see that no harm comes to the lad, it is likely he will send him away to his estates for a time. For he strives always to avoid quarrels and disputes, and though he will not give way a jot in matters where it seems to him that the good of the realm is concerned, he will go much farther lengths than most men would do in the way of conciliation. Look how he has borne with Tostig and with the Earls of Mercia. He seems to have no animosity in his nature, but is ready to forgive all injuries as soon as pardon is asked."

The smith was not far wrong in his opinion as to what was likely to happen. As soon as Wulf returned to the palace he was told that the earl desired his presence, and he proceeded at once to the apartment where Harold transacted public business. It was a hall of considerable size; the floor was strewed with rushes; three scribes sat at a table, and to them the earl dictated his replies and decisions on the various matters brought before him. When he saw Wulf enter he rose from his seat, and, beckoning to him to follow, pushed aside the hangings across a door leading to an apartment behind and went in. Wulf had no fear whatever of any severe consequence to himself from his quarrel with Walter Fitz-Urse, but he was ashamed that his thoughtlessness should have given the slightest trouble to the earl, for, popular as he was among all classes of men in southern England, Harold was an object of love as well as respect to his dependents, and indeed to all who came in close contact with him.

The earl was now forty-one years of age. He was very tall, and was considered the strongest man in England. His face was singularly handsome, with an expression of mingled gentleness and firmness. His bearing was courteous to all. He united a frank and straightforward manner with a polished address rare among his rough countrymen. Harold had travelled more and farther than any Englishman of his age. He had visited foreign courts and mingled with people more advanced in civilization than were those of England or Normandy, and was centuries ahead of the mass of his countrymen. He was an ardent advocate of education, a strong supporter of the national church, an upholder of the rights of all men, and although he occasionally gave way to bursts of passion, was of a singularly sweet and forgiving disposition.

King Edward was respected by his people because, coming after two utterly worthless kings, he had an earnest desire for their good, although that desire seldom led to any very active results. He was a member of their own royal house. He was deeply religious. His life was pure and simple, and although all his tastes and sympathies were with the land in which he had been brought up, Englishmen forgave him this because at least he was a Saxon, while his predecessors had been Danes. But while they respected Edward, for Harold, their real ruler, they felt a passionate admiration. He was a worthy representative of all that was best in the Saxon character. He possessed in an eminent degree the openness of nature, the frank liberality, the indomitable bravery, and the endurance of hardship that distinguished the race. He was Earl of the West Saxons, and as such had special claims to their fealty.

London, it was true, did not lie in his earldom, but in that of his brother Leofwyn, but Leofwyn and Harold were as one — true brothers in heart and in disposition. The gentleness and courtesy of manner that, although natural, had been softened and increased by Harold's contact with foreigners, was not only pardoned but admired because he was England's champion against foreigners. He had fought, and victoriously, alike against the Norwegians, the Danes of Northumbria, and the Welsh, and he struggled as sturdily, though peacefully, against Norman influence in England. Already the dread of Norman preponderance was present in the minds of Englishmen. It was no secret that in his early days Edward had held out hopes, if he had not given an actual promise, to William of Normandy that he should succeed him. Of late the king had been somewhat weaned from his Norman predilections, and had placed himself unreservedly in Harold's hands, giving to the latter all real power while he confined himself to the discharge of religious exercises, and to the supervision of the building of his abbey, varied occasionally by hunting expeditions, for he still retained a passionate love of the chase; but men knew that the warlike Duke of Normandy would not be likely to forget the promise, and that trouble might come to England from over the sea.

Harold, then, they not only regarded as their present ruler, but as their future king, and as the national leader and champion. Edward had no children. The royal house was extinct save for Edward the Atheling, who, like the present king, had lived all his life abroad, and could have no sympathy with Englishmen. There being, then, no one of the royal house available, who but Harold, the head of the great house of Godwin, the earl of the West Saxons, the virtual ruler of England, could be chosen? The English kings, although generally selected from the royal house, ruled rather by the election of the people as declared by their representatives in the Witan than by their hereditary right. The prince next in succession by blood might, at the death of the sovereign, be called king, but he was not really a monarch until elected by the Witan and formally consecrated.

It had been nine months after he had been acclaimed to the throne by the people of London that King Edward had been elected king by the Witan, and formally enthroned. Thus, then, the fact that Harold did not belong to the royal family mattered but little in the eyes of Englishmen. To them belonged the right of choosing their own monarch, and if they chose him, who was to say them nay?

Wulf felt uncomfortable as he followed the stately figure into the inner room, but he faced the Earl as the door closed behind him with as fearless a look as that with which he had stood before the haughty prelate of London. A slight smile played upon Harold's face as he looked down upon the boy.

"You are a troublesome varlet, Wulf, and the Lord Bishop has been making serious complaint of you to the king. He says that you brawled with his page, Walter Fitz-Urse; that you used insolent words against his countrymen; and that you even withstood himself. What have you to say to this?"

"The brawling was on the part of the bishop's page and not of mine, my lord. I was running out to carry the message with which you charged me to Ernulf of Dover when I ran against Fitz-Urse. That was not my fault, but a pure mischance, nevertheless I expressed my regret in fitting terms. Instead of accepting them, he spoke insolently, talked of chastising me, and put his hand on the hilt of his dagger. Then, my lord, I grew angry too. Why should I, the page of Earl Harold, submit to be thus contemptuously spoken to by this young Norman, who is but the page of an upstart bishop, and whom, if your lordship will give permission, I would right willingly fight, with swords or any other weapons. Doubtless, in my anger, I did not speak respectfully of Walter's countrymen, and for this I am sorry, since it has been the ground of complaint and of trouble to you."

"In fact, Wulf, you spoke as a quarrelsome boy and not as the page of one who has the cares of this kingdom on his shoulders, and whose great desire is to keep peace between all parties," the earl put in gravely.

For the first time Wulf hung his head:

"I was wrong, my lord."

"You were wrong, Wulf; it is not good always to say what we think; and you, as my page, should bear in mind that here at court it behoves you to behave and to speak not as a headstrong boy, but as one whose words may, rightly or wrongly, be considered as an echo of those you may have heard from me. And now to the third charge, that you withstood the prelate; a matter that, in the king's eyes, is a very serious one."

"The bishop would give ear to nought I had to say. He listened to his own page's account and not to mine, and when I said in my defence that though I did use the words about the Normans, I did so merely as one boy quarrelling with the other, he said I ought to have my ears slit. Surely, my lord, a free-born thane is not to be spoken to even by a Norman bishop as if he were a Norman serf. I only replied that before there was any slitting of ears your lordship would have a say in the matter. So far, I admit, I did withstand the bishop, and I see not how I could have made other reply."

"It would have been better to have held your peace altogether, Wulf."

"It would, my lord, but it would also surely have been better had the bishop abstained from talking about slitting ears."

"That would have been better also, but two wrongs do not make a right. I was present when the bishop made his complaint, and upon my inquiring more into the matter, his version was somewhat similar to yours. I then pointed out to him that if holy bishops lost their tempers and used threats that were beyond their power to carry into effect, they must not be too severe upon boys who forget the respect due to their office. Nevertheless, I admitted that you were wrong, and I promised the king, who was perhaps more disturbed by this incident than there was any occasion for, that I would take you to task seriously, and that to avoid any further brawl between you and young Fitz-Urse, you should for a time be sent away from court. I did this on the agreement that the bishop should, on his part, admonish Walter Fitz-Urse against discourteous behaviour and unseemly brawling, and had I known that he had put his hand on his dagger, I would have gone further. Have you any witnesses that he did so?"

"Yes, my lord; I saw the smith Ulred among those standing by, and doubtless he would see the action."

"That is well," Harold said. "I shall acquaint the bishop with the fact when I tell him that I have ordered you to leave for your estate at Steyning, and that if his page denies it, I have witnesses to prove the truth of your assertions. I think in that case he will be glad to drop the matter, for were I to mention the fact to the king, he, who has a horror of the drawing of weapons, would order Walter Fitz-Urse to be sent back to Normandy. So your exile is not likely to be of long duration. You understand, Wulf, that I am not seriously angered with you in this matter. You are but a boy, and one cannot expect that you will behave as a prudent man; but remember, lad, even a boy's words may do mischief, especially when placed as you are. There may come a time when you shall show by deeds and not by words your feelings against the Normans, but till then bear yourself prudently. We Saxons are over given to hasty words, and this is a fault. I myself, as all men know, have no love for the Normans, but no one has heard me speak against them. The king loves them, as is but natural, seeing that he was brought up amongst them, and I have not withstood his wishes in the matter, trying only that a certain amount of preferment in the land should be bestowed upon those who are its owners and not strangers to it and its tongue. You will ride this afternoon for Steyning, Wulf, but I hope it will not be long before you are back again. If I had my own way in the matter, I should think that sufficient had already been said and done in so trifling a matter as a boys' quarrel; but as it has been brought before our king by a bishop, it is in the king's eyes a serious business, for assuredly he himself would have borne a reproof from William of London more meekly than you did, and having therefore become a church matter, it is altogether beyond my power to interfere. At any rate, a short sojourn on your estate will do you no harm; it is sometime since you were there, and it is a good thing that the lord of the soil should be well known by those over whom he is placed."

Wulf bowed deeply and withdrew. The prospect of a visit for a few weeks or even months to Steyning was not a terrible one. It was some years since he had stayed there for any time. He had been two years at Waltham, and since his father's death had been for the most part with Harold, and the thought of an unrestricted life and of spending his time as he chose, hunting and hawking, and going about among his tenants, was by no means unpleasant. He was quite satisfied that Harold was not seriously angered with him, and for anything else he cared little.

As he understood that his duties as a page were at present at an end, he thought he would first call upon Ulred the smith, to ask him if he had seen Walter Fitz-Urse handle his dagger, and also to tell Osgod that he was going away for a time. He found the smith at work.

"Good morning, Master Wulf; though this is not the first time I have seen you today, for I was at hand when you had that quarrel with the Norman page."

"Yes, I caught sight of your face, Ulred. It was about that I have come to you. The bishop has made complaint against me to the king, and Earl Harold has ordered me to go down to Steyning for a time. Of course I acted wrongly in speaking as I did to the bishop, but so far as Walter Fitz-Urse is concerned I maintain that I did no wrong. I told my lord as much, and that the Norman put hand upon his dagger. The earl said that if I could prove that it would benefit my case. I told him that I had seen you close by, but that I did not know whether you saw the page do it."

"Assuredly I did," the smith replied, "and had my cudgel in readiness to tap him on the wrist if he had drawn his dagger. I would testify the same before King Edward himself."

"Thank you, Ulred, I will tell my lord so."

"I am sorry you are to be sent away from court. That is a bad job, Master Wulf, and Osgod here will miss you greatly."

"That shall I," the lad said. "Could you not take me down with you, young master? You could teach me there how to comport myself as your squire, so that when the time comes that you need one, I should know my duties. Besides, you could practise on me with sword and battle-axe."

"I could not do much in the way of teaching you, Osgod, seeing as yet I am myself but a learner, but I should be glad, in truth, to have you with me, and it would be good for me to keep up my practice in arms. I shall feel almost like a stranger there, and should like to have one I know with me. I could ask Earl Harold to let me have a horse for you from his stables, where he has two or three score doing nothing."

"With your favour, sir, I would rather trust to my own feet. I am a stout walker, and though I shall not be able to keep up with you, I think that each night I can get to the hostelrie where you may put up; but, if not, it matters little, I can make my way after you and join you there—that is, if my father will give me permission to go."

"You may as well go sooner as later," the smith said. "Since you have taken into your head that you will be Master Wulf's man, I see not that it will benefit you remaining in the forge. You know enough now to mend a broken rivet and to do such repairs to helm and armour as may be needed on an expedition; therefore, if the young thane is minded to take you I have naught to say against it."

"Then so shall it be," Wulf said, "I shall see my Lord Harold before I start, and will tell him that you are minded to be my man, and that I am minded so to take you. He will not object, I am sure, but it were best to ask him, since, when I return to court, I shall have you about me."

"When do you start, Master Wulf?"

"I am ordered to go to-day; therefore, as soon as I have seen the earl again I shall be off."

"Where will you sleep to-night?"

"I shall ride to Guildford this afternoon."

"Then you had better lay aside your hammer at once, Osgod," the smith said, "and don fresh clothes, and make your best suit into a bundle and start without delay; it is but ten o'clock, and you may be at Guildford before sunset. 'Tis but thirty miles, and eight hours' walking will take you there. If the young thane tells you that Lord Harold makes objection to his taking you, you can turn your face backward to-morrow and no harm will be done."

"I shall overtake you before you are half-way, Osgod, and can then take you up behind me on my horse; and now I will go back to the palace. I may have to wait some time before I can see Earl Harold.

From sunrise to sunset he has but a few moments to himself, and I shall have to watch my time to get a word with him."

It was not, indeed, until two o'clock in the afternoon that Wulf had a chance of speaking to the duke. Then, seeing that he was for the moment alone, he entered the room and stood with bowed head waiting for Harold to address him.

"So you have come to say good-bye, Wulf," the latter said kindly; "it is best so, boy. A time in the country will do you good, and there will be much for you to do down there. I have ordered two of my men to be in readiness to mount and ride with you, for I would not that you should go unattended. One of them will bear a message from me and a letter under my hand to the steward, and will tell him that although you will, of course, remain as my ward until you come of age, you are in all respects to be treated as if you were already my sworn man, and thane. It would be well if you could gather among your tenants twenty stout men as house-carls. The steward is ordered to pay to you whatever moneys you may require, and to account for them to me when he sends me in his checkers. These house-carls will, of course, be paid. There must be ample store of armour at Steyning for them, for your father was followed by forty house-carls when he went with me to the Welsh wars. One of the men who goes with you is a stout man-at-arms and is one of my own house-carls; he will remain with you and will instruct your men in arms and teach them to fight shoulder to shoulder. There may be bad times ere long, and it is upon trained troops and not upon hasty levies that we must most depend. In time I trust you will be able to place fifty such men in the field, but at present twenty will suffice. Have you aught to say to me before you go?"

"Yes, my lord; first, to thank you for your kindness, and to say that I will carry out your instructions; secondly, to tell you that Ulred the smith saw Walter Fitz-Urse handle his dagger, and was standing ready to knock it from his hand did he draw it. Lastly, that Ulred's son Osgod, who is a stout lad a year older than myself, and for his age well accustomed to arms, desires to be sworn as my man and to serve me in hall and in field. I like him much and have almost daily practised with him in arms, and I should be glad to have him with me if you see no objection."

"Not at all, Wulf; it is well that a man should have at his side one in whom he can altogether trust, be he of gentle blood or simple man-at-arms."

"Then I may take him down with me, my lord?"

"Yes, if it pleases you. Can he ride?"

"Not as yet, my lord, I will see that he is instructed down at Steyning. He started to walk this morning, understanding that if you refused him permission to be my man he would at once return. We shall overtake him on the road."

"Bid one of your escort take him up behind," the earl said, "I like his spirit. See that he is fittingly apparelled. You shall hear from me ere long."

Half an hour later Wulf mounted, and with his two followers rode from Westminster.

CHAPTER II. — COUNTRY LIFE.

Far from being depressed, Wulf felt his spirits rise as he rode away on his banishment from court, for instead of feeling it a disgrace he regarded it as a step forward in life. Earl Harold could certainly, had he been so inclined, have smoothed down the angry prelate, and could have retained him at court; but by the way he had spoken, Wulf was convinced that the earl let him go because he thought that it was good for him to be away. For four years he had been under tutelage, first at Waltham, and then at the court. In the last position his life had indeed been a pleasant one, for as one of Harold's pages he had mixed with all the noble youths of the court, and had had a place at every festive gathering. Still, he had been but a page, and treated as a boy. Now he was to go forth, and to learn his duties as his father's successor.

Harold's steward, who had since the thane's death acted as the earl's agent in the management of the estate, would instruct him doubtless in his civil duties, while the soldier who rode behind him would teach him how to lead men in battle, and how to make the fighting force of the estate efficient. Beyond these duties his time would be his own. He would have responsibilities, but they would be the responsibilities of a thane towards his tenants, and not of a page towards his master. He was going away a boy, but if it pleased Harold that he should remain away for two years he would return a thane. A young one, indeed, but one who had learned the duties of his station, and who, if needs be, could take his place in the field of battle at the head of his followers. For, even putting aside the Normans, from whom the earl seemed to think the greatest danger would come, there was never any long cessation of fighting in England.

There were the Welsh, who were always turbulent; the Danes of Northumbria, who were still a distinct people, although throughout the rest of England their identity was fast being merged into that of the Saxons. There were the Norsemen, still ready to take every opportunity of interfering in the affairs of England, or, if none offered, to plunder and harry the coast. There were the earls of Mercia, who bore no great love to the house of Godwin, and who resented the ascendency of the West Saxons. Lastly, there was Harold's brother Tostig, a fiery and turbulent noble, now Earl of Northumbria, who was jealous of Harold, ever ready to join in plots, and in close alliance with Norway already; he had several times withstood the royal authority, and would assuredly again become a fomenter of trouble should he see a favourable opportunity. At the king's death, if not before, that opportunity would be sure to present itself. Harold would be certainly chosen king by the people of London and by the West Saxons, but almost as certainly would his claim be disputed by the earls of Mercia on one hand, and by Tostig and the Danes on the other. Wulf was sure, therefore, that the work spent in preparing his tenants to take the field when called upon to do so, would not be wasted.

Full of these thoughts he rode for some miles from Westminster without addressing himself to the two men behind him; then, bethinking him that these were trusted followers of the earl, and had been specially told off by him to accompany and stay with him, he called them up to his side. Wulf had donned a riding suit instead of court attire, which, in deference to the king's partiality for the Normans, was, even among the staunchest opposers of the foreigners, a compromise between Saxon and Norman fashions. He now wore a tunic of a bright green cloth, girded in at the waist and reaching only to the knee. Over this was worn a garment closely resembling the Roman toga, though somewhat less ample. The folds in front fell below the waist, but it was looped up at each shoulder by a brooch, leaving the arms bare. His legs were clad in tightly-fitting trousers, and his feet in somewhat high shoes. On his head he wore a cap in shape closely resembling the Phrygian bonnet. He was armed with a dagger, and a short sword, which hung by a leather strap, two or three inches long, from his belt. The outer garment had a hood which could in bad weather be drawn over the head.

The man who was the bearer of Harold's orders to the steward wore a civilian dress, not unlike that of Wulf's. He occupied the position of a confidential scribe to Harold. The other wore the garb of a soldier. He was clothed from head to foot in a tight fitting leather suit, upon which were sewn iron rings overlapping each other, and strongly resembling in appearance the chain-armour of later days. His casque, with a curtain of leather similarly covered and affording a protection to the neck, cheeks, and throat, hung from his saddle-bow, and he wore a cap with a long projecting peak, while a cloak was thrown over his shoulders and fell almost to his feet.

"I am afraid you will find it but dull time with me, Leof," Wulf said as they came up abreast of him, "for the earl says that he has charged you to remain with me at Steyning."

"I shall not be sorry for that," the soldier said bluntly, "for I shall be right glad to be away from these Normans who fill every place at court and swagger there as if Englishmen were but dirt under their feet. Moreover, I love not London nor its ways, and shall be glad to be down again among honest country folk, though I would still rather be following my lord the earl in the field."

"And you, Master Gurth, will your stay down at Steyning be a long one?"

"No, indeed. I have but to bear my master's wishes and instructions to the steward, and to stay for a few days to see that they are carried out according to his desires. I am not like Leof, for I prefer life in London, where one meets with learned monks and others, can obtain sometimes the use of a choice manuscript, and can hear the news from beyond the seas, whereas in the country there is nought to talk about save beeves and sheep. I like the journey well enough, though I would that the animal I bestrode were more gentle in his paces. He has for the last half-hour been fretting on the rein to place himself by the side of yours. Horses are well enough for nobles and fighting men, but for a peaceful scrivener like myself a chair makes a far more comfortable seat."

The soldier gave a contemptuous grunt, and Wulf laughed. "It is well that we have not all the same tastes, but for my part a seat in a chair tires me more than one in a saddle, and I am never more happy than when galloping briskly along," and he shook the reins, a signal which the horse had been expecting for a considerable time, and at once responded to by breaking into a canter.

"Stay you, I pray, Master Wulf," the scrivener cried in great tribulation as his horse followed the example of its companion. "Even if the animal does not break my neck he will jolt the life out of me. I pray you curb him in if you would not see me prone in the dust; and if I am disabled, who is to carry the earl's message to the steward?"

Wulf reined in his horse. "Pardon me, good Gurth. I had forgotten that you are not accustomed to journey on horseback. I was scarce conscious, indeed, that I touched my horse, but he is used to travel more rapidly, and was so eager to be off at the slightest hint that I was willing that he should do so. We will try and journey soberly for the rest of the distance."

Osgod was overtaken, plodding steadily along the road, fifteen miles from town. Leof took him up on his horse, and they reached Guildford just as the sun was setting. The inn, which stood in the principal street of the town, was a low building built with a massive framework filled in with bricks. The ground-floor was occupied by a single room. At one end was the great fireplace where, over a pile of blazing logs, were hung many cauldrons and pots. Round the room ran a raised bench some six feet wide on which the guests disposed themselves for sleep at night; rough tables and benches occupied the rest of the room. Some twenty or thirty travellers were seated at these. Few were eating, but the greater portion had horns of beer or mead before them. As Wulf and his companions entered, after giving over their horses to one of the helpers, the host, seeing by his attire that he was of condition above the ordinary, came forward and led him to the end of the room nearest the fire, where the floor was raised a foot and a half above the general level, forming a sort of dais where travellers of distinction could take their meals apart from the rest of the guests. Leof was now spokesman.

"We will have supper, and of your best, master host, for we have ridden from London. We are in the service of Earl Harold, and are riding with this young thane, Wulf of Steyning."

The name of Earl Harold was sufficient to gain for them the best attentions of their host, and in twenty minutes supper was served, consisting of trout broiled over the fire, swine's flesh, and a stew of fowls and smoked bacon flavoured with herbs. Wulf took the head of the table, and the other three sat a short distance below him. The dishes were handed round, and each with his dagger cut off his portion and ate it on his wooden platter with the assistance of dagger and fingers only, for the utility of forks was at that time a matter undreamt of. After the meal was over, the host brought a ewer of water with a napkin, and each dipped his fingers into the water, an operation necessary even for the most dainty feeder. Presently a glee singer came in, and for an hour amused the guests with songs, for the most part of a patriotic character.

Wulf was then conducted by the host to a small chamber upstairs, where there was the luxury of a bed stuffed with straw. The rest of the travellers, including Wulf's companions, merely wrapped themselves in their cloaks and lay down on the raised bench which ran round the room.

On the afternoon of the third day the party arrived at Steyning. It was four years since Wulf had been at home, and he gave a shout of pleasure as his eye fell on the long low house with its background of trees, and touching his horse with his heel he left his companions behind and galloped towards the door. An old servitor came out.

"Why, Cedric, do you not know me? I am Wulf, whom you first taught to play single-stick and to draw a bow."

"Why, surely it is my young master," Cedric said, taking the hand that Wulf held out to him and placing it to his lips; "this is a glad day indeed for us all. We have longed sorely for a sight of you, for though I say nought against Master Egbert the steward, who is well liked by all, it is not the same as having our lord with us. You have come to stay, I trust."

"For a time at any rate, Cedric. Earl Harold wishes me to learn my duties as a thane and to fit myself to lead my people in the field if it be necessary."

"I trust that it never will be so," Cedric said, "but as we fought under your father so will we all be ready to fight under you should it be needful. The men of Steyning were never backward when there was fighting to be done, and in my young days there was no lack of that, though we have had quiet times since King Edward came to the throne."

The house was not built for the purpose of resistance, for, unlike the Normans, the Saxons did not deem it necessary to convert their houses into castles. It was, however, massively framed, the windows on the ground-floor were barred, the door was strong and solid, and after nightfall none could come in or go out without the knowledge and consent of the master. Wulf's companions came up just as the steward himself appeared at the door. He knew both Gurth and Leof, having himself been in the service of Harold before being deputed by him to manage the estates of Steyning during the earl's guardianship of its thane.

"The earl sends his greetings to you, Egbert," Gurth said, "and he has sent us hither with the young thane, who, as the letter I bring from the earl will inform you, has come down to take up his position as lord here, and to learn from you all things connected with his estate."

"Welcome to Steyning, thane," the steward said, doffing his cap; "it is well that you should be here. I have done my best to carry out the earl's commands to keep all things in readiness for your coming, and to be just and fair to the tenants, seeing that they pay their dues, and yet not pressing too hardly upon them if things go not well with them; but it is always best that the master should be in his own place, and right willingly do I give over my authority to you."

"The authority has been in good hands, I know well," Wulf said, "and right heartily do I thank you for having so well filled my place; but I would not take up my thaneship as yet I am but a boy, and have to learn my duties from you, and shall account myself but as your pupil. I know something of the ways of court, but nothing at all of those of the country, and it will be long before I am fit to take the control of things into my own hands."

They had by this time entered the great hall which formed the common room of the establishment. Its arrangement was similar to that of the room at the inn, with its raised dais for the master, his family, and guests, while the rest of the room was devoted to the retainers and servants. The cooking, however, was carried on in a room apart. There were two fireplaces, one upon the dais and the other in the body of the hall. On the walls hung trophies of the chase and arms of all sorts. The wooden roof was supported by massive beams, and with the exception of the trophies on the walls there was no attempt at decoration of any kind. During the residence of the family at the house, however, the hangings of tapestry, the work of generations of dames of Steyning, their daughters and maids, hung upon the walls round the dais.

The news quickly spread of the arrival of the young thane, and a score of men and eight or ten women and maids flocked into the hall to welcome him, and as he stood on the dais each in turn came forward to kiss his hand and salute him.

"I think my first order must be," he said to the steward, "that a cask of your best ale be broached."

"That shall be done at once," Egbert replied; "there is never a lack of drink here, but the best is none too good for the occasion. And who is this youth with you?" he went on when he had given the necessary orders, pointing to Osgod, who was standing somewhat shyly apart.

"He is my friend, and is going to be my body attendant and squire," Wulf said. "He, like myself, knows nothing as yet of his duties, but that he will be faithful and trusty I know full well, and the earl himself said that I did wisely to bring him with me."

"I will myself instruct him in his duties," Egbert said, "which indeed are not hard to learn by one of willing mind. He will stand behind you at table, will hand you your cup and take your orders. In the old times it would have been his duty to see that you were not struck down by a traitorous blow while you drank, but those days are passed. When in the field he will carry your helmet till you need to put it on; will keep close to you in the fight and guard you with his shield from arrows, and with his sword from attacks from behind; he will carry your banner, and see that as long as he has strength to hold it, it floats fairly out as a rallying point for your men. In the field indeed his duties are numerous, but at home in peace, beyond seeing that your arms are bright and clean, and that your orders are carried out properly, he will have but little to do. It is well that you brought him with you, for otherwise you would have had to choose one of the sons of your tenants, and the choice would have been a difficult one, for each would have desired the honour, and whichever you chose there would have been sore jealousy among the others."

The next day there was a great gathering in the hall. The whole of the tenants attended, and took the oath to be Wulf's men, as they had been those of his father, to obey his orders, and to follow him in the field with the due number of men according to the size of their holdings; while Wulf on his part swore to protect them from all wrong and oppression, to be a just master, calling upon them only for such service as he was entitled to demand, and exacting no feus or payments beyond those customary. A bullock had been killed, and after the ceremony was over all present sat down to a banquet at which much ale was drunk and feasting went on till nightfall.

The next morning Wulf, accompanied by Leof and Egbert, rode round the estate, choosing among the sons of the tenants thirty stout young men willing to enrol themselves as house-carls, receiving a regular rate of pay, and ready at all times to give service under arms, and to remain in the field as long as they might be required, whereas the general levy could only be kept under arms for a limited time. He had already gone into the matter with Leof, who pointed out that, as at present he had no wish to keep up any show or to have a body of armed men in the house, it would suffice if the men were exercised every day for a month, and after that merely practised with sword and battle-axe for two or three hours once a week. On these terms he had no difficulty in obtaining considerably more than the number he asked for, and finally fifty men were enrolled.

For those carls helmets were bought and coats of ringed armour made, and for a month they exercised daily. Of manoeuvring there was little indeed. The Saxons and Danes alike fought in line, with but room enough between them to swing their battle-axes. Each carried a spear as well as an axe, and when repelling the assault of an enemy closed up so that their shields well-nigh touched each other. Their exercise was generally either to engage in combats between chosen pairs, or, dividing into two parties, to fight line against line with blunted poles for spears and with stout cudgels for axes. Leof in these combats acted as judge, decided which side had gained the victory, praised the skilful, and chided the careless and sluggish. He gave lessons in the use of the sword and battle-axe to Wulf and Osgod, sometimes pitting them against each other, sometimes fighting himself against Wulf, and teaching Osgod how to assist his master by covering him with his shield.

Sometimes he would order three or four of the men to shoot with blunted arrows at Wulf, whom he taught to catch them on his shield or to sever the shafts with a blow of his sword, while Osgod standing by helped to cover him when two or three arrows flew at him together. This was a daily exercise, and even after the month's regular work was over some of the men came up every day to shoot, until Wulf had attained such coolness and skill that he could in the great majority of cases cut the shafts in two with his sword.

But the whole day was by no means given up to warlike exercises. Wulf rode out with the steward inspecting the houses and farms, learning what there was to be learned of the rude processes of agriculture, investigating the complaints of the depredations committed by errant herds of swine or by neighbours' cattle and sheep, seeing what was required in the repairs of farmhouses, and learning from Egbert to discriminate between those who were unable to pay their dues owing to misfortune, illness, or murrain among the animals, and those whose losses were due to their own sloth or carelessness. Upon these visits, too, the arms of the tenants were inspected to ascertain that they could properly fulfil their service if summoned to take the field.

The lands embraced by Wulf's feof were of considerable extent, reaching down to the sea, where they were some eight miles broad, and running back twelve miles beyond Steyning. Several small hamlets lay within it, and in case of war he could summon more than three hundred men to his banner. Several of the neighbouring thanes rode in as soon as they heard that Wulf had returned to fill his father's place at Steyning, and these visits were duly returned. But accustomed as Wulf had been to the orderliness of the court of the ascetic King Edward the rude manners and nightly revelry of these rough thanes by no means pleased him, so that he was glad when the visits were over, and he could remain quietly at home, where he was not without frequent guests.

The most regular of his visitors was the prior of the monastery at Bramber, which had been founded by the piety of one of Wulf's ancestors. The prior had, though Wulf was ignorant of it, received a letter from Earl Harold asking him to befriend Wulf, to encourage him to keep up the studies he had followed at Waltham, and to see that he did not fall into the drinking habit so common among the Saxons. The priest was well fitted for the mission. He was by no means a strict disciplinarian, but the monastery had the reputation of being one of the best managed in Sussex, and among the monks were many of good blood. He was passionately fond of art, and encouraged its exercise among the monks, so that the illuminated missals of Bramber were highly prized, and added largely to the revenues of the monastery.

The prior had been one of the monks at Waltham, and owed his elevation to the influence of Earl Harold with the late thane of Steyning. He was well taught in all the learning of the day, and having been for a time at Westminster, knew more of court life than the majority of the priors of isolated monasteries, and could suit his conversation to his hearer. Harold had said in his letter, "The lad has good parts. He is somewhat full of mischief, and has got into a scrape here by a quarrel with a Norman page, and by failing somewhat in the respect due to William of London, who took his compatriot's part with too much zeal. But Wulf is shrewd, and benefited greatly by his stay at Waltham, and both for the lad's own sake and for my friendship with the good thane, his father, I would fain that he grew up not only a sturdy Englishman, as to which I have no manner of doubt, but one who may some day play his part at court, and be a worthy friend and counsellor of an English king. Therefore I pray you, father, to keep an eye on the lad, and spare him what time you can from your duties. Tell him not that I have written to you, for it is the nature of youth to be averse to anything that looks like guardianship."

Such a request from Earl Harold was regarded by the prior as an order, and a few days after Wulf was installed at Steyning the prior rode over on his palfrey, accompanied only by the almoner of the convent.

"Peace to you, my son," he said, as Wulf bowed respectfully to him, "I have called not only as the prior of the monastery founded by the piety of one of the thanes of Steyning, but to welcome one who was a pupil at Earl Harold's college of Waltham, in which I at one time was a preceptor. Not when you were there, for I was installed here just before your good father's death."

"I left there two years since," Wulf said, "in order to be one of Earl Harold's pages; but I have not forgotten my reading, for the earl insists that his pages give two hours a day to study."

"'Tis a good rule," the prior said, "for learning is like a weapon, it soon becomes rusted when thrown aside. You will, I hope, continue the habit."

"I should wish to do so, father, but there are no manuscripts here."

"In that at least I can supply your wants," the prior said. "My monastery has a good library, and it will be quite at your service, and also my advice in any matters that may concern you. My almoner here, brother John, knows pretty well the circumstances of most of your people, and may be able to tell you where your alms may be well bestowed, and where they would do more harm than good. The worthless are ever the most importunate, and for every honest man in need there are twenty rogues abegging."

The ice once broken, the prior came over frequently. His conversation was bright and interesting. He himself was engaged in writing a history of the Saxon and Danish monarchs from the times of Alfred, and had stores of anecdotes of people and events of whom Wulf had before heard only vague traditions from the wandering singers and story-tellers who travelled the country, and were welcome guests in every household. As Wulf was urged by the prior to come over whenever time hung on his hands, his visits to the monastery were naturally very much more frequent than those of the prior to Steyning. Sometimes he would sit in the private apartment of the prior, but more often he spent his time studying the rare manuscripts, or watching the monks at their work of copying and illuminating. If he went in the evening he generally sat in the refectory, where the monks for the most part spent their evening in talk and harmless amusement, for the strict rules and discipline that prevailed in monastic establishments on the Continent had been unknown up to that time in England, although some of the Norman bishops were doing their best to introduce them into the establishments in their dioceses,—a proceeding that caused great discontent, and was strongly opposed by the English monks. These had, hitherto, regarded monastic life as one of work for the good of the poor, and as affording for those who wished it a tranquil retirement from the trials of the world. Moreover, it offered special attractions to those of quiet and studious tastes, since the monasteries provided the architects and the painters, the teachers and the writers, and it was here alone that learning was maintained and fostered. Consequently, at Bramber there was none of that monastic asceticism that prevailed abroad, and later became the rule in England also.

During the day the monks had their pursuits according to their tastes. There were those who worked in the copying and painting room. There were some who drew plans for churches or the dwellings of the wealthy, and who sometimes went out and superintended the carrying out of their designs. Some were in charge of the garden, where the work was chiefly done by the lay servitors, and where the herbs and simples were grown that were used in the concoction of the medicines distributed among the sick, and highly prized throughout the country round. Two or three were skilled in music, and these taught and conducted the choir, while two acted as teachers to youths, the sons of thanes and others, who, moved by the ardour with which their earl advocated learning, intrusted their sons to the monks for education. Then when the day's work was done, and vespers sung in the chapel, the monks gathered in the refectory. The conversation was of a bright and varied description, and as Wulf moved about from group to group he listened to the talk with far greater pleasure than he had ever derived from that at court, and largely increased his knowledge in many respects.

National matters were discussed with keen interest, for the monks were all English, and viewed with bitter hostility the elevation of foreigners to the chief dignities of the church, not only because they were foreigners, but because they introduced innovations of all kinds, and sought to reduce the Church of England to subjection to Rome, whereas previously it had been wholly independent of Papal authority. In secular matters, too, there were dangers that threatened the tranquillity of the country. Chief among these were the turbulence and ambition of Tostig, and the menace to the kingdom by his extensive earldom of Northumbria with its alien Danish population, which was rendered more serious by his alliance with the kings of Norway.

Then, too, it was doubtful whether the great central earldom of Mercia could be relied upon to act cordially with the West Saxons; Griffith of Wales was still restless and turbulent; and lastly, there was the ever-present menace of the Norman duke. Had England been united it could have laughed at the pretensions of the Duke of Normandy; but with Northumbria ready at any moment to break into civil war, and with Mercia doubtful, the claim of Normandy, however shadowy and indefensible, could not but be considered as a grave element of danger.

Listening to the talk of the monks Wulf learned much more as to the actual situation than he had done in the court of the Normanized king, and his feelings of patriotism became more and more developed and strengthened, while he applied himself with even greater ardour to his military exercises, as he recognized more fully the necessity that might arise for every West Saxon to be ready to take his place in the line of battle. The evenings that he spent at home were by no means dull. It was only in considerable towns that there were inns for the accommodation of travellers. Everywhere else these were dependent upon hospitality, and no door was ever closed in their faces. It was seldom that less than five or six travellers rested for the night at Steyning, and often that number was largely exceeded. Besides the wayfarers there were the professional wanderers, the minstrels, the story-tellers, and occasionally a troupe of buffoons.

All these were welcome, for they brought the news from without; the last rumours in London concerning the quarrels of the earls; the movements of the Danish ships that were harrying the coast, and those of the vessels Earl Harold despatched to cope with them; the prices of wool and hides in the chief markets; and even reports of what was happening beyond the seas. Leaving the dais, Wulf would go down and listen to the talk of the travellers, or, when they were of a degree above the common, have them up beside him, and question them as to their journeyings, the places they had visited, and the personages they had seen. Thus his hours were fully occupied from morning until night. He found far less time than he had expected for sport, and although he occasionally went out with his falcons or hunted the stag in the forest, which covered a wide extent of country beyond the hills, it was but seldom that he could find leisure for these amusements.

"It seems to me that you are always doing something, Wulf," Osgod said one day. "It is not at all the sort of life I should have thought a young thane would live. Why, you work many more hours a day than I did in my father's forge. It is either books, or the affairs of the tenants, or visiting the monastery all day when you are not at work with your sword exercises. When I have done with my work with Leof I like to lie down in the sun and take it quietly, and I cannot understand how you can be for ever on foot."

"I have so many things to do, Osgod; there is so much to learn, and I do not wish to grow up a mere beer swiller like Edmund of Angmering or Ethelred of Arundel. Their lives are, as far as I can see, no whit higher or more worthy than that of their own serfs, from whom they differ only that they eat more, drink more, and sleep on softer beds. Earl Harold expects better things than that of me, and I want to make myself worthy of being one of those in whom he can place confidence and on whom he can depend in case of trouble. I have heard him say how bad it is for England that our thanes are, in learning and culture, so far behind the nobles of other countries, and that if England is ever to take her place among great nations it must be by her thanes first raising themselves to the level of the nobles abroad, who are the counsellors of their kings. I can never hope to be anything like Earl Harold, who is the wisest and greatest of Englishmen, but I do hope so to fit myself that some day he may think me worthy of trust and confidence."

"Well, master," Osgod said lazily, "every one to his liking. I hope to be a good soldier and your true servant, but as for all this thinking and learning it would weary me to death."

CHAPTER III. — AT COURT.

Two months after Wulf had gone down to Steyning one of Harold's men brought a short letter from the earl himself. "I am glad to hear, Wulf," it began, "from my steward, Egbert, that you are applying yourself so heartily to your work. I have also good accounts of you from the Prior of Bramber, who sometimes writes to me. He is a good and wise man, as well as a learned one, and I am right glad to hear that you are spending your time so well. I told you that you should hear if there was any alteration in your affair. Some change was made as soon as you had left; for, two days later, meeting William of London in the presence of the king, I told him that I had inquired further into the matter, and had found that you were by no means the aggressor in the quarrel with young Fitz-Urse, for that he had fingered his dagger, and would doubtless have drawn it had there not been many bystanders. I also said that, with all respect to the bishop, it would have been better had he not inclined his ears solely to the tale of his page, and that under the circumstances it was scarcely wonderful that, being but a boy, you had defended yourself when you were, as you deemed, unjustly accused.

"The prelate sent at once for his page, who stoutly denied that he had touched the hilt of his dagger, but I too had sent off for Ulred, the armourer, and he brought with him a gossip who had also been present. I asked the king's permission to introduce them, and they entirely confirmed your story. Fitz-Urse exclaimed that it was a Saxon plot to do him harm, and I could see that the bishop was of the same opinion; but the king, who is ever anxious to do justice, declared at once that he was sure that the two craftsmen were but speaking the truth. He sternly rebuked Fitz-Urse as a liar, and signified to the bishop that he would do well to punish him severely by sending him back to Normandy, for that he would not tolerate his presence at court—an order which the bishop obeyed with very bad grace. But at any rate the lad was sent away by a ship a week later.

"After the bishop had left the audience-chamber the king said that he was afraid he had acted with harshness to you, as it seemed that the fault was by no means wholly on your side, and that I could at once recall you if I wished to do so. I thanked his majesty dutifully, but said I thought it were best in all ways that for a time you should remain away from court. In the first place, you deserved some punishment for your want of respect for the bishop, to whom you should have submitted yourself, even if you had thought him unjust. In the second place, as Fitz-Urse had been sent away, it would create an animosity against you on the part of his countrymen at court were you to reappear at once; and lastly, that I considered it would be to your benefit to pass at least some months on your estates, learning your duties as thane, and making the acquaintance of your people. Therefore, I wished you to continue at Steyning. It will assuredly be pleasant for you to know that you are no longer to be considered as being there in consequence of having fallen under the king's displeasure, but simply because it is my wish that you should for a time dwell among your people, and fit yourself to be a wise lord to them."

Wulf was much pleased at the receipt of this letter, partly because the fact that he had been sent away in disgrace stung him, and he had felt obliged frankly to acknowledge to the neighbouring thanes that he had been sent down on account of a quarrel with a Norman page; but chiefly because it showed the kindly interest that Harold felt in him, and that although absent he had still thought of him.

It was nigh ten months before he heard again. During that time he had grown a good deal, and although he would never be tall, his frame had so widened out that it was evident he would grow into an exceptionally powerful man.

At sixteen he was still a boy, and although his position at Steyning, where, although still under the nominal tutelage of the earl's steward, he was practically lord and master, accustomed to play the part of host within its walls, and that of feudal lord over the wide estates, had given him the habits of authority and the bearing of one who respected himself, the merry expression of his face, aided by a slight upward turn of his nose, showed that in other respects he was unchanged. He had learned with his weapons all that Leof could teach him. He could wield a light battle-axe, and with his sword could turn aside or sever an arrow however sharply shot at him, provided that he had time to mark its flight. With a quarter-staff he was a match for any youth on the estate, and he could hurl a dart with unerring aim.

Osgod had sprung up into a powerful young fellow, taller than his master by well-nigh a head, and his equal in exercises requiring strength rather than quickness and skill. His duties at table had been delegated to another, for there was a certain clumsiness in Osgod's strength that no teaching could correct; and in his eagerness to serve his master he so frequently spilled the contents of a cup, or upset a platter, that even Egbert acknowledged that it was hopeless to attempt to make a skilful servitor of him.

The earl's second letter contained only the words:

"Come up to London as soon as you receive this. Leave Egbert in charge of everything as before."

Although the time had not seemed long, and his occupations were so varied that he had never felt dull since he had come down, Wulf was delighted to receive the summons. He had, unconsciously to himself, begun to feel restless, and to wonder whether Earl Harold had altogether forgotten his existence.

"We are going back to London, Osgod," he shouted.

"I am right glad of it," the young giant said, stretching his arms lazily. "I am grievously tired of the country, and had it not been that nothing would induce me to leave your service, I have thought sometimes that I would gladly be back again in my father's smithy, hammering away on hot iron. I used to think it would be the grandest thing possible to have nothing to do, but I have found that one can have too much of a good thing. Certainly I am glad to be going back, but I am not sure whether it won't be worse at court than it is here."

"Perhaps we may not be staying there," Wulf said encouragingly. "Maybe the earl is going to start on some expedition; though we have heard of no trouble, either in the North or in Wales. But even if I stay at court, Osgod, you will often be able to be away, and can spend some hours a day at the smithy, where, if you like, you can take off your smock and belabour iron to your heart's content. I should say you would be a rare help to your father, for, as Leof says, for a downright solid blow there are not many men who could surpass you."

Osgod laughed. "Leof has not forgiven that blow I dealt him a month ago, when I flattened in his helmet with my blunted axe and stretched him senseless on the ground; in faith, I meant not to hit so hard, but he had been taunting me with my slowness, and seeing an opening for a blow at his head I could not resist it, and struck, as he was always telling me to do, quickly."

"You well-nigh killed him," Wulf said, shaking his head; "he has not taken an axe in his hand since, at least not with either of us. He said to me the first time I invited him to a bout, it was high time a man should give up teaching when he came to be struck senseless by a boy."

"Not much of a boy," Osgod replied, "seeing that I stand over six feet high, and got my muscles hardened early at the forge. However, he bears me no ill-will; all he ever said to me on the matter was, 'I am glad to see that you can shake off your sluggishness sometimes, Osgod; I should have been less earnest in my advice to you to strike more quickly if I had thought that you were going to do it at my expense. Keep those blows for your master's enemies, lad. If you deal them to his friends you will lessen their number.'"

"Have my horse brought round at once, Osgod, have the wallets packed, and be ready to start in an hour's time. I cannot go without riding over to say good-bye to the prior and some of the monks. Do you, when you have packed, follow me; it is not greatly out of the way, and I shall meet you on the road. A short half-hour will suffice for me there."

"So Harold has sent for you, Wulf?" the prior said, when the young thane told him that he was on the point of starting for London. "'Tis as well. Come back when you may, you will now be fit to rule at Steyning, and to rule well, but I foresee that we are likely to have you but seldom down here. You are in good train to rise high among Englishmen. You already possess the favour of Earl Harold, who is, in all respects but name, King of England. You possess far more learning than most young men of your rank, and as Harold rightly thinks much of such knowledge, you are likely, if you live, to learn more. But better than this, so far as your prospects are concerned in the troubled times that may be coming, you are quick witted and ready. I hear that you are already very proficient in arms, and a match for most grown men. Best of all, so far as your future happiness is concerned, you have a kind heart and a good disposition. You could scarce be a page of Earl Harold's and not be a true Englishman and patriot; therefore, my son, I think that I can predict a bright and honourable future for you if Harold lives and reigns King of England. Be steadfast and firm, lad. Act ever in what your heart tells you is the right; be neither hasty nor quarrelsome. But,"—he broke off with a smile, "you have had one lesson that way already. Now I will detain you no longer. Pax vobiscum, may God keep and guard you! If opportunity offer, and a messenger comes this way, write me a few lines; news of you will be always welcome at Bramber."

Leaving the prior, Wulf paid a hurried visit to the chambers where the monks were engaged in their various avocations, and then started at a canter and met Osgod coming along with a sumpter-horse carrying the wallets, a store of provisions for the way, and Wulf's arms and armour fastened to the crupper of his saddle.

"You have done well, Osgod," Wulf said as he turned his horse, and at a quieter pace proceeded beside him. "I forgot to give you any directions or to speak about your bringing a pack-horse with you, but I am glad you thought of it, for our steeds would have been heavily burdened had all that baggage been divided between them."

"We go back more heavily laden than we came," Osgod remarked. "My wardrobe was then of the scantiest, and your own has been considerably added to since we came here. Truly, Wulf, I feel that I have changed mightily in this year, and can scarce believe that it is but a twelvemonth back since I flung down my hammer and started on my tramp to Guildford with a change of clothes dangling from the end of my cudgel. I was glad when you and your party overtook me, for I was badly scared once or twice when I met a rough fellow or two on the way, though, fortunately, they did not deem me worth robbing. We could give a good account of four or five of such knaves now."

"There has been a change indeed, Osgod, and in me as much as in you, though I have not shot up into such huge proportions. I was a page then, and had learned but to obey. I am a boy still, but I have begun to learn to rule; at any rate, to rule myself. I have not conquered my fault of hastiness altogether."

Osgod smiled broadly.

"You are quick in temper still, Wulf. You remember it was but yesterday that you rated me soundly because I had fed your hawks early, and they were too lazy to fly when you wanted them."

"Well, it was annoying," Wulf laughed; "and you deserved rating, since you have been told over and over again that the hawks were not to be fed early in the morning. Besides, the rating did you no harm."

"None at all, master. I know that you mean not what you say, and hard words break no bones. I should have thought no more of it had you yourself not remarked that you were still somewhat hasty of temper."

"I was wrong, Osgod," Wulf said, holding out his hand, "but you know that I love you, and that though your carelessness and forgetfulness chafe me sorely at times, I mean not what I say."

"I know it, master, and I would not have you other than you are. I suppose it is the thickness of my skull that prevents me from taking in all that I am told, and perhaps if I had more to do I might do it better. I shall be able to play my part when it comes to hard blows, and you must remember that no one can excel in all things. A staghound is trusty and sure when on the chase, but he could not be taught to fetch and to carry and to perform all sorts of tricks such as were done by the little mongrel cur that danced to the order of the mountebank the other evening. My father always said I was a fool, and that, though for a piece of rough hammering I was by no means amiss, I should never learn the real intricacies of repairing fine armour. Everything has its good, you see, Master Wulf; for had my father thought better of me in his trade, I doubt if he would ever have given me leave to quit it, and go as your man."

"I have no doubt that is so, Osgod, and heartily glad am I that you showed no genius for smith's work. Nature evidently intended you to damage casques and armour rather than to repair them. You have not got all my clothes with you," he added, as he looked round at the led horse.

"No indeed, Wulf," Osgod said, "nor a quarter of them, for in truth your wardrobe has grown prodigiously since we came here. I had to talk it over with Egbert, having but little faith in my own wits. He advised me to take the two suits that were most fitted for court, saying that if he heard you were going to remain there he would send on the rest in charge of a couple of well-armed men."

"That is the best plan, doubtless," Wulf agreed. "My hawking suit and some of the others would be useless to me at court, and it would have been folly to have burdened ourselves with them if we are likely to return hither shortly."

"Where shall we stop to-night?" Osgod asked.

"At the monastery of the Grey Friars, where we put up on our way from London. It will not be a long ride, but we started late. To-morrow we shall of course make a long day's journey to Guildford. I don't know what travellers would do were it not for the priories."

"Sleep in the woods, Wulf, and be none the worse for it. For myself, I would rather lie on the sward with a blazing fire and the greenwood overhead, than sleep on the cold stones in a monk's kitchen, especially if it happened to be a fast-day and one had gone to rest on a well-nigh empty stomach."

"It is never so bad as that," Wulf laughed; "as a rule, however much the monks may fast, they entertain their guests well."

"If it is an English monastery they do," Osgod admitted, "but not where there is a Norman prior, with his new-fangled notions, and his vigils and fasts and flagellations. If I ever become a monk, which I trust is not likely, I will take care to enter a Saxon house, where a man may laugh without its being held to be a deadly sin, and can sleep honestly without being wakened up half a dozen times by the chapel bell."

"You would assuredly make but a bad monk, Osgod, and come what will I do not think you will ever take to that vocation. But let us urge on our horses to a better pace, or the kitchen will be closed, and there will be but a poor chance of supper when we reach the priory."

"Well, Osgod," Wulf asked the next morning as they rode on their way, "how did you fare last night?"

"Well enough as to the eating, there was a haunch of cold venison that a king needn't have grumbled at, but truly my bones ache now with the hardness of my couch. Couch! there was but the barest handful of rushes on the cold stone floor, and I woke a score of times feeling as if my bones were coming through the skin."

"You have been spoilt, Osgod, by a year of sleeping softly. I marked more than once how thickly the rushes were strewn in that corner in which you always slept. How will it be when you have to stand the hardships of a soldier's life?"

"I can sleep well on the ground with my cloak round me," Osgod said steadily, "and if the place be hard you have but to take up a sod under your hip-bone and another under your shoulder, and you need not envy one who sleeps on a straw bed. As to cold and wet, I have never tried sleeping out of doors, but I doubt not that I can stand it as well as another. As to eating and drinking, they say that Earl Harold always looks closely after his men, and holds that if soldiers are to fight well they must be fed well. At any rate, Master Wulf, I shall be better off than you will, for I have never been accustomed, as you have, to such luxuries as a straw bed; and I doubt whether you ever went hungry to bed as I have done many and many a time, for in the days when my father hoped to make an armourer of me I was sent off supperless whenever I bungled a job or neglected his instructions. I wonder what the earl can want you for in such haste?"

"I do not suppose he wants me in any haste at all. He may have spoken to the king about me, and when Edward again spoke of my returning he would simply send for me to come at once."

Such indeed proved to be the case. When he waited on Harold as soon as he arrived the latter held out his hand; "I am glad to see you back again, Wulf. A year of country air and exercise has done wonders for you, and though you are not as tall as you might be, you have truly widened out into fair proportions, and should be able to swing a battle-axe of full weight. Thinking it was time for you to return here, I spoke to the king, who was in high good-humour, for he had been mightily pleased that morning at some of the figures the monks have wrought in stone for the adornment of his Church of St. Peter; therefore he not only consented to your return, but chided me gently for not having called you up to town before. 'The matter had altogether slipped my mind,' he said; 'I told you that he might return directly it was shown that it was the bishop's page who was in fault, and from that day I have never thought of it.'

"I told the king that I had purposely kept silence, for I thought the day had come when you should learn your duties down there instead of dawdling away your time at court. You need not put on a page's attire any more. You will remain here as my ward, and I have had so good an account from the good prior of Bramber that in a short time I shall be able to receive your oath as Thane of Steyning. You will attend me to court this evening as one of my gentlemen, and I will then present you to the king, whom it is well that you should thank for having pardoned you. I hear from the prior that the varlet you took down with you has grown into a big man, and is well-nigh as tall as I am already. He must have lodging with my followers while you are here."

Finding that he was to remain for the present at Westminster, Wulf sent off a messenger at once to request Egbert to forward the rest of his clothes immediately. That evening the earl took him into a chamber, where the king was seated surrounded by a few of his favourites.

"This is Wulf of Steyning, my lord king," Harold said, "the youth who was unfortunate enough to incur your royal displeasure a year since, and who has upon your order returned from his estates. I have had excellent accounts of him from my good friend the prior of Bramber, who speaks well alike of his love of study and his attention to the affairs of his estate. I have also heard from other hands of his progress in military exercises, and that he bids fair to become a valiant and skilful soldier of your majesty. He has prayed me to express his thanks to your majesty for having pardoned him, and having authorized me to enrol him again in the ranks of my followers here."

The king nodded pleasantly in answer to the deep bow that Wulf made. "I was somewhat hasty in your matter," he said graciously, "and dealt out somewhat hard measure to you, but doubtless, as Earl Harold said, your stay in the country has been for your good, and I am glad to hear that the worthy prior of Bramber speaks so well of you."

The earl gave a little nod to Wulf, and the latter, gathering that his case was concluded, and that he could now go at once, retired with another deep obeisance.

Leaving the palace he made his way to the armourer's, whither he had sent Osgod as soon as they arrived. The smith doffed his cap as he entered. "I am right glad to see you back again, young master. My son gave me a rare surprise, for truly when he walked in I did not know him again, not having had him in my thoughts or having heard of his arrival. The varlet saw that I did not know him, and said, 'Canst mend me a broken dagger, master armourer?'

"'That can I,' I answered, and would have said more, when a laugh came from his great mouth that well-nigh shook the house, and I knew that it was my son, though the note was deeper than his used to be, and was, as I told him, more like the bellow of a bull than the laugh of a young fellow of eighteen. His mother looked in from behind the shop and said, 'Surely that must have been Osgod's laugh.' 'It was,' I said, 'and there he stands before you. The impudent rascal has topped me by over half a head, though I am a fair height myself.' Then she carried him away, and I saw no more of him until I had finished my work. Since supper he has been telling me somewhat of what he has been doing down with you, which, as far as I can learn, amounts to nothing, save the exercising of his arms and the devouring of victuals."

"He did all there was to do, Ulred, except that he could not bring that long body and those loose arms of his to offer me cup or platter without risk to my garments, and even Egbert was forced to agree that he should never be able to make a courtly servant of him; but save in that matter Osgod has got on right well. He has always been ready when I wanted him, and prepared at once to start with me either on foot or horseback whenever I wished to go out. He is growing into a mighty man-at-arms, and well-nigh broke the skull as well as the casque of the captain and teacher of my house carls. Another two years, if he goes on as he has done and we go into battle again, no thane in the land will have a stouter body-guard."

"Are you going to stay in London, Master Wulf?"

"Yes; that is, while the earl is here. When he is away hunting or attending to the affairs of the state I suppose I shall go with him. Osgod of course will go with me. While here I shall have but little use for his services, and he can be at home most part of the day."

"Then I trust you will soon be off," the smith said bluntly, "for to have a youth six feet and a hand in height hanging about doing nothing would set all the men thinking it well that they too should be idle. Osgod was always ready enough for a talk, though I do not say he could not work when it was necessary, but now that he is in your worship's service and under no orders of mine, his tongue will never cease wagging."

"Oh, I am ready to work a bit, father. I know how long it took me to hammer out a bar before, and I shall be curious to find out in what time I can do it now."

"I doubt you will spoil more than you make, Osgod. Still, I too shall be curious to see how many strokes you can give with the big hammer, and how quickly you can beat a bar into a blade."

The stay in town was, however, of short duration, for four days later the earl told him that he was going down to his house at Bosham, and that he was to accompany him.

"'Tis three months since I was away from London," he said. "The king is going down into Hereford to hunt, and I am therefore free for a while, as there are no matters of state that press at present, though I fear that ere very long the Welsh will be up again. I hear that their King Griffith, not content with the beating he had a short time since, is again preparing for war. Still it may be some time before the storm bursts, and I am longing to be down again among the green woods or afloat on the water."

Harold took with him a large party of personal friends, his brother Wulfnoth, and his nephew Hakon. Among the party was Beorn, a young thane, who also was a ward of the earl. He was two years older than Wulf, but there had been a close friendship between them at Edward's court. Shortly after Wulf's departure Beorn had also been sent by the earl to his estates in Hampshire, and had been recalled at the same time.

Beorn was far less strong and active than Wulf, having been very weakly during the early years of his life, nor had he had the same advantages of education, as he only became Harold's ward a year after Wulf was installed as a page at Westminster. He was a youth of good and generous disposition, and looked with feelings of admiration upon the strength and skill in arms of the younger lad, and especially at his power of reading.

"I can never be like you there, Wulf," he would say, "but I hope I may some day grow as strong as you and as skilful in arms."

Beorn's stay in the country had done much for him, his thin tall frame had filled out and there was a healthy colour on his cheek. He had practised diligently at military exercises, and although he found when, on the first day after Wulf's arrival in London, he challenged him to a trial in arms, he was still very greatly his inferior in skill and strength, he bade fair to become a gallant fighter.

"It is a disappointment to me, Wulf," he said as he picked up the battle-axe that had been struck from his hand and sent flying across the hall by a sweeping blow of Wulf's weapon. "I have really worked very hard, and I did think that I ought to have caught you up, seeing that I am two years the elder. But you have gained more than I have. I did as well as the other youths who were taught with me by the house-carl Harold sent down with me, but I am sure I shall never be as quick or hit as strongly as you do."

"Oh yes, you will, Beorn. Age is nothing. You see you were sick and ailing till you were fifteen years old, so those years counted for nothing, and instead of being two years older than I am you are many years younger. In another four or five years you will come to your full strength, and will be able to strike a far heavier blow than I can now; although I do not say heavier than I may be able to do then, as you are neither so wide nor so deep chested as I am. But what does it matter, one only fights sometimes. You have other advantages, you are gentler in speech and manner and have a handsome face. When we were pages together the bower-maidens of the queen always made much of you, while they called me impudent, and would give me many a slap on the cheek."

"Well, you deserved it richly, Wulf, for you were always playing tricks upon them—hiding their distaffs or tangling their thread, and giving them pert answers when they wanted you to do their errands. Well, I hope we shall be always great friends, Wulf. Your estates lie not far from mine, and though we can scarce be called neighbours we shall be within a day's ride of each other, and I trust that we shall fight together under the good earl, and often spend our time at each other's houses, and hunt and feast together."

"I hope we shall be much together, Beorn," Wulf said warmly, "and that we shall be sworn friends; but as for feasting, I care but little for it. We Saxon thanes are too fond both of food and wine-cup, and though I am no monk I would that our customs could be altered. I hate foreigners, but their ways are in many respects better than ours. The Normans, it is true, may not be much better than we are, but then they are but Northmen a little civilized; but I have heard the earl say that the French, and still more the Italians, are vastly ahead of us in all arts, and bear themselves with a courtesy and gentleness to each other that puts to shame our rough manners."

"We should be neither happier nor better that I can see, Wulf, did we adopt the manners of these Italians you speak of instead of our own."

"Perhaps not, Beorn, but we should be able to make the people happier and better if we could raise them."

"I will not even grant that, Wulf. Think you that the smith and the shepherd, the bowmaker and the weaver, would be any the happier could they read or even write than they are as they sing Saxon songs over their work? I should like to be able to read, because Harold thinks much of it, but except for that I see not that it would do me much good. If the king makes me any further grant of land it will be doubtless properly made out, and I can get a clerk or a monk to read it to me. My steward will keep the tallies of the tenants' payments. I can learn the history of our forefathers as well from the songs and tales of the gleemen as from books."

"You are as bad as my man Osgod," Wulf said indignantly.

"Well, you need not get hot about it, good Wulf," Beorn laughed. "When you come to see me I will have gleemen to sing the deeds of our fathers to you. When I come to you I will sit as mum as a mouse while you read to me from some monk's missal. I will force you neither to eat nor to drink more than it pleases you, and you shall give me as much to eat and drink as it pleases me, then we shall be both well satisfied. As for your man Osgod, I wish I had such a fellow. He will be well-nigh a giant one of these days, and in strength may come to rival the earl, who is said to be the strongest man on English soil."

"He is a good fellow, Beorn, and I could wish for no better to hold a shield over me in the day of battle or to stand back to back with me in a hand-to-hand fight."

"You should get him to stand in front of you," Beorn laughed. "He would be a rare screen against arrows and javelins."

The friends were well pleased when they heard they were both to accompany Harold to Bosham, which was one of the favourite abodes of the Earls of Wessex. It had originally been built as a hunting-seat, but Godwin had grown to love the place, with its woods extending for miles back and its quiet landlocked harbour, and additions had been made until it had grown to be, in point of size at least, a residence worthy of the great earls, and Harold preferred it to any of the many mansions belonging to him. It was a large and gay party that rode down the road through the quiet woods of Surrey and Sussex. They put up each night at the houses of thanes, where, as notice had been sent of their coming, they were royally entertained, and those selected were proud to afford hospitality to the earl.

For a week they stayed at Bosham, hunting in the forests, going off in parties under the guidance of the foresters, some who cared not for hard labour, hunting in the woods between Bosham and the hills, while others went far inland into the weald, which was for the most part covered by a great forest, with but a few scattered hamlets here and there. Smoke rising among the trees showed where the charcoal-burners were at work, or where the furnaces were glowing, converting the ore into the tough iron that furnished arms and armour for the greater portion of the men of the south. At the end of the week the earl announced to his guests that he had provided a new diversion for them.

"You see those three ships in the harbour," he said. "They were brought here last night, and three hundred men have been at work all day preparing them for our reception. I propose that we all embark with our dogs and servants, and sail along the coast, landing where we please and taking our sport. As we sail eastward there are abundant forests, and the game is far more plentiful than here, and our trip will partake of the character of an adventure in thus dropping upon unknown places. Tents have been stored on board the vessels, with abundance of good cheer of all kinds, so that we can establish ourselves where we will, and sleep on shore instead of rocking uneasily on the waves."

The proposal was received with acclamation, and the following morning the whole party embarked upon the three ships. The largest was occupied by Harold himself, his brother and nephew, and six or seven of his principal thanes. In this craft too went Wulf and Beorn with their men. On issuing from the harbour the ships' heads were turned to the east. The wind was light and fitful, the sails therefore were not loosed, and they proceeded under oars. There was but little tide until they reached the extremity of the long point of Selsea, past which they were hurried at great speed by the rapid current. Rowing closer inshore they got into quieter water, and continued their way until tide turned, when they anchored, and landing with their dogs hunted in the woods for some hours.

On their return to the sea-shore they found the tents erected and supper prepared, and the sport having been good they remained another day. The tide took them the next day past the shore of Wulf's estate, and he begged the earl to land there and to pass a day or two with his company at Steyning; but all were bent upon the chase, and they kept on until they reached the point where the white cliffs began to rise from the edge of the water. Here they landed again, and spent two or three days in hunting. Neither Wulf nor Beorn had been to sea before, and the quiet motion of the ships with their bellying sails and banks of sturdy oarsmen delighted them. There had been scarcely any motion, and neither had felt the qualms which they had been warned were generally experienced for a while by those who went upon the sea for the first time.

When the journey was resumed Wulf was struck with surprise and almost awe by the mighty cliffs that rose up from the water's edge. Neither he nor Beorn had seen anything like this, for although both their estates bordered the sea, the shores were flat, and vessels, if needs be, could be hauled up on shore.

"What would happen if a gale were to burst upon us here?" Wulf said to his companion. "If the waves were to dash us against those white rocks the ships would be broken up like egg-shells."

"Your question is answered," Beorn said, as a bay suddenly opened to their sight. "You see we are going in here, and shall anchor snugly somewhere up this river in front of us, which is truly the best haven we have seen since we left Bosham." Half an hour later the vessels were moored to the bank, close to a wooden bridge which spanned the little river.

CHAPTER IV. — A STORM.

After hunting for two days in the forests lying behind Newhaven, and in the valley in which Lewes lies, they again embarked. The master of Harold's ship had expressed some doubts as to the weather, but as he stated that it was but some eight miles round the great cliff that they saw to the east, and that beyond this the rocks ceased and there was a bay in which they could ride at anchor, or if necessary beach their vessels, it was determined to proceed, as Harold had the day before been visited by a thane whose house lay but two miles from the shore, and had accepted his invitation for the party to take up their abode there for a few days, as he promised them good sport in the forest. The cliffs rose higher as they proceeded. They kept closer inshore, and although they could see that the clouds were flying rapidly overhead they felt no breeze whatever, being protected from the wind by the lofty cliffs. The master was evidently uneasy, for he urged the rowers to exert themselves to the utmost. Wulf and Beorn stood looking with amazement at the cliffs towering up beside them.

"Is it not strange that they should rise like this—like a wall from the water?" Wulf said. "Had they been built up by human hands they could scarcely have been more erect and regular. I have never seen anything at all like it on land."

"Then it must be something formed by the sea, Wulf. Do you see those caverns at the foot of the cliff, and in some places you see there is a mound of rocks as if newly formed? It may be that this white stone is soft, and that the sea beating against the foot wears it away in time, and then the rock overhead gives way by its weight and so leaves an upright wall. Perhaps, long back, these hills were like other hills, sloping gradually down into the sea; but in time, perhaps many, many years before the Romans landed here, the sea began to eat them away, and has continued to do so ever since, until they are as we see them."

"That may be so, Beorn. My father has told me that he could remember when our estates stretched a good half-mile farther seaward, but had since been eaten away by the waves, and he says that his father had told him the same thing; therefore, as you say, in many hundreds of years even hills, if the stone were soft, might also be worn away. There we are rounding the point, and beyond there are no more cliffs; doubtless it is in this bay that the Shipmaster Edred thinks to anchor."

At that moment their conversation was cut short by a tremendous gust of wind rushing down the sloping hill into the bay striking them with such terrible force that the ship heeled over until the water rushed above the bulwark. The men were thrown against each other, and several fell down to leeward. The confusion was heightened by the fact that the great sail, which was but loosely furled to its yard, burst the ropes, and the wind catching it buried the craft still further, and she would have filled and sunk had not the ship-master seized the tiller, and aided by the two sailors there pushed it up, and so the boat's head payed off from the wind and ran before it.

The master shouted to the men to lower the sail, which was bellying and flapping violently, but before his orders could be obeyed there was a crash. The mast snapped off at the slings of the yard, and the wreck fell over the bow of the boat. All hands were employed for some minutes in getting the sail on board and furling it to its yard, which was laid lengthways along the thwarts. It was found that three men standing in the bows had been killed, and several others badly hurt. The vessel was by this time some distance from shore. Nothing could be done until she was freed of the water, with which she was nigh half-full, and all hands were employed in bailing it out.

The squall had increased rather than lessened in fury, and by the time the water was cleared out they were two miles from the headland. Orders were then given to man the oars again but it was found that several of these had been lost, having been washed away when the men leapt up, believing that the boat would capsize, or had slipped from the rowlocks unnoticed while they were engaged in getting in the sail. This was a serious misfortune, for every oar was needed to force her through the water in the teeth of the wind, which was blowing directly off shore. The remaining oars were all double-banked, Harold himself and his thanes taking their places among the rowers.

For an hour they laboured their hardest, but at the end of that time they were farther from shore than when they began, the force of the wind acting on the poop and broad hull driving her seaward faster than the rowers could force her shoreward. The sea, too, was now getting up, and the motion of the vessel rendered it increasingly difficult to row. Edred left his place at the tiller and went forward to Harold.

"My lord," he said, "it is useless. In spite of your efforts we are drifting farther and farther out, and from the look of the sky I fear that we are going to have a great gale, and there is nothing to do but to set a little sail and to run before it. Maybe there will presently be a shift of wind, which may enable us to make for shore. At present you are but exhausting yourselves in vain, and the sea will soon get up so much that it will be impossible to use the oars."

"So be it," Harold replied; and at the master's orders the oars were laid in, and the men prepared to get sail upon her. A sailor climbed up the mast and fastened the stays close to the point which was broken off. Then another joined him, and a block was lashed to the mast just below the stays, and the halliards were rove through it; then Edred brought out a small sail, and this was hoisted, and the vessel, which had before been rolling heavily, began to glide swiftly through the water. They had had the satisfaction of seeing that their consorts, although like themselves nearly capsized by the squall, had suffered no damage, but after lowering their sails and yards to the deck, had succeeded in rowing into the bay, their lighter hull and draught enabling the oars to drive them through the water in the teeth of the wind.

"She is going along finely now," Wulf said.

"Yes," Beorn agreed; "but before night there is like to be a sea that will try her."

Harold held a consultation with the master, and presently all the men were called to work. The great sail was unrolled from its yard and a portion cut off, somewhat wider than the beam of the boat, and in length reaching from the bow to the mast. Nails and hammers were brought up from the little cabin, and the canvas was stretched from bulwark to bulwark and strongly nailed to the wood on either side, oars being first lashed across at short intervals to support it.

"I suppose that is for us to lie under, Master Wulf?" Osgod said. "It is a pity it was not erected before, for there is not a man on board who is not drenched to the skin."

"It is not put there to keep you dry, Osgod, but to keep the waves from coming into the ship. But she goes over them well. The wind is getting up, Osgod, and we shall have a great sea presently."

"Then why don't we turn and sail back again? It seems to me to be folly to be running away from the land if such is going to be the weather."

"How can we sail back again? Do you not see that it is the wind that is blowing us off, and the vessel must go as the wind takes her. One can go a little this way or that, but no man ever yet sailed in the teeth of the wind."

"This is the first time I have ever been to sea," Osgod said, "and I trust it will be the last. The tossing of the ship makes me strangely giddy, and many of the servants are downright ill with it. Why men should go on the water when they can walk upon the land is more than I can say. I think I will go and lie down under the shelter of the sail, for indeed I feel as if I were about to die."

Wulf himself was feeling strangely uncomfortable. As long as they had been at work he had not felt unwell, for the necessity of holding on to the bulwarks or ropes, and the excitement of their strange position, had saved him from experiencing many qualms; but both he and Beorn were soon glad to follow Osgod's example, and to lie down on the boards under the rowers' benches. Fiercer and fiercer blew the wind, more and more violent became the motion of the ship; masses of water fell on the canvas forward, as she plunged into the waves, and would have soon beaten it in had it not been for the support of the oars. By evening most of the men were lying under the shelter, while Harold's brother and friends had retired to the little cabin in the stern. The earl himself remained by the side of the ship-master, who had taken his place close to the tiller, which was worked by four men.

"Think you that she will weather it, Edred?"

"I have little fear about that, my lord. She is a staunch boat, and I have been aboard her in seas as heavy as this. Besides, that thought of yours of stretching the canvas across her bow has greatly improved her chances. The water runs off as fast as it falls on it, and none comes on board. Had it not been for this every man would have had to bail all night. No, I have no fear of her weathering the gale. What I am afraid of is, that if this wind continues to blow we shall assuredly be lost on the coast of Normandy."

"That would be an ill fortune, indeed, for I know that the Normans count all that are cast on their shores as lawful prey; and even if we reach the land in safety and escape murder at the hands of the lord of the soil and his people, I may fall into the hands of Duke William, who is assuredly no friend of mine, seeing that I stand in the way of his designs upon the throne of England. Truly it was an evil moment when the thought of taking to the sea occurred to me, and I would give a broad slice of my earldom to be back at Bosham."

Hour by hour the waves increased in size and violence, and often poured in over the sides. The number of men on board was too great for all to work effectively. They therefore were divided into two parties, one being engaged in bailing while the other lay under cover, the change being made every hour. Wulf preferred working to lying still, for as the craft rolled the water washed over them, while the din of the waves striking the ship's side, and the cataracts of spray falling on to the canvas above were deafening, and it was impossible to get a moment's sleep. All were glad when morning broke, although the scene that met their eyes was the reverse of comforting. Small as was the amount of sail the vessel tore through the water under the pressure of the following wind. Great waves with white crests pursued her, and as they neared her stern it seemed to Wulf that they must inevitably fall over and crush her. The spray torn from the crest by the wind filled the air. The wind shrieked in the cordage, and the vessel creaked and groaned as she rolled from side to side.

"I would not have believed if I had not seen it, that the sea could be so violent and ill-behaved," Wulf shouted to Osgod, who was then standing beside him.

"If my clothes were but dry and my stomach full I would not mind so much," Osgod replied; "but to be drenched in water all night and to have nought to eat in the morning, takes the courage out of one mightily. How long, think you, will this go on?"

"That no one can say. It may last two or three days."

"And no food all that time!" Osgod exclaimed in dismay.

"We could stand that well enough, Osgod; but I do not think there is much chance of our being called upon to do so, for I heard one of the sailors say that unless the storm abates marvellously we are likely to be cast upon the French coast before nightfall."

"I should be glad to be cast anywhere so it were out of this. At least, whether it be France or England, there must be food to be had on shore."

"You do not understand, Osgod. Unless we happen to be cast upon a shelving coast with sand or gravel the craft may be dashed to pieces, and all lose their lives; for assuredly none could swim long in such a sea as this."

"Well, we must hope that we shall find a shore such as you speak of," Osgod said tranquilly; "but for my part, I am content to take the risk rather than wait another three days before getting anything to eat."

"And I would rather fast for a week than run the risk of the ship being broken up on the rocks," Wulf replied. "I can swim but little even in calm water, and I am sure that I could do nothing among those waves."

"I can swim, and will look after you," Osgod said confidently. "I used to swim every day in the Thames."

Wulf shook his head. "I daresay you might look after me if I fell into the Thames, Osgod, but it is a very different thing in a sea like this. These waves would dash a swimmer hither and thither as if he were but a chip of wood; besides, the spray would smother him. Even at this height above the water it is difficult to breathe when one turns round and faces the wind. I think that our only hope lies in running upon a flat shore, where the waves will wash the vessel up so high that we may be able to leap out from the bow on to the land beyond the reach of their fury."

Late in the afternoon one of the sailors on the poop astern shouted out that land was visible, and it was not long before it could be seen from the deck. All eyes were directed anxiously towards it.

"It is a rocky coast," Edred said, "but the rocks are not high, and if we can manage to direct the vessel between two of them we may escape. At present it is needful that most of the crew should keep in the stern, but when we are about to strike they must all run suddenly forward, so as to leap out as soon as she touches the ground. There will be but little time given to them, for assuredly the seas will batter her to pieces the moment she falls among the rocks."

Harold issued the order. All were to remain at their posts until he gave the word, and were then to run forward. The master scanned the shore anxiously.

"See you, my lord, that opening right ahead of us? It seems to me barely the width of the ship, but if I can direct her truly between the rocks methinks that most of the crew will gain the land. I shall myself take the helm. That is my duty and my right, and should I not succeed in making the shore, I shall at least die well contented with the thought that you who are the hope of England will be saved."

"I would fain stay with you, Edred."

"That cannot be, my lord. As it is my duty to stay by the ship to the last, so it is your first duty to save your life for England. I need no aid, for the vessel steers well, and by the help of a rope round the tiller I can manage her alone. Farewell, my lord, if we are not to meet again on earth. A very few minutes will decide our fate."

"Swimming will be of no use there, Osgod," Wulf said. "Look how the spray dashes itself against the black rocks."

"I thought not that it would be so bad," Osgod replied. "I wonder the master does not cast anchor."

"The ropes would not hold for a moment," Wulf said, "and when they broke we might drift broadside on to the rocks, which would mean destruction for all. The master is steering for that narrow opening between these two great rocks ahead. It will be but two or three minutes now before our fate is decided."

At this moment Harold shouted:

"Let each man make his peace with God." And baring his head he stood silently for a minute or two, imitated by all on board. Then Harold again raised his voice in a shout that was heard above the storm:

"Move forward now all of you, but not further forward than the mast; for if her head were too far down the master could not hold her straight. Moreover, the mast will assuredly fall forward and crush those in front of it. Therefore, let no man go forward of it until the ship strikes."

The sailors had already cut away the canvas stretched across the bow, and all on board clustered just aft the mast. Wulf looked back, and saw the master standing alone on the poop, with his eyes fixed in front of him and a look of grim resolve on his face. Then he turned again to look ahead. The scene was terrible. On either side extended a long line of white foam. Great masses of water were hurled against the rocks with a thundering crash, and the spray flew high up into the air, and then, caught by the wind, was carried far inland. The rocks were now but a few lengths ahead, and the passage between them looked terribly narrow, so narrow that he doubted if the ship could possibly pass through them. Not a word was spoken on board as the ship neared the opening. Now she swerved a little to one side, now a little to the other, as the waves lifted her stern and swept her along, but the hand of the master checked her immediately, and brought her head back to the line.

She was but a length away from the passage when there was a crash that shook her from stem to stern; then another great wave lifted her, and Wulf saw a black wall of rock gleaming with the water that streamed down it. The wall of rock flashed past the bulwarks so closely that he could have touched it. A moment later the ship struck again, this time with a force that threw many off their feet, while the mast fell over the bow. Then once more she lifted, shot a few feet further, then struck with tremendous force and remained stationary.

There was a grinding and splintering of planks, as the men rushed forward, and then a wave swept over the vessel, carrying all on deck before it into the cove beyond the rock, rolling them over and over up a sandy shore behind. Some managed to dig their hands and feet into the sand and to scramble out; more were sucked back again by the receding waters. As Wulf found himself in the water he felt his arm clutched, and Osgod shouted in his ear: "Do not struggle, I can keep you up!"

When thrown up on the sand Wulf tried in vain to resist the backward rush of the water; he and Osgod were borne out again.

When the next wave again swept them up Wulf saw the earl standing knee-deep in the water, and as he was swept past, Harold seized him and Osgod, and with tremendous strength lifted them right out of the water. "Keep still!" he shouted; "your weight will help me to keep my feet." Wulf felt his supporter quiver as the water rushed out, for he was waist-deep now; but directly afterwards he set them both down on their feet, saying, "Run before the next wave comes." Ten yards farther and they were beyond the reach of the sea. Harold was with them, and directed those who had got ashore to form lines, taking hold of each other's hands, and so to advance far into the surf and grasp their comrades as they were swept up. Many were saved in this way, although some of the rescuers were badly hurt by floating pieces of wreckage, for the vessel had entirely broken up immediately after her course had been arrested.

As soon as all who could be seen were brought ashore it was found that ten men were missing, among whom was the master of the ship, most of them having probably been struck by floating timbers. As soon as it was certain that no more would come ashore alive Harold called the men together. Rough litters were made of oars and pieces of sail, for the conveyance of those who had broken limbs or were too much injured to walk, and the party prepared for a start. By this time several men, apparently of the fishing class, had approached, but stood a short distance away, evidently waiting for the departure of the party before beginning the work of collecting whatever the sea might cast up. Harold went over to them, and asked in the Norman tongue:

"What shore is this, and how far is it to the nearest town where we can obtain shelter and assistance?"

"You are in Ponthieu, in the territories of Count Conrad. The town of St. Valery is but two miles along the coast. There you can obtain all you need."

Returning to his men, Harold ordered the wounded to be raised, and the party at once set out. Harold had already taken off his gold chain and rings, and had told his companions to do the same, in order that the cupidity of the natives might not be excited nor their rank guessed at. As soon as they started Wulf went up to him.

"My lord," he said, "I fear that you have already been recognized by one of the fishermen. I saw him looking earnestly at you, and then whisper to one of his companions. After doing so he hurried away."

"That is bad news, Wulf; but I could hardly expect that I should be long unrecognized. There are many vessels come and go between the northern ports and our own, and in St. Valery there must be numbers of sailors and fishermen who have seen me in London. Besides, we are sure to be questioned by the count as to our rank and condition, and even could we conceal it for a while, the news is certain to be brought ere long from England of our having been blown off the coast, and when it was known it would be speedily guessed that we were the missing party. Hark you, Wulf; I have never heard aught good of Count Conrad, and one cannot say what steps he may take to force us to pay a heavy ransom, but it is like enough that he will do all he can to prevent the news of my being in his hands from reaching the ears of the duke. It is likely that you and Beorn, being but lads, will be watched less rigorously than the rest of us. Should this be so, try, if you find an opportunity, to send the news to the duke that we are all held prisoners here. I shall, of course, endeavour to communicate with him, but some chance may occur by which you can do so more readily than I can."

"I will try to do so, my lord; but I trust this Norman count will treat you with all due honour and courtesy."

Wulf then fell back to Beorn's side, and half an hour later the shipwrecked party entered the gates of St. Valery. The townspeople flocked round them, and as soon as they learned that they were a party of shipwrecked Saxons who had been blown by the gale from England, they were led to the house of the officer in command of the town. He asked them a few questions, saying, "I must refer the matter to the count. By the usages of our land all who are cast upon it become his prisoners, to be put to ransom or otherwise as he may decide. However, food shall be supplied you at once, but you must be content to remain under guard until his pleasure is known."

They were accordingly at once placed in a disused granary, under the charge of a strong guard. Food was brought to them, and as soon as they had consumed this, most of the men threw themselves on the ground, worn out by their long exertions.

"This is a sorry welcome, Wulf, after our escape from the sea," Beorn said. "Truly the land seems as inhospitable as the ocean."

"It is not pleasant, Beorn, but at present I feel so thankful for my escape from those terrible waves that even the thought that we are all prisoners to this petty noble does not greatly concern me. Doubtless William of Normandy, who is the liege lord of the land, will speedily take us out of his hands. Were we alone it may be that we should suffer a long stay in his dungeons, but Harold and his brother are far too important personages to be allowed to remain in the hands of one of the duke's vassals."

"It is shameful," Beorn said indignantly. "I do not say that those who are cast on our shores may not be often pillaged and ill-treated by the common folk, but surely none of gentle blood would fail to show them kindness and hospitality."

"That is so on our coast of Sussex, but I have heard that further west, and certainly among the Danes of Northumbria, vessels cast on the coast are considered as gifts from the sea, and even the lives of those who gain the shore are not often respected. I regret much that Harold should be with us. It is true that his being here will doubtless shorten the term of our imprisonment, but it is unfortunate that he should fall into the hands of William, who is as famous for craft and subtlety as he is for bravery and skill as a leader."

"But what can he gain from Harold?" Beorn asked. "Our earl is well-nigh as much known throughout Europe as William of Normandy, and all Christendom would cry out with shame were he treated with ought but courtesy by the duke."

"I doubt not that he will treat him with courtesy, Beorn, but he may well wring some concessions from him before he lets him depart. He may bargain that the Normans may be again allowed to hold land in England, and to build their castles, as they did before Godwin and his sons returned from exile, and the Normans had to fly the land, save those around the person of the king. He may beg so many bishoprics for Norman priests. There is no saying what concessions he may extort. Of all princes in Europe I had rather Harold had fallen into the hands of any other than into those of William of Normandy."

"Truly I have never troubled my head about such matters, Wulf, and thought that it would be time to do so when I became a thane, and had a vote at the Witan."

"I have heard much of them from the prior of Bramber, who is a true Englishman, and though a priest, learned in all matters that appertain to the history of times past and of our own; he impressed upon me that just as a boy must practise arms if he is to bear them worthily as a man, so he should study the story of our kings, and learn what is passing, not only in our own country but in others, if he is ever to raise his voice in council."

Harold and his thanes sat apart discussing the position, their conclusion being very similar to that arrived at by Wulf. Chivalry had but slight influence as yet in the West of Europe. Kings and princes cared little as to the means by which they attained an end. Rivals to a throne were put out of the way without scruple; the profession of arms was a business like any other, carried on for gain; a captured foe was valued chiefly for the amount of ransom that could be obtained for him; petty barons and powerful nobles alike levied exactions on those who might fall into their hands, unless previously provided with a safe-conduct. Years later, when King Richard was made a prisoner on his return from the Holy Land, it was only because of his great exploits for the recapture of the Holy Sepulchre that any feeling of reprobation was excited against his captors. Thus then, although Normandy was at peace with England, it did not seem an unnatural thing to Harold and his companions that the noble into whose hands they had fallen should demand a heavy ransom, or that the Duke of Normandy himself should utilize the opportunity for his advantage.

On the following morning they heard a large body of horsemen ride up. A minute later the governor accompanied by a Norman noble entered. They were followed by a number of men-at-arms, among whom was a fisherman.

"Now, fellow," the count said to this man, "which is the Saxon Harold?"

"I am," Harold said, advancing a step before his companions. "I am Harold, Earl of Wessex. I have with my companions been cast on your shores. I expect honourable treatment, and am willing to pay any reasonable ransom should you demand one."

"We will talk of that afterwards," the count said roughly; "for the present you go with me to my castle at Beaurain. But first do you and your men hand over all valuables that you may possess; they are forfeited to me, being cast up on my land."

Without a word Harold produced his chain of office and other ornaments, and dropped them into a helmet which a soldier at the orders of the count held out for them. His companions did the same, the thanes first and then the two lads.

"That will do," the count said to the soldiers. "That is my share, you can search the rest yourselves."

"I protest against this robbery," Harold said haughtily, "and will proclaim you in all the courts of Europe as one who is false to his station, and who condescends to pillage those whom fortune has cast on his shores."

"You can wait until you get an opportunity to do so," the count sneered; "it is not likely to come for some time. You can do as you like to the others," he went on to the governor, "I want not to be cumbered with them. You can doubtless find work for them on the fortifications, but if you can put them to no use or they are troublesome, cut their throats and throw them into the sea."

The Saxons fingered their knives, but Harold said in their own tongue, "Resistance would be folly, the time may come when we may turn the tables on this fellow." The soldiers now closed round Harold and the thanes and led them out of the house. Here they were ordered to mount each behind a soldier, and as soon as they had done so they rode out from St. Valery, and crossing the river Somme at Abbeville, and the Authie by a ford near Crecy, reached the fortress of Beaurain on the river Canche near the town of Hesdin before nightfall. On the road Wulf watched anxiously for a chance to escape, but none offered itself. Soldiers rode on both sides of the captives, and had he slipped from the horse he could not have hoped to make his escape across an open country. As soon as they entered the fortress Harold and the thanes were all consigned to dungeons, but the count, learning that the two lads had been Harold's pages, said they should wait on himself. "And see," he said to them, "that your service is good, if you do not wish to dangle over the moat at the end of a rope."

"It is a shame that such a man should be a nobleman," Beorn exclaimed indignantly to Wulf, as he saw that the soldiers were placing chains upon Harold before they led him away.

"He is a hateful-looking villain," Wulf said. "It is but lately that he revolted against William. I heard of it from the prior. His brother, the last Count of Ponthieu, joined France in an invasion of Normandy. He fell in an ambush at St. Aubin, and this man became count. For a time he was held prisoner by the duke, but afterwards he was freed, and received back his dominions as a vassal. His face is at once cruel and base. I told you the instructions Harold gave me, Beorn; the need for carrying them out has arrived, and I will try to make my escape without loss of time from this fortress to bear the tidings to the duke."

"I will escape with you, Wulf; two can get on better than one."

"That is so, Beorn, and I would gladly have you with me, but maybe I shall be detected in attempting to escape and be slain, or I may fall into the hands of peasants and be brought back here, and if we were together all hope of letting the duke know of our lord's captivity would be at an end. Therefore it were best that I made the attempt first. If I fail, which is like enough, then do you in turn try to get away and bear the news to the duke."

Beorn did not like to stay behind, but he saw that Wulf's plan was best, and accordingly fell in with it.

"Will you go at once?" he asked.

"No; I will stay for a day or two to lull suspicion. They may watch us just at first, but if they see that we do as we are ordered with goodwill they will cease to regard us so narrowly; moreover, it will be needful to know the place well before I devise a plan of escape."

CHAPTER V. — ROUEN.

For the next two days the lives of the two young Saxons were well-nigh unbearable. At meals the count by turns abused and jeered at them, and his companions, following his example, lost no opportunity of insulting them in every way.

"If this goes on, Wulf," Beorn said as they threw themselves down on the ground late that night, when the carousal was ended, "I shall snatch the count's dagger from his belt and bury it in his heart, though they put me to death by torture afterwards."

"I thought of doing so myself, Beorn, to-night, when he threw a cup of wine over me. But I said to myself my life is not my own, Harold's rescue depends on it. We are bound as his men to suffer in patience whatever may befall us. In another hour I shall try to make my escape. When it was your turn to wait this evening I stole away for a time, and went to the shed where they keep the war-engines and took thence a coil of rope, which I have hidden in the courtyard. You know that we noticed last night where the sentries were placed, and decided where I might best drop from the wall unobserved. Fortunately the moat is dry at present, though they can turn water into it from the stream at will, so that once down I shall have no difficulty in getting away. Now I want you to go to sleep directly, I shall not stir until you do so, then when you are questioned in the morning you can say that I was by your side when you went to sleep, and that when you woke in the morning the place was vacant. You can say that I told you during the day that I could not suffer these insults much longer, and that you suppose that after you had gone to sleep I must have got up and either killed myself or in some way made my escape."

Beorn lay quiet for a time and then Wulf said suddenly, "I have changed my mind, Beorn; we will go together. I feel it is likely that in his wrath at my escape the count may slay you, and thus the object with which you remained behind would come to nothing, therefore it is best that you go with me."

"I was thinking so myself, Wulf, though I would not say it; but in truth I think the risks we may run in making our way to Rouen are small compared to those of staying here."

"We must lose no time, Beorn. The castle is quiet now, and we must be many miles away from here before morning, for you may be sure the count's horsemen will scour the country far and wide in pursuit of us."

They had that morning, before the count was up and their services were required, wandered about the fortress, apparently paying no attention to anything, but really closely observing the approaches to the walls and the general features of the country outside. They now stole out, keeping in the shadow of the building, until they reached the staircase leading up to the battlements, close to the point Wulf had fixed upon for making their descent. This had been chosen chiefly because no sentry was placed on that part of the wall, the watch generally being careless, as Normandy was at present at peace with its neighbours. When they reached the top of the steps they listened for a short time, but everything was silent. Then they stepped out on to the narrow pathway along the battlements, fastened one end of the rope round a piece of stonework and let the other end drop down into the fosse.

"Shall we both go down together, the rope is strong enough?" Beorn asked.

"It is strong enough, but we had better go separately, Beorn; we are neither of us accustomed to climb ropes, and if the upper one were to slip down too fast he might knock the other off the rope. It makes no matter who goes first. I will if you like, only mind if you hear a footstep approaching let yourself down at once whether I am off the rope or not. Be sure and twist your legs tightly round it, or it will run through your fingers."

Taking hold of the rope he at once swung himself over, and without much difficulty reached the bottom in safety. He had scarcely done so when Beorn came down beside him with a rush.

"What made you come down like that, you narrowly missed coming on my head?"

"I believe I have cut my fingers to the bone," Beorn groaned; "I feel as if I were holding a bar of hot iron. You had scarcely started before I heard voices; they were evidently those of men going their rounds, so I caught hold of the rope and swung myself off, but before I got my legs fairly round the rope I began to slip, and though I gripped it as hard as I could I could not stop myself, but slid down like lightning."

"Hush!" Wulf whispered, "they are coming along above." The voices came nearer until they sounded directly overhead Wulf knew that it was very unlikely they would notice the rope in the dark, but he felt much relieved as he heard them pass on. He waited until they could no longer be heard.

"Now, Beorn, we can safely be off."

It was muddy at the bottom of the fosse, but not so deep as they thought it would be, and they scrambled up the opposite side and then struck across the country south. Presently they came upon a road, which they followed, until after three hours' walking they reached the Authie river, at a spot where the bank was broken down.

"This must be a ford, we had best try to wade across. Anyhow there cannot be very many yards to swim, and we can both manage that."

They found that the bottom was pebbly, and that even in the middle the water was not much above their waists.

"That is something done, at any rate," Beorn said. "Now which way shall we go? This road we are on seems to lead south and we cannot do better than follow it, the stars give us light enough, now that our eyes are accustomed to the darkness."

"Yes, we can keep this road, which is no doubt that by which we travelled before, as far as the village which I heard them call Noyelle, then we shall have to strike off to the left, for that place was not far from Abbeville, and shall have to follow the Somme up some distance, unless we can find means of crossing it."

"I should think we had better leave the road before we get to the village, so as to be well away from it. If any peasant were going to work early and caught sight of us he would be sure to mention it to any horseman who might come along searching for us. I noticed that there were several woods on our right as we rode along."

"That would be the safest way, no doubt," Wulf agreed. "Fortunately we can do without food for to-morrow"—for both had managed to get some supper after they had finished in the hall,—"and having made up my mind to escape to-night I hid away a large piece of bread under my smock. We can manage very well on that."

Accordingly after an hour's walking they left the road and bore to the south-west. But little of the land was cultivated, and they were fortunate in not coming upon any woodland until light began to break in the sky. Then they made their way to the nearest wood, went in for some distance and then threw themselves down, and in a few minutes were fast asleep. Accustomed to judge time by the position of the sun, they saw when they awoke that it was already past noon, and after eating a few mouthfuls of bread they continued their journey. For the most part their course lay among woods, and they did not venture across an open piece of country until after a careful examination to see that no one was in sight.

Shortly after starting they caught sight of a village in the distance, which they afterwards learned was St. Riguier, but with these exceptions saw no human habitation. Late in the afternoon they came down on the bank of the Somme. This was thickly covered with long reeds and rushes, and among these they sat down and ate the rest of their bread, confident that however vigilant the search they would not be traced.

"This is a very different matter to the last crossing," Beorn said. "This is a wide river, and I fear that I could not swim across it."

"Nor should I like to try. But fortunately there is no occasion for us to trust to swimming; for we can pull up or break off a number of these great rushes and make them into two bunches; these will give us ample support for our passage."

"So they will, Wulf; I should never have thought of that."

Two large bundles were soon made, the reeds being tied together by a tough climber that wreathed itself everywhere among them, and as soon as it was quite dark they went down to the water's edge, and found to their satisfaction that the reeds possessed ample buoyancy for their purpose. Wading in they started swimming, resting their chests on the reeds and striking out with their legs, and in a few minutes were on the southern bank of the river.

"Now we must make to the east of south," Wulf said. "I should say if we walk steadily all night we shall be beyond the territory of this vile count. I hope before long we shall strike on some road leading in the right direction, for if we get among the woods again we shall be able to make no progress. But any road we may come upon going at all in the right direction is likely to lead to Rouen."

"How far is it, do you think?"

"I have a very vague idea. The prior had a map of Normandy, and on this he pointed out to me how the duchy had grown since William came as a boy to be its duke. I can remember the general position of the town, but not more than that. I should think from the Somme to Rouen must be over seventy miles and less than a hundred, but more closely than that I cannot guess."

They came upon no road before morning, but as the country was open they made good progress, and when they lay down in a thicket as the day was breaking they calculated that they must be nearly thirty miles south of the Somme.

"I feel that I want sleep," Beorn said, "but still more that I want food. If it is another sixty miles to Rouen I know not how we are going to travel the distance fasting."

"No, we must get some food to morrow or rather to day, Beorn. We have nothing of any value to offer for it. They searched us too closely for anything to escape them. We dare not go into any town or village until we are quite sure that we are beyond the count's territories, but we might enter some solitary hut and pray for a piece of bread for charity, or we can walk all day, by which time we shall surely be well beyond the Count of Ponthieu's territory, and could boldly go into a town. If we are seized, we can demand to be sent to Rouen, saying we are bearers of an important message to Duke William, and even if they do not send us straight on, they would hardly keep us without food."

After sleeping for four or five hours they again started, and after walking some miles came upon a herdsman's cottage The man was out, and his wife looked with surprise at the two lads, whose garments, though stained by sea water and travel, were evidently those of youths of a class above the common. Beorn addressed her in her own language, and told her that they were wayfarers who had lost their road and were grievously in need of food. She at once invited them to come in, and set before them some black bread and some cheese made from goats' milk. They learned to their satisfaction that they had long passed the limits of Ponthieu, and that Rouen was distant about fifty miles.

"The road from Amiens lies five miles to the east," she said; "but it would be shorter for you to keep due south, for it inclines in that direction. You will strike it after seven miles' walking, and after that you cannot miss your way."

After warmly thanking the woman for her hospitality the lads again started, feeling greatly strengthened and refreshed by their meal; but want of sleep told upon them, and when they got within sight of the road they again lay down, and slept until the sun was setting. Resuming their journey they followed the road, and before morning crossed over a range of hills, and presently arrived at a small hamlet close to which was a monastery. Towards this they directed their steps, and seating themselves on the ground near the door, waited until it was unbarred.

"You are early wayfarers, my sons," the monk who opened the gates said as they went up, "and you seem to have travelled far."

"That have we, father, and are sorely in need of food."

The hospitality of the monasteries was unbounded, and the monk at once led them into the kitchen, where bread, meat, and wine were placed before them.

"Truly you were hungry," the monk said smilingly as he watched their onslaught upon the joint.

"We were well-nigh starving, father. For two days we have had nought to eat save a crust of bread we had brought with us, and some that a shepherd's wife bestowed upon us out of charity, and we have walked from near Hesdin."

"I do not ask out of curiosity, my sons," the monk said after a pause, "and you know it is not our custom to question wayfarers who come in to ask our hospitality; but it is strange to see two youths, who by their dress and manner seem to belong to a superior station, in so pitiable a state as you are, and wandering alone, as it would seem, penniless through the country. I ask not your confidence, but if you chose to give it maybe we might aid or advise you. Our prior is a kindly man and very gentle with the faults of others."

"We are Saxons, father. We were wrecked four days since near St. Valery, and are now bound on an errand of high importance to Duke William, to whom it is urgent we should arrive as soon as possible. We have run sore peril on the way, and have been stripped of our money and valuables."

"Is your mission of importance to the duke as well as to yourselves?" the monk asked gravely.

"It is of great importance to him. I am sure that he would consider that any one who assisted us on our way had done him good service."

The monk look earnestly at them. "I will speak to the prior," he said. He returned in a few minutes and bade them follow him.

The prior was a tall, gentle old man. "I have heard your story from brother Gregory," he said, "and I wished to see you that I might judge for myself whether so strange a tale, as that two shipwrecked boys should have important business with our duke, could be believed, before I did aught to help you forward. You look to me honest of purpose and of gentle blood, and not, I am sure, belonging to the class of wayfarer who will trump up any story for the purpose of gaining alms. Whether your errand with the duke is of the importance you deem it I cannot say, but if you give me your word that you consider it an urgent matter, I will aid you to proceed at once."

"We do indeed consider it most urgent, father, and we are sure that the duke will so regard it. We should not have walked well-nigh a hundred miles in two days and nights, and that almost without food, had we not deemed it so."

"Brother Gregory," the prior said, "bid lay-brother Philip at once prepare three palfreys, and tell him he is to ride himself with these two Saxon youths to Rouen. The distance is thirty miles," he went on as the monk left the room. "It is not yet six o'clock, and though our palfreys are not accustomed to travel at rapid speed, you will be there this afternoon in time to have audience with the duke."

The lads returned their warm thanks to the prior. "We would gladly tell you the purport of our mission," Beorn said, "but we are only the bearers of news, and the duke might be displeased did he know that we had confided to any before it reached his own ear."

"I wish not to learn it, my son. It is sufficient for me that you have a mission to our duke, and that I am possibly furthering his interest by aiding you to reach him. But, in sooth, I am more moved by the desire to aid two stranger youths, whom the sea and man alike seem to have treated hardly. Is it long since you left England?"

"We have well-nigh lost account of time, father, so much has taken place in a few days. 'Tis but a week since we were sailing along the English coast with a large company in three ships, when a sudden tempest arose, carried away our sail, blew us off the shore, and then increasing in fury drove us before it until we were wrecked on the coast of Ponthieu, near St. Valery. Since then we have been prisoners, have escaped, and have journeyed here on foot."

"Truly a bad week's work for you," the prior said. "Were all your ships wrecked?"

"No; our two consorts, being lighter and more easily rowed, regained the land when we were blown off it."

"Conrad of Ponthieu is an evil man," the prior said. "Had you come ashore twenty miles farther south you would have been beyond his jurisdiction. I fear that all the seacoast people view the goods obtained from vessels cast ashore as a lawful prey, but your company would assuredly have received fair hospitality if cast on the shores of Normandy itself. But now methinks I hear the patter of the palfreys' hoofs. Farewell, my sons, and may God who has protected you through these dangers give you his blessing."

The lads knelt before him as he placed his hands on their heads and gave them his benediction. As they rose brother Gregory entered to say that the horses were ready, and with renewed thanks to the prior they followed him to the courtyard, mounted, and rode off with the lay-brother, glad indeed to find their journey on foot thus abridged. Impatient as they were to reach Rouen, the gentle pace at which the palfreys ambled along fretted them very much. Brother Philip kept up a constant string of talk on the monastery, its estates, the kindness of the prior, the strictness of the subprior, and other matters of great interest to himself, but of none to the boys, whose thoughts were with Harold, chained and in prison. The palfreys, however, made very fair progress, and it was but three o'clock when they rode into the streets of Rouen, whose size and grandeur would at any other time have impressed them much, for it was an incomparably finer city than London.

"That is the duke's palace," brother Philip said, as they approached a stately building. "I will put up the horses at the convent at the farther corner of this square, and will then go with you to the palace, as I have orders to tell any officer who may make a difficulty about you entering, that I am bid by the prior of Forges to say that you are here on urgent business with the duke, and to pray that you may have immediate audience with him."

In those days great men were easy accessible, and one of the ushers, on receiving the message from the prior, at once led the boys to an apartment in which the duke was sitting. He looked up in some surprise on seeing the two lads standing bareheaded at the door, while the usher repeated the message he had received.

"Advance," he said. "What is this business of which the prior of Forges has sent me word?"

The two boys advanced and knelt before the duke. He was a man of about the same age as Harold, with dark hair and complexion, less tall than the earl, but of a powerful figure, and a stern, resolute face. The boys had discussed among themselves which should be the speaker. Wulf had desired that Beorn, being the elder, should deliver the message, but Beorn insisted that as Wulf himself had received it from Harold, it was he who should be the one to deliver it to the duke.

"My Lord Duke," Wulf said, "we are Saxons, pages of Earl Harold, and we bring you by his orders the news that the vessel in which he was sailing along his coast had been blown off by a tempest and cast on the shore of Ponthieu, near St. Valery, and that he and his companions have been villainously ill-treated by Conrad, Count of Ponthieu, who has seized them and cast them into dungeons in his fortress of Beaurain, Harold and his companions being fettered like malefactors."

The duke was astounded at the news. No greater piece of good fortune could have befallen him, for he had it in his power to lay his great rival under an obligation to him, to show himself a generous prince, and at the same time to obtain substantial benefits. He rose at once to his feet.

"By the Host," he exclaimed, "but this is foul treatment indeed of the noble earl, and brings disgrace alike upon the Count of Ponthieu and upon me, his liege lord. This wrong shall be remedied, and speedily. You shall see that I waste no moment in rescuing your lord from this unmannerly count." He struck his hand on the table, and an attendant entered, "Pray the knights Fitz-Osberne and Warren to come hither at once. And how is it, boys," he went on, as the attendant hurried away, "that you were enabled to bear this message to me?"

"While Harold and his thanes were cast into prison," Wulf said, "the count kept us to wait upon him; not for our services, but that he might flout and ill-treat us. We obtained possession of a rope, and let ourselves down at night from the battlements, and made our way on foot as far as Forges, where the good prior, learning from us that we had a message of importance to you, though nothing of its import, sent us forward on palfreys, so that no time might be lost."

"When did you leave Beaurain?"

"It will be three days come midnight," Wulf said.

"And how did you live by the way?"

"We took a piece of bread with us, and once obtained food at a shepherd's hut, and this morning we were well entertained at the convent of Forges."

"You have proved yourselves good and trusty messengers," the duke said. "Would I were always as well served. As you are the earl's pages you are of course of gentle blood?"

"We are both his wards, my lord, and shall be thanes when we come of age."

"And how is it that you, young sir, who seem to be younger than your companion, are the spokesman?"

"It happened thus," Wulf said modestly. "Some fishermen came up just after we had gained the shore with the loss of many of our company. I marked that one of them started on seeing Earl Harold, and whispered to a companion, and feeling sure that he had recognized my lord, I told the earl of it as we walked towards St. Valery. He then charged me if he was taken prisoner by the count to endeavour to bear the news to you, and to give the same orders to my comrade Beorn, saying it was likely that we might not be so strictly watched as the men of the company, and might therefore succeed in slipping away, as indeed turned out to be the case. I was desirous that Beorn should tell you the tale, being older and more accustomed to the speech of the court than I was, but he held that the message, being first given to me, it was I who should deliver it."

"He judged rightly," the duke said, "and deserves credit for thus standing aside."

At this moment two knights entered. "Fitz-Osberne, Warren," the duke said, "a foul wrong has been done by Conrad of Ponthieu to Earl Harold of Wessex, the foremost of Englishmen next to the king himself, who has, with a company of his thanes, been cast ashore near St. Valery. Instead of receiving honourable treatment, as was his due, he has been most foully seized, chained, and with his friends thrown into prison by the count, who has sent no intimation of what has taken place to me, his lord, and had it not been for these two brave and faithful youths, who effected their escape over the battlements of Beaurain in order to bring me the news, the earl might have lingered in shameful captivity. I pray you take horse at once, with twenty chosen spears, and ride at the top of your speed to Beaurain. There express in fitting terms to Conrad my indignation at his foul treatment of one who should have been received as a most honoured guest. Say that the earl and his company must at once be released, and be accorded the treatment due not only to themselves, but to them as my guests, and bid the count mount with them and ride to my fortress of Eu, to which I myself will at once journey to receive them. Tell Conrad that I will account to him for any fair ransom he may claim, and if he demur to obey my orders warn him that the whole force of Normandy shall at once be set on foot against him. After having been for two years my prisoner, methinks he will not care to run the risk of again being shut up within my walls."

"We will use all haste," Fitz-Osberne said. "Conrad's conduct is a disgrace to every Norman noble, for all Europe will cry shame when the news of the earl's treatment gets abroad. That Conrad should hold him to ransom is only in accordance with his strict rights, but that he should imprison and chain him is, by the saints, almost beyond belief."

As soon as the knights had left, the duke sent for his chamberlain, and ordered him to conduct Beorn and Wulf to an apartment and to see that they were at once furnished with garments befitting young nobles, together with a purse of money for their immediate wants. Then taking a long and heavy gold chain from his neck he placed it on the table, and with a blow with his dagger cut it in sunder, and handed half to each of the lads.

"Take this," he said, "in token of my thanks for having brought me this news, and remember, that if at any time you should have a boon to ask that it is within my power to grant, I swear to you upon my ducal honour that it shall be yours. Never have I received more joyful news than that the great Earl of Wessex will shortly be my guest."

The lads bowed deeply, and then followed the chamberlain from the apartment.

"Well, what think you of it, Beorn?" Wulf said, when they found themselves alone in a handsome chamber.

"So far as rescuing Harold from the power of the Count of Ponthieu we have surely succeeded even beyond our hopes. As to the rest, I know not. As you were speaking I marked the satisfaction and joy on the duke's face, and I said to myself that it was greater than need have been caused by the thought that Earl Harold was to be his guest."

"So I thought myself, Beorn. There can be no doubt that, as he said, he deemed it the best news he had ever received, and I fear greatly that Harold will but exchange one captivity for another. It will doubtless be a more pleasant one, but methinks Harold will find himself as much a prisoner, although treated as an honoured guest by William, as he was while lying in the dungeon of Conrad. It is a bad business, and I greatly fear indeed that Harold will long rue the unfortunate scheme of hunting along the coast that has brought him to this pass."

In a short time an attendant arrived with ewers, water, and four suits of handsome garments, belts embroidered with gold thread, and daggers, together with two plumed caps and purses, each containing ten gold pieces; he informed them that two horses had been provided for their use, and that they were to take their meals with the duke's household, and to consider themselves in all respects as his guests.

"We look finer birds than we did when we rode in with brother Philip," Beorn laughed when they had attired themselves in their new garments. "The more sober of these suits are a good deal gayer than those we wore at home even at court ceremonies."

"King Edward objects to show," Wulf said, "and his own pages are so sober in their attire that the earl likes not that we should outshine them, and we usually cut a poor figure beside those of William of London and the other Normans of his court."

In a short time the chamberlain came in and informed them that supper was served, and conducted them to the hall, where he presented them to the duke's gentlemen and pages as William's guests, and wards and pages of the Earl of Wessex. The news of Harold's shipwreck and imprisonment travelled quickly, for orders had already been issued for the court to prepare to start early the next morning to accompany the duke to Eu, in order to receive with due honour William's guest and friend, Harold of England; and while the meal went on many questions were asked as to the shipwreck and prisonment of the earl, and the liveliest indignation was expressed at the conduct of Conrad of Ponthieu.

"Truly all Normans will be reckoned churls," one of the gentlemen exclaimed indignantly. "The fame of Harold's bravery, wisdom, and courtesy to all men is known in every court in Europe, and that the duke's vassal should have dared to imprison and chain him will excite universal indignation. Why, the rudest of our own Norse ancestors would not have so foully treated one so noble whom fate had cast into his hands. Had we been at war with England it would be shameful, but being at peace there are no words that can fitly describe the outrage."

When the meal was over, one of the duke's pages who was about the same age as Beorn asked him what they were going to do with themselves.

"If you have nothing better," he said, "will you ride with me to my father's castle, it is but five miles away? My name is De Burg. I can promise you a hearty welcome. My father was one of the knights who accompanied the duke when he paid his visit to England some fifteen years ago, and he liked the country much, and has ever since spoken of the princely hospitality with which they were received by your king. He did not meet Earl Harold then."

"No, the earl with his father and brothers was away in exile," Wulf said rather shortly, for that visit had been a most unpleasant one to Englishmen. It had happened when the Norman influence was altogether in the ascendant. The king was filling the chief places at court and in the church with Normans, had bestowed wide domains upon them, and their castles were everywhere rising to dominate the land. Englishmen then regarded with hostility this visit of the young Norman duke with his great train of knights, and although at the return of Godwin and his sons the greater portion of the intruders had been driven out, their influence still remained at court, and it was even said that Edward had promised the duke that he should be his successor.

It was true that Englishmen laughed at the promise. The King of England was chosen by the nation, and Edward had no shadow of right to bequeath the throne even to one of his sons much less to a foreign prince, who, although related to himself by marriage, had no drop of English blood in his veins. Still, that the promise should ever have been made rankled in the minds of the English people, the more so as the power of Normandy increased, and the ambition as well as the valour of its duke became more and more manifest According to English law the promise was but an empty breath, absolutely without effect or value. According to Norman law it constituted a powerful claim, and Duke William was assuredly not a man to let such a claim drop unpressed.

Wulf had heard all this again and again, and the prior of Bramber had explained it to him in all its bearings, showing him that little as Englishmen might think of the promise given by Edward so long ago, it would be likely to bring grievous trouble on the land at his death. He might perhaps have said more in reference to William's visit had not Beorn at once accepted the invitation to ride with young De Burg to his father's castle.

CHAPTER VI. — RELEASE OF THE EARL

In a few minutes the three horses were brought out. Wulf and Beorn were much pleased with the animals that had been placed at their service. They were powerful horses, which could carry a knight in his full armour with ease, and seemed full of spirit and fire. They were handsomely caparisoned, and the lads felt as they sprang on to their backs that they had never been so well mounted before.

"You would have made the journey more quickly and easily if you had had these horses three days ago," young De Burg laughed.

"Yes, indeed. There would have been no occasion to hide in the woods then. With our light weight on their backs they would have made nothing of the journey."

"You must not expect to see a castle," De Burg said presently, "though I call it one. In his early days the duke set himself to destroy the great majority of castles throughout Normandy, for as you know he had no little trouble with his nobles, and held that while the strength of these fortresses disposes men to engage either in civil war or in private feuds with each other, they were of no avail against the enemies of the country. My father, who is just the age of the duke, was his loyal follower from the first, and of his free will levelled his walls as did many others of the duke's friends, in the first place because it gave the duke pleasure, and in the second because, had only the castles of those opposed to the duke been destroyed, there would have been such jealousy and animosity on the part of their owners that matters would never have quieted down in the country. Thus it is that throughout the land you will find but few castles remaining. The nobles felt it strange at first to be thus dwelling in houses undefended against attack, but they soon learnt that it was far more convenient than to be shut up within massive walls, and the present dwellings are much larger and more comfortable than those of former days. The duke said rightly that the abolition of fortresses well-nigh doubled his fighting power, for that so many men were required to garrison them as to greatly diminish the number their lords could take with them into the field. You do not have castles in England, do you?"

"No, we live in open houses, and hold that it is far better and more pleasant to do so. There is no fighting between neighbours with us. The great earls may quarrel and lead their forces into the field, or may gather them against Danish and Norwegian pirates, but except on these occasions, which are rare, all dwell peaceably in their homes."

The horses were fresh, and the five miles quickly passed over.

"There is the house," De Burg said, pointing to a large building standing on an eminence. It was castellated in form, and much of the old building had been incorporated with the additions, but the outer wall had been pulled down and the moat filled up. Broad casements had replaced the narrow loopholes, and though the flag of the De Burgs still waved over the keep, which stood a little apart from the rest, the family no longer dwelt in it.

"It is chiefly used as a storehouse now," Guy De Burg explained; "but there, as you see, the old loopholes still remain, and in case of trouble it might be held for a time. But of that, however, there is little chance; the duke's hand is a heavy one, and he has shown himself a great leader. He has raised Normandy well-nigh level with France, and so long as he lives and reigns there is no fear of domestic trouble."

The gate stood open and they rode into a courtyard, when several men came out and took the horses. Guy de Burg ran up a broad staircase to the entrance of the house itself, and passed beneath a noble entrance with a lofty pointed arch supported by clustered pillars. Inside was a spacious hall paved with stone, and from this De Burg turned into an apartment whose walls were covered with rich hangings. Here a lady was at work embroidering, surrounded by several of her maids similarly engaged. A girl some fourteen years old was reading a missal, while the master of the castle was sitting in a chair with low arms, and was playing with the ears of a hound whose head was lying on his knee.

"Well, Guy, what is your news?" he asked as his son entered. "Half an hour since I received a message from the duke desiring me to appear with ten men-at-arms in their best trappings to ride with him to Eu. Is Conrad of Ponthieu giving trouble again, and who are these young gentlemen with you?"

Guy went down on one knee to kiss his father's hand, and then did the same to his mother, then he said, "I will with your permission answer the last question first, father. My friends are young Saxon thanes, pages to Earl Harold, and at present guests of the duke."

"You are bearers, doubtless, of some message from the king to our duke?"

"No, my lord," Beorn said, "we were bearers of a message from Earl Harold."

"It is to meet him, father, that we are to ride to Eu to-morrow. He has been wrecked on the shores of Ponthieu, and has been foully imprisoned and even fettered by Count Conrad. Beorn and Wulf escaped from the prison and brought the news to the duke, who this afternoon dispatched Fitz-Osberne and Warren at full speed to bid the count at once free his prisoners, and deliver them over to him at Eu under pain of his direst displeasure."

"Harold in Normandy and a prisoner! This is strange news indeed. We shall surely make him welcome, for he is in all respects a great man, and save our own duke has a reputation second to none in Europe."

Wulf thought as he looked at the speaker that at least he had no second thought in his mind. It was a frank honest face, martial in its outline, but softened by a pleasant smile.

He had spoken in a genial tone of affection to his son, and Wulf thought, that although no doubt he was ready to take the field at the summons of his lord, he preferred a quiet life in this stately home.

"This is news for you, wife," he went on. "You will have to furbish up your gayest attire, for we shall be having grand doings in honour of this great English earl, and our dames will have to look their best in order that he may carry home a fair report of them to the Saxon ladies. And how did you manage to escape, young sirs, and when did you arrive with the news?"

Beorn, who as the elder was specially addressed, shortly related the story of their escape and journey.

"You have done well," the baron said when he had concluded. "Guy, you may learn from these young Saxons that even pages may be called upon to do work of more importance than handing wine-cups and standing behind their lord on state occasions. Had it not been for their readiness and courage Harold might have lain weeks in prison, maybe months, while the count was striving to wring the utmost ransom from him. The lads would doubtless have been slain had they been detected in making their escape or overtaken on the way, and the attempt was therefore one that required courage as well as devotion to their lord. I doubt not that you would exhibit both qualities did opportunity offer, but I question whether you could have walked the distance they did, and that on such scanty fare. We Normans are too apt to trust wholly to our horses' legs to the neglect of our own, and although I have no doubt that you could ride as far as a horse could carry you, I warrant that you could hardly have performed on foot the journey from Beaurain in twice the time in which they did it. They must have exercised their legs as well as their arms, and although in a campaign a Norman noble depends upon his war horse both on the march and on the day of battle, there may often be times when it is well that a knight should be able to march as far as any of the footmen in the army. Well, Agnes, and what have you to say to these Saxon youths? Methinks your eyes are paying more attention to them than to your missal."

"I can read my missal at any hour, father, but this is the first time that I have seen young Saxon nobles. I thought there would have been more difference between them and us. Their hair is fairer and more golden and their eyes bluer, but their dress differs in no way from our own." She spoke in a matter-of-fact and serious air, as if it were a horse or a dog that she was commenting upon, and both Beorn and Wulf smiled, while Guy laughed outright.

"It is little wonder that their attire is like ours, Agnes," he said, "seeing that they were furnished with it by the duke's orders. You do not suppose that after being tossed about on the sea and well-nigh drowned in landing, and being made prisoners, and then travelling through the country and sleeping in the woods, Beorn and Wulf would arrive here with their garments new and spotless. That would indeed have been a miracle."

"But, indeed," Beorn said, "our garments differ not greatly from those we now have on, for Norman fashions are prevalent at King Edward's court, and we had no choice but to conform to them. Your language is always spoken there, and methinks that were you to visit Westminster you would see but little difference between King Edward's court and that of your own duke."

"And your sisters, do they too dress like us?"

"Queen Edith's ladies dress like her in Norman fashion, but away from the court the attire is different and more simple. Sisters, Wulf and I have none; we are orphans both, and wards of Earl Harold, who holds our estates until we are of age to take the oaths to him and to lead our men in battle."

"And will you be barons like my father, or counts, or simple knights?"

"We shall be none of these things, Lady Agnes. We have our great earls as in France you have your great dukes, but below that we have no titles. We are thanes, that is land owners, who hold their land direct from our earls. Some have wider lands than others, but as free thanes we are all equal. As to knights, we have not in England the titles and ceremonies which are so much thought of in France and in other courts."

"That is a pity," the girl said gravely, "for the vows of knighthood make a knight courteous and gentle to enemies and friends alike."

"Or rather, Agnes," her mother put in, "they should do so; but in truth, looking round at the cruel wars we have had in Normandy, I do not see that men have been more gentle or courteous than they would have been had they never taken the vows or had knightly spurs buckled on; and in truth it seems to me from the news of what has taken place beyond the sea, that in the civil troubles they have had in England men are much more gentle with each other, and foes are far more easily reconciled than with us in Normandy, who are supposed to be bound by the laws of chivalry. Had our duke been cast upon the shores of England as Harold has been cast upon that of Ponthieu, I think that he would not have been so dishonourably treated by one of the English thanes as Harold has been by Count Conrad. When Godwin and his sons returned from the exile into which they had been driven, and again became all powerful, there was not, as I have heard from your father, a single drop of blood shed, nor any vengeance taken upon the men who had brought about their exile. It would have been very different had such things happened here."

"You speak rightly, wife. The English are of a more gentle disposition than we are, though nowise backward in battle. But now, Guy, it is time that you were returning. You have already made a longer stay than usual. I shall see you again to-morrow when we start for Eu. Young sirs, I hope that on your return you will often ride over here when your lord does not require you. We shall always be pleased to see you, and although the forest lies some miles away, Guy can show you good hunting, though not so good as that which, as I hear, you can get in England, where the population is not so thick as it is in this part of Normandy."

The horses were brought round, and the three lads rode into Rouen just as night was falling.

Long before daybreak there was a stir in the streets of the city, as parties of knights and nobles rode in with bodies of their retainers in obedience to the orders of the duke. All in the palace were awake early. A hasty breakfast was eaten, while just as the sun rose the duke mounted his horse, and at the head of an array, composed of some twenty barons and knights and four hundred men-at-arms, rode out of the city.

"There is a good deal more pomp and show here than there was when we rode with Harold from London," Wulf said. "In truth these Norman nobles make a far braver appearance in their armour and robes, and with their banners carried behind them, than we do. Were the king himself to ride in state through London he would scarce be so gaily attended."

"Duke William does not look as if he cared for show," Beorn said.

"Nor does he," Guy, who was riding beside them, put in. "For himself he is simple in his tastes, but he knows that the people are impressed by pomp, and love to see a brave cavalcade, therefore he insists on the observance of outward forms; and his court here on state occasions vies, as they tell me, with that of Henry of France."

"Where shall we rest tonight?" Wulf asked. "Methinks from the appearance of the sky that we shall have rain, and unless we sleep under shelter, many of these fine robes that we see are like to be as much dabbled in mud as were those in which we arrived."

"We shall sleep in no town, for there is no place on the road between this and Eu that could receive so large a party; but soon after we rode out yesterday a train of waggons with tents and all else needful started from Rouen, and half-way to Eu we shall find the camp erected and everything in readiness for our reception."

This was indeed the case. The camp had been erected in a sheltered valley, through which ran a stream that supplied the needs of man and horses. The tents were placed in regular order, that of the duke in the centre, those of his chief nobles in order of rank on either side. Behind was a line for the use of the court officials, pages, and knights of less degree, while the soldiers would sleep in the open. As the party rode up a chamberlain with three or four assistants met them. Each was provided with lists containing the names of all the duke's following, and these were at once conducted to the tents alloted to them, so that in a few minutes all were housed without the slightest confusion or trouble. The squires of the knights and nobles and the attendants of the officers and pages at once took the horses and picketed them in lines behind the tents, rubbing them down and cleaning them with the greatest care, and then supplying them with forage from the piles that had that morning been brought in from the neighbouring farms. Fuel in abundance had also been stacked. A number of cooks had come on with the tent equipage, and supper was already prepared for the duke and his party, while animals had been slaughtered and cut up, and the men-at-arms soon had the joints hanging over their bivouac fires.

"This is all wonderfully well managed, Beorn," Wulf said. "I doubt whether it could be done so well and orderly with us at home."

"What does it matter?" Beorn said contemptuously. "It makes no difference whether one sups five minutes after arrival or an hour."

"It matters nothing, Beorn; but what is but a question of an hour's waiting in a small party is one of going altogether supperless to bed when it is a large one. The Normans have been constantly fighting for the last twenty years, and you see they have learned how important it is that everything should be regular and orderly. If they manage matters with a large force as well as they do with a small one, as it is probable that they do, see what an advantage it gives to them. Were two armies to arrive near each other with the intention of fighting in the morning, and one knew exactly what to do, and could get their food in comfort and then lie down to rest, while the other was all in confusion, no one knowing where he should go or where to bestow himself, and, being unable to obtain food, forced to lie down supperless, the first army would obtain a great advantage when they met the next morning, especially if it had breakfasted well while the other went into the fight still fasting. Look at ourselves how weak we were that morning when we had lain down hungry and got up fasting, while on the morning when the woman gave us that food, simple as it was, we stepped out boldly and in spirits."

"That is true enough, Wulf, but you know that among us it is said that Earl Harold is always most careful for the comfort of his soldiers."

"Yes, the earl always thinks of those around him. As I have never been in the field I know not what the arrangements are, but I cannot think they would be so well ordered in a great gathering of Englishmen, or that we should manage matters as well as the Normans with all their experience have learnt to do."

"Well, Wulf," Beorn laughed, "you had best study the matter, and then ask the earl to appoint you to take charge of the arrangements when he takes the field."

"One could hardly have a more useful office," Wulf said earnestly; "but it would need a man of experience and of high rank and position, for our Saxon thanes are not accustomed to discipline as are these Norman barons, and only one of great authority could induce them to observe regulations and carry out any plan in due order."

Beorn nodded. "That is true enough, Wulf, and it is therefore clear that a good many years must pass before you can properly fill the post of chief chamberlain to the army. For myself, I shall be well content to do what fighting is required, and to leave all these matters in your hands."

"Yes; but it can't be left in the hands of one officer," Wulf said warmly, "unless all give their aid willingly to carry out his plans."

"Well, you need not be angry about it, Wulf. There will be time enough for that when you get to be grand chamberlain. You know what the Saxon thanes are—how ease-loving, and averse to trouble themselves with aught save the chase. I would as soon marshal a flock of sheep in military order and teach each to keep its place as get the thanes to conform to strict orders and regulations."

"And yet, Beorn," said Baron De Burg, who had just entered the tent unnoticed by them in order to speak to his son, who with another page shared it with them, "unless all will conform to strict orders and regulations an army is but a mere gathering of armed men, animated not by one will, but by as many wills as it contains men. Such an army may be valiant; every man may be a hero, and yet it may be shattered to pieces by another which gives itself up wholly to the direction of one will. That is why we Normans have so badly beaten the French. Every mail has his place in battle. He charges when he is ordered to charge, or he is held in reserve the whole day, and the battle ended without his ever striking a blow. We may fret under inaction, we may see what we think chances of falling upon the enemy wasted, but we know that our duke is a great leader, that he has a plan for the battle and will carry it through, and that disobedience to his orders would be an offence as great as that of riding from the field. Hence we have learned to obey, and consequently we have always been victorious against men as brave as ourselves, but each obeying his own feudal lord, and so fighting in detached bodies rather than as a whole. Your young companion is in the right. In a duel between two men strength and skill is everything; in a struggle between two armies obedience to orders is a virtue even higher than bravery and skill at arms. Where is Guy?"

"He is in attendance on the duke, my lord," Beorn said. "We presented ourselves also at his tent, but he told us that he required no duty from us."

"Let him come to my tent when he returns," the baron said; "that is as soon as he has finished supper. I shall be glad if you will also come, unless the duke sends for you, which methinks he is not likely to do. He is in thoughtful mood to-day, and will probably be alone."

Two or three other knights were assembled in Baron de Burg's tent when the three lads went in. De Burg said a few words to his companions, explaining who they were, and then continued his conversation with the others. Beorn and Wulf, as they stood behind the chairs and listened to the talk, could not help being struck with the difference between it and the conversations they had heard at the houses of Saxon thanes.

With Harold they had been accustomed to hear matters of state touched on. The church and the struggle going on between the Norman prelates and monks on the one hand and the English clergy on the other was one that was frequently talked over, as were also the projects Harold had at heart for encouraging the spread of education and raising the condition of people generally. At the houses of the thanes, however, the evenings were passed in feasting and song, and it was seldom that there was anything like discussion upon general affairs. Indeed, between men heated with wine and accustomed to state their opinions bluntly anything like friendly argument was well nigh impossible. De Burg and his companions made no allusion at all to public affairs, but discussed gravely and calmly, and with a courteous respect for each other's opinions, questions connected with the art of war, hunting, the changed conditions brought about by the demolition of castles, the improvements gradually being introduced in armour, and other kindred topics. The other nobles were men of about the same age as De Burg, and although the latter's page from time to time carried round wine the goblets were rarely emptied.

Certain topics were touched upon only to be dropped at once, and Wulf saw that subjects upon which there was any disagreement among them were carefully avoided.

When the boys returned to their tent Wulf said, "Their talk reminds me of the evenings I spent with the prior, his almoner, and two or three other monks, rather than of those at the houses of Saxon thanes."

Beorn nodded. "I am not so much against our customs of feasting and merriment as you are, Wulf, and should not care to spend my evenings often in listening to such grave talk, but truly these Norman barons and knights are far more courteous in their speech than our own thanes, and seem to care but little for the wine cup. I admit that such men must be far wiser advisers for a king than are our Saxons, saving of course Harold and his brothers."

"The Normans are not all so abstemious as my father and those you saw with him," Guy laughed. "Listen. You can hear songs and loud laughter from many of the tents, ay, and might hear quarrels too did you listen long enough. But those you saw were all men high in the confidence of the duke. They have fought together under his banner in many a field, and are all powerful barons. They are content to hold their own, and have nothing to gain at the expense of others. Their value is well established, and I believe that all of them would be well pleased were they never called upon to set lance in rest again. Methinks this evening they avoided all public questions chiefly because we were present; and you see no word was spoken of the unexpected accident that has thrown Harold on our shores, although it must have been in all their minds; and doubtless they talked it over as they rode hither to-day. I should not be surprised if my father had us in his tent for the very reason that your being there would prevent more being said about it. I do not suppose any of them know exactly what is in the duke's mind — possibly he has not even made it up himself; and it is assuredly wise here in Normandy to express no strong opinion until the duke's own mind is manifest."

"I daresay you are right, Guy. I rather wondered why your father had asked us as well as you to his tent when he had others with him; but it is like enough that he thought our presence would prevent any discussion on delicate topics."

The next morning the cavalcade mounted early, and in the afternoon rode into the fortress of Eu. It stood upon the river Bresle, and had, previous to the conquest of Ponthieu, been the frontier guard of Normandy on the north. It lay only some ten miles from the spot where the Saxon galley had been wrecked. A messenger had arrived there early in the day from Fitz-Osberne saying that Conrad of Ponthieu had assented to the demand of the duke for the surrender of his captives, that these had been at once released from their confinement, and were now honourably entertained. They would start on the following morning from Beaurain, and would be accompanied by Conrad, who desired to come to Eu to pay his respects to the duke.

Although it had been certain that Conrad would not venture to refuse the command of his powerful over-lord, Wulf and Beorn were greatly delighted to hear that Harold and his companions had at once been released from their imprisonment, and that they would so speedily arrive at Eu. In the afternoon of the following day a messenger arrived stating that the cavalcade was but an hour's ride away, and preparations were at once made to receive it with all honour.

The garrison of the castle in their bravest attire lined the courtyard, hangings brought from Rouen were disposed round the walls of the great hall, two chairs of state were placed on the dais, the men-at-arms who had come from Rouen were drawn up on either side of the great entrance, and here William with his nobles assembled when the cavalcade approached the castle.

The procession was headed by the Norman men-at-arms of Fitz-Osberne and Warren. After them rode Conrad of Ponthieu with Harold by his side. Both carried hawks on their wrists, and were, apparently, on the most amiable terms. Behind them rode Harold's brother and nephew and the two Norman barons; they were followed by the Saxon thanes and the officers of the count's household. Behind these came on foot the Saxons of inferior degree who had been left at St. Valery, and who had by Conrad's orders been sent to join the cavalcade where it crossed the Somme at Abbeville; the procession was closed by a strong body of the count's men-at-arms. They rode through the double line of spearmen until they reached the entrance. Then as Harold dismounted, the duke descended the steps and embraced him with the warmest expressions of satisfaction at thus meeting the most illustrious of Englishmen.

Harold replied in suitable terms, and the duke then turned to Conrad and thanked him warmly for having acceded to his request.

Ponthieu was but newly conquered, and might yet be a thorn in the side of Normandy in the event of a renewal of war with France. It was therefore to William's interest to treat Conrad's obedience to his orders as if it had been a voluntary submission, and to ignore his discourteous treatment of his captives. In order to eradicate all sense of injury on the part of his vassal, he not only paid him the ransom for Harold but gave him a considerable grant of territory. The duke now presented his nobles and principal officers to Harold, and then with his arm placed familiarly on his guest's shoulder led him into the hall, and placed him in the chair of state beside his own, other seats being placed for Wulfnoth and Hakon and for some of the principal Norman barons, while the rest mingled with the Saxon thanes in the body of the hall. As soon as the reception was over Wulf hurried out into the courtyard to speak to Osgod.

"Right glad am I to see you again, Osgod; I have been troubled as to how you were faring."

"In truth we have fared badly enough, master; we have been working like beasts of burden, without having food that would suffice for an ass. However, it was not for long, and will do us no harm, though there are more than one of those fellows at St. Valery with whom I would gladly have ten minutes play with cudgel or quarter-staff. You may guess how surprised we were yesterday evening when we were suddenly called out from the shed where we were sleeping, and with many professions of regret and apology for our treatment conducted to better quarters, where a good honest meal was set before us, and we were then told that the duke himself had just arrived at Eu, and that Harold and all his following were there to be given up to him. We had fresh rushes for our beds, and a hearty breakfast this morning, and were then placed in boats and taken up to Abbeville. We had been there but an hour when the earl arrived with the thanes, and glad were we, as you may imagine, to see his face again. They stopped there for an hour to rest their steeds and to dine, and then we marched hither as you saw. I had missed you and Beorn from Harold's party, and made shift to approach the earl and humbly ask him what had become of you. 'No harm has befallen your master and his friend, good fellow,' the earl said. 'They have indeed done me good service, for they made their escape from Beaurain and carried the news of our detention to Duke William, and it is thus that we have all obtained our liberty.' You seem to have fared bravely, Wulf, judging from your attire."

"Yes, we were in sore plight when we arrived at Rouen, but the duke saw that we were provided with clothes and with horses for our journey here."

At this moment an attendant came out from the hall and informed Wulf that the duke desired speech with him. Beorn was already at the entrance, and they were conducted on to the dais.

"Here are your two pages," the duke said to Harold. "I hold myself to be greatly their debtor for having carried me the news that has brought about this meeting, and given me the pleasure of having you as my guest. They are faithful lads and quick-witted, for no men could have carried out the mission better or more promptly than they did."

"Still more am I indebted to them," Harold said as he held out his hand to the two lads, who bent on one knee while they kissed it. "I knew not of their going until I learnt from your barons that they had reached Rouen with the news. They are wards of mine, and although at one time my pages they have ceased to be so for more than a year, and have both been down upon their estates learning the duties of their station, which I deemed better for them than wasting their time and getting into mischief at court."

The duke nodded. "The result shows that your course was a wise one. At court youths learn but little good. The atmosphere is not healthy for men still less for boys, and these youths will shortly be of an age when they will be fit to render men's service, as indeed they have already done." The lads now retired from the dais.

"It has been a fortunate week's work for us," Beorn said. "We have obtained the freedom of our lord and have gained his approbation and that of Duke William; though, indeed, it matters not greatly as to the duke."

"I don't know, Beorn; one cannot look into the future, and there is no saying what may happen. Anyhow, even now it may be of advantage to us. Honourably as the duke is treating Harold, the earl is still wholly in his power, and until we hear something of his intentions we are all just as much prisoners as we were to Conrad, although I admit the captivity is a very much more pleasant one."

CHAPTER VII. — THE OATH.

From Eu the party travelled back to Rouen where there were feastings and entertainments in honour of Harold. Nothing could be more courteous than the duke's manner to his guest. He professed an almost fraternal affection for him, and handsome lodgings were assigned in the town to his thanes. A solemn court was held, at which Harold was knighted by William himself with much state and ceremonial, according to the rites of chivalry, which had then been but recently introduced, and had not as yet extended into England. There were great hunting parties in the forest, and to all outward appearance the friendship between William and Harold was of the warmest and most sincere nature. Harold himself was really gratified at the pains that William took to show the esteem in which he held him, and his thanes were all well satisfied with the attentions bestowed upon them by the Norman barons.

Beorn and Wulf had nothing to do save to make friends with young Normans of their own age, to visit their castles and to join in the hunting parties. The duke lost no opportunity of showing the sincerity of the feelings of gratitude he had expressed to them for bringing him the news of Harold's presence in his dominions, and they were always specially invited to all court ceremonials, enjoying themselves exceedingly. Wulf occasionally expressed his surprise to his companion that no word was said as to their return to England, but Beorn's answer always silenced him.

"The earl himself seems well satisfied, Wulf. Why should you be more anxious for him than he is for himself?"

Once indeed he replied, "Harold is of so open and generous nature, Beorn, that he would be the last person to suspect another of dishonourable motives. Moreover, it is not because he is apparently well content here that we must judge him to be without uneasiness.

Whatever he felt it would be impolitic to show it, and we see but little of him now save when in company of the Normans. He cannot but know that his presence is required in England."

It was a matter of satisfaction to Wulf that Walter Fitz-Urse was not at the court, he having a few weeks before returned to England, where he was again in the suite of the Norman bishop of London. He himself had become firm friends with Guy de Burg, and often rode over with him to his father's residence, where they hunted in the forest together or rode out with falcons on their wrists, Agnes de Burg often accompanying them on her pony.

Three weeks after their arrival at Rouen the Bretons broke out in insurrection, and the duke invited Harold to accompany him on an expedition to subdue them, courteously saying that he should obtain great advantage from the military experience of his guest.

Harold accepted the invitation, and with his thanes set out with the duke. Against the disciplined forces of Normandy the Breton peasants had no chance whatever in the open field, but their wild and broken country, well-nigh covered with forest, afforded them an opportunity for the display of their own method of fighting by sudden surprises and attacks, and they defended their rough but formidable intrenchments with desperate valour. Harold's experience gained in his warfare with the Welsh was of much utility, and the duke committed to his hands the formal command of the troops engaged, averring that he himself knew comparatively little of warfare such as this.

Harold conducted the operations with equal vigour and prudence. Stronghold after stronghold was attacked and captured, a small portion of the force only being engaged in active operations, whilst the rest were posted so as to repel the attempts of the Bretons to aid the besieged. By his advice clemency was always shown to the garrisons when the fortresses were stormed, and they were permitted to return unharmed to their people, bearing the news that the duke bore no ill-will towards them, and was ready to show mercy to all who laid down their arms. Wulf and Beorn were permitted to share in the assaults, and with the Saxon thanes followed Harold, as he led the way on foot up to the intrenchments at one point, while the duke with a party of his barons attacked at another. More than once the English banner was carried into the heart of the Breton fortress before the Normans had fought their way in, and on each of these occasions the duke warmly expressed his admiration for the courage of his English allies. At last there remained but one formidable stronghold to be captured, and so strong was this by nature, and so desperately defended, that for some time the efforts of the besiegers were fruitless.

One evening Guy de Burg had been with Wulf in his tent. Beorn was out spending the evening with some of his Norman friends. When Guy rose to go Wulf said that he would walk with him to his father's tent, which was situated some little distance away. As there had been strict regulations that none were to move about without arms, he buckled on his sword and put on his helmet before starting. Osgod, who was lying outside the tent, rose when they issued out and followed them at a short distance. They went along at the rear of the tents, when Wulf suddenly said:

"It seems to me that I hear sounds in the forest, Guy."

"De Launey's men are posted behind us," Guy said carelessly; "there is no fear of an attack."

"Not if they are vigilant," Wulf agreed. "But the Bretons have for some time abstained from night surprises, and De Launey's men may be keeping a poor watch."

Suddenly there was a loud cry, followed immediately by the Breton war-shout, and by a confusion of shouts, cries, and the sound of the clashing of arms.

The lads drew their swords and ran towards the scene of conflict, when, from some bushes a short distance from them, a number of wild figures sprung out. It was a party of the enemy who had made their way through De Launey's sleeping men unobserved, and who now, knowing that further concealment was useless, were rushing forward towards the tents. Wulf's first impulse was to turn back, but young de Burg, shouting his father's battle-cry, ran forward, and without hesitation Wulf followed him. A moment later they were engaged with the Bretons.

"Back to back, Guy!" Wulf exclaimed, as he ran his sword through the first man who attacked him.

He had scarcely spoken when Osgod ran up and joined them, and wielding the heavy axe he carried as if it had been a featherweight, struck down several of the Bretons who ventured within its swing.

Wulf defended himself as firmly, but had to shift his ground continually to avoid the blows of the heavy spiked clubs with which his assailants were armed. Presently he heard his name shouted, and an instant later a crash, as Guy de Burg was struck down.

"Stand over him, Osgod!" he shouted, and with a bound was beside his companion, cutting down a Breton who was about to thrust his spear into him. At the same moment a club descended on his helmet, bringing him for a moment to his knee. He sprang up again, Osgod striking his opponent to the ground before he could repeat his blow.

For two or three minutes the fight went on. Wulf received more than one stab from the Breton knives, as two or three of them often rushed in upon him at once, but each time when he was hard pressed Osgod's axe freed him from his assailants, for so terrible were the blows dealt by the tall Saxon that the Bretons shrank from assailing him, and thus left him free at times to render assistance to Wulf. But the combat was too unequal to last long. A pike-thrust disabled Wulf for a moment, and as his arm fell a blow from a club stretched him beside Guy. Osgod had also received several wounds, but furious at his master's fall he still defended himself with such vigour that the Bretons again fell back. They were on the point of attacking him anew, when there was a shout, and William and Harold, bareheaded as they had leapt from the table, and followed by a score or two of Norman barons and soldiers, fell upon the Bretons. The latter with cries of alarm at once fled.

By this time the Norman trumpets were everywhere sounding, and the troops hastening out to repel the attack, which a few minutes later ceased as suddenly as it began, the Bretons flying into the forest, where pursuit by the heavily-armed Normans was hopeless. Returning to the tents, the duke and Harold paused where Osgod, who had sunk to the ground as soon as the Breton attack had ceased, was sitting by the side of his master.

"Whom have we here?" the duke asked. "Whoever they are we owe our safety to them, Harold, for had it not been for the resistance they made, the Bretons would have been among our tents before we had time to catch up our arms. Bring a torch here!" he shouted; and two or three soldiers came running up from the tents with lights.

"Methinks it is one of my men," Harold said, and repeated the duke's question in Saxon.

"I am Osgod, my lord, the servant of Wulf of Steyning, who with his friend, Guy de Burg, lies here beside me, I fear done to death."

"I trust not, indeed," Harold said, stooping over the bodies.

At this moment the men came up with the lights. "By the rood," William exclaimed, "but they fought stoutly, whoever they are. The ground round them is covered with the bodies of these Breton rascals. There must be at least a score of them, while so far as I can see there are but three of our men. Who are they, Harold?"

"One is Guy, son of the Baron de Burg," Harold replied. "Another is young Wulf, and this stout fellow is his man."

"Right gallantly have they done," the duke exclaimed, "and I trust that their lives are not spent. Let someone summon De Burg here quickly. Carry his son to his tent, and bid my leech attend at once to his wounds and to those of these brave Saxons."

"I will carry Wulf to his tent myself," Harold said, raising the lad and carrying him off, while four soldiers followed bearing Osgod. They were laid down together in Wulf's tent. As the young thane's helmet was removed, he opened his eyes and looked round in bewilderment as he saw, by the light of the torches, Harold and several others standing beside him.

"What has happened?" he asked faintly.

"The best thing that has happened is that you have come to yourself and are able to speak, Wulf," Harold said. "But do not try to talk, lad, until the leech comes and examines your wounds. You have done us all a rare service to-night, for thanks to the carelessness of De Launey's men, most of whom have paid for their error with their lives, we should all have been taken by surprise had it not been for the brave stand you made. Now we will take off your garments and see where you are wounded. They seem to be soaked everywhere with blood."

"I received three or four gashes with their knives," Wulf said feebly, "and I think a spear wound. How are the others?"

"I know not about Guy," Harold said, "but your man is able to speak, and has not, I hope, received mortal injuries."

"Don't trouble yourself about me, Master Wulf," Osgod put in. "I have got a few pricks with the knaves' knives, and a spear-thrust or two, but as I was able to keep on my feet until the earl arrived with help, I think the wounds are of no great consequence."

"If aught happens to me," Wulf said to Harold, "I pray you to see to him, my lord, and to take him as one of your own men. Had it not been for him the Bretons would have made short work of us."

He could barely utter the words, and again became insensible from loss of blood.

When he recovered the leech was kneeling beside him, pouring oil into his wounds and applying bandages.

"Do not try to talk," he said quietly, as Wulf opened his eyes. "Lie quite still, the least movement might cause your wounds to break out afresh. They are serious, but I think not of a mortal nature."

"Guy?" Wulf whispered.

"He is in a more perilous condition than you are, but it is possible that he too may live. As for your man here, I have as yet but glanced at his wounds; but though cut sorely, I have no fear for his life. Now drink this potion, and then go off to sleep if you can."

Wulf drank off the contents of the goblet placed to his lips, and in a few minutes was fast asleep. When he woke it was broad daylight, and Beorn was sitting by his side. The latter put his finger to his lips.

"You are not to talk, Wulf. The leech gave me the strictest orders when he was here a short time since, and said that you seemed to be doing well. Osgod he says will surely recover, and be none the worse for the letting out of some of his blood. The Bretons were too hasty with their strokes, and although he has a dozen wounds none of them are serious. Guy de Burg is alive, but as yet the leech can say nothing. It has been a bad business. It seems that De Launey's men were most of them killed whilst they were asleep. The bodies of the sentries were found at their posts, but whether they were asleep, or whether, as is thought more likely, their foes stole up and killed them before they had time to utter a cry, we know not. The Bretons attacked at two or three other points, but nowhere with such success, though many Normans have fallen. Everyone says that the party which passed through De Launey's men would have reached the tents and probably killed most of those in them had they not stopped while some of their number attacked you and Guy de Burg. The duke and Harold have both said that your bravery saved us from a great disaster. I would that I had been with you, but the tent I was in was the farthest along the line, and the Bretons were in full flight before we came upon the scene."

Presently the Baron de Burg came to the side of the pallet on which Wulf was lying. "I cannot say that I owe you the life of my son," he said, laying his hand gently upon Wulf's, "for I know not as yet whether he will live, but he was sensible when we brought him to my tent, and he told me that you had stood over him and defended him from the Bretons until you too fell. He was sensible all the time, though unable to move."

"It was Osgod who did most of the fighting, my lord," Wulf said.

"He did much, Wulf, and it will be my pleasure to reward him, but the duke, who is full of admiration at the slaughter done by three alone, has caused the bodies to be examined. Twelve of them were killed with axe wounds, nine by sword wounds. Guy tells me that he knows that only two fell to his sword, therefore you must have slain seven. Truly a feat that any man might be proud of, to say nothing of a lad of your age. Guy is anxious to have you with him, and the leech said that if you keep quiet to-day, and none of your wounds break out afresh, it will do you no harm to be carried to my tent."

Accordingly the next day Wulf was carried across to Lord de Burg's, and his pallet set down by the side of Guy's. The latter was a little better, and the leech had faint hopes of his recovery. His right arm had been broken by a blow with a club, and so badly fractured that it had already been taken off near the shoulder. His most dangerous wound was a pike-thrust on the left side, which had penetrated his lungs. He smiled faintly as Wulf was placed by his side. Wulf tried to smile back again, but he was too much shocked at the change in his friend's appearance. His cheeks had fallen in, and his face was deadly pale. His lips were almost colourless, and his eyes seemed unnaturally large. Wulf made an effort to speak cheerfully.

"We did not expect to come to this so soon, Guy," he said. "We have often talked about fighting, but we never thought that our first serious fight would end like this."

"You have nothing to regret," Baron de Burg said. "You have both done your duty nobly, and one of gentle blood can wish for no better end than to die doing his duty against great odds. God grant that you may both be spared, but if it be otherwise, death could not come to you more gloriously than in giving your lives to save your lords from surprise."

Wulf's recovery was comparatively rapid. He was greatly pleased when, a week after his removal, Osgod was brought into the tent by Harold. He was still pale and feeble, but was able to walk, and assured his young lord that he should soon be ready for another fight with the Bretons.

"There will be no more fighting," Harold said. "Yesterday their chiefs came in to make their submission and ask for mercy, and on this being granted their fortress has surrendered this morning. They will pay a heavy fine in cattle, and their two strongest fortresses are to be garrisoned by Norman troops. A considerable slice of their territory is to be taken from them. In a week I hope we shall all be on our way back to Rouen."

Guy was mending very slowly. Even yet the leech could not say with certainty that his life would be saved, and warned his father that in any case he would for a very long time be an invalid. In another week the camp was broken up. Wulf declared that he was well enough to sit a horse, but the leech insisted that he should be carried on a litter.

"In another fortnight," he said, "you may be able to ride, but it would not be safe to attempt to do so now. You are going on as well as could be wished, and it would be madness to risk everything by haste."

Accordingly he and Guy were transported in litters to the baron's residence, where Wulf steadily recovered his health and strength. Osgod, who had received a heavy purse of gold from the baron, had at the end of that time entirely recovered; Guy still lay pale and feeble on his couch.

"I scarcely wish to live," he said one day to his father. "I can never be a warrior now. What have I got to live for?"

"You have much to live for, Guy," his father said, "even if you never bestride a war-horse. You have made a name for yourself for bravery, and will always be held in respect. It is not as if you had been from your birth weak and feeble. You will in time, I hope, come to be lord of our estates and to look after our people, and be beloved by them; and, if you cannot yourself lead them in the field, you can see that they go well equipped, and do honour to your banner. There are other things besides fighting to live for."

"I would that you had had another son, father, and that Wulf had been my brother. I should not so much have minded then that I could not myself carry the banner of De Burg into the field."

"Had he been one of ourselves, Guy, that might have come about," his father said, "for if I have no other son I have a daughter. But this young Saxon has his own estates in his own country. He would not settle down here as a Norman baron, and I would not lose Agnes nor be willing that she should go from us to dwell in a foreign land. But no one can say what the future will bring about. The duke has promised one of his daughters to Harold, and should the marriage come off it will bind the two peoples more closely together. Besides, you know, Edward of England has promised to Duke William that he should succeed him."

"I was speaking to Wulf about that one day, father, and he said that Edward had no power to make the gift, for that the people of England chose their king themselves, and that Edward's promise would go for nothing with them. It is not with them as it is with us, where a prince can name his successor."

"That may be Saxon opinion, Guy, but it is not Norman, and assuredly it is not the duke's; and friendly as are the relations between him and Harold, it is clear that until this question is settled no permanent friendship can be looked for between the two nations."

Wulf was sorry when the time came that he could no longer linger at Baron de Burg's chateau. The earl had more than once sent over to say that his presence was looked for at court as soon as he was sufficiently recovered to attend there, but he stayed on until he felt so thoroughly strong and well that he could not make his health any longer an excuse. On leaving, De Burg and his wife both pressed him to come over whenever he could spare time.

"You know, Wulf," the former said, "how warm is the affection Guy has for you, and he will look very eagerly for your visits. Just at present he has very few pleasures in life, and chief among them will be your comings. We are all dull here, lad, and Agnes will miss you sorely."

"I will ride over whenever I can. I should be ungrateful indeed did I not do so, after the great kindness you and Lady de Burg have shown me; but even putting this aside I will come every day if I can, if only for half an hour's talk with Guy."

"I am glad to see you back again, Wulf," Earl Harold said as the lad entered his room. "You look strong and well again, and might, methinks, have come to us before now."

"I could have done so, doubtless, my lord, but it pained me to leave Guy, who is still on his couch, and will, I fear, never be strong and well again."

"We heard but a poor account of him from the duke's leech," Harold said. "It is a sad thing; for one, who as a lad has shown such bravery, would have turned out a gallant knight. I should have let you linger there for some time yet, but the duke has frequently asked after you, and I thought it were best that you came over; though, in truth, there will be little for you to do here, and you will be able to ride and see your friend when you will."

"Are we likely to go back to England soon, my lord?"

"I trust it will not be long. I have spoken of it more than once to the duke, but he chides me for being weary of his company; which indeed I am not, for no man could have treated another better than he has done me. Still," he said, walking up and down the room, "I am impatient to be off, but I am no more free to choose my time here that I was at Beaurain. It is a velvet glove that is placed on my shoulder, but there is an iron hand in it, I know right well."

"Is there no possibility of escaping, my lord?"

Harold looked keenly at the boy. "No, Wulf, treated as I am as a guest I cannot fly without incurring the reproach of the basest ingratitude, nor even if I wished it could I escape. Under the excuse of doing me honour, there are Norman soldiers at the gate, and a Norman sentry stands at my door. I must go through with it now, and if need be promise all that William asks. This time there is nowhere to send you to fetch aid for me. You have heard, I suppose, that William has promised me his daughter in marriage?"

"Yes, my lord, I have heard it. Is the marriage to take place soon?"

Harold smiled. "The duke will not wish it to take place until he sees that he can secure my services by the marriage. If that time should never come I shall probably hear no more of it. Engagements have been broken off before now many a time, and absolution for a broken promise of that kind is not hard to obtain. You must attend the court this evening, Wulf."

Wulf bowed and withdrew, and in the evening attended the court in the suite of Harold. As soon as the duke's eye fell upon him he called him up.

"Messieurs," he said to the barons present, "this lad is Wulf, Thane of Steyning, and a follower of Earl Harold. He it was who, with the young Guy de Burg, and aided only by a Saxon man-at-arms, withstood the first rush of the Bretons, and so gained time by which I myself and my barons were able to prepare ourselves to resist the attack. Had it not been for them we should all have been taken by surprise, and maybe slain. The Saxon and the two lads, Wulf and De Burg, all fell wounded well-nigh to death, but not before twenty-one Bretons lay dead around them. This was indeed a feat of arms that any of you, valiant knights and barons as you are, might have been proud to perform.

"Already I had promised him any boon that in reason he may ask for having borne to me the news that Earl Harold, my honoured guest and brother-in-arms, had been cast on our shores, and I promise him now, that should at any time it happen that I have any power or influence in England, his estates shall remain to him and to his heirs free from all service or dues, even though he has withstood me in arms;—nay, more, that they shall be largely added to. Should such issue never arise, and aught occur to render him desirous of crossing the seas hither, I promise him a baron's feu as a token of my gratitude for the great service he rendered me; and I am well assured that, whether to a King of England or to a Duke of Normandy, he will prove himself a true and faithful follower. I call on you all here to witness this promise that I have made, and should there be need, to recall it to my memory."

The Normans above all things admired valour, and when Wulf, after kneeling and kissing the duke's hand, retired shamefacedly to a corner of the room, where he was joined by Beorn, one after another came up to him and said a few words of approbation.

"You have done well, young sir," Fitz-Osberne, one of the duke's most trusted councillors said to him. "The duke is not given to overpraise, and assuredly no one of your age has ever won such commendation from his lips. After making so fair a commencement, it will be your own fault indeed if you do not make a great name for yourself in the future. There is not one of us who was in the duke's camp that evening but feels that he owes you much for the few minutes' delay that saved us from being taken altogether by surprise. You are young, and may think but little of the promise the duke has given you this evening, but the day may come when you will find it stand you in good stead."

Harold said nearly the same thing to Wulf when he saw him the next morning.

"But there is no chance of the duke ever having power in England, my lord," Wulf said.

"I trust not, Wulf, but there is no doubt that his whole mind is bent upon obtaining the throne of England. He has spoken to me openly about it, and has more than hinted to me that I, if married to his daughter, would still, as Earl of Wessex, be the foremost man in the land next to its sovereign should he ever gain the kingdom."

"And what said you, my lord, if I may be so bold as to ask?"

"I said but little, lad. I am a prisoner, and I am well assured that I shall never return to England until William thinks that he can depend upon me. It is needful that I should return, and that quickly, for I hear that there is fresh trouble in Wales, and I have received an urgent message from the king to hasten to his side. It is hard to see what it is best to do."

Four days later a grand ceremony was announced to take place, but few knew what its nature was to be. That it was something beyond the ordinary was certain by the number of barons and knights that were bidden to attend. A dais was erected in the courtyard of the palace, and on this a table covered with a cloth was placed.

"I don't like this business," Wulf said to Beorn, as with the other Saxons they took their place near the dais. "There is something very mysterious about it, and I believe that at last we are going to see what William's full intentions are."

A religious ceremony was first held, and then the duke rose to his feet and addressed the barons. He first recalled to them the promise that Edward of England had made to him, and then went on: "The saints have worked in my favour," he said, "by sending here as my guest my well-beloved brother-in-arms, the great Earl of Wessex. Between us there is the closest friendship, and to cement and make even closer the bonds between us, he has become betrothed to my daughter, and through the lands I shall bestow upon her he will become a baron of Normandy. Relying upon his affection and friendship, I have called you here together to hear him swear in public that which he has already told me privately — that he will be my faithful feudatory, and will in all ways aid me to gain my lawful rights."

Harold changed colour. The matter had come upon him as a surprise. Doubtless he had in a vague way when discussing his future relations as son-in-law to the duke, expressed his warm friendship and a general willingness to be of service to him, but to be called upon to take an oath publicly was a different matter. Most of those present had taken oaths of allegiance to William and had broken them again and again, and William himself had not less frequently broken his feudal oaths to his suzerain, the King of France. But Harold was a man with a deep sense of religion, and did not esteem as lightly as these Norman barons an oath thus sworn; but he felt that he had fallen into a trap, and that resistance would but consign him to a prison, if not a grave.

He at once understood how hollow had been the pretended friendship of his host; but he was in William's power, and unless as a friend the duke would never permit so formidable a rival to quit his shores. As he hesitated he saw a movement on the part of the Norman knights near the dais, and understood that they had been previously informed of William's intentions, and were there to enforce them. Their brows were bent on him angrily as he hesitated, and more than one hand went to the hilt of the wearer's sword. There was no drawing back, and placing his hand on the table he swore the oath William had dictated. When he concluded William snatched the cloth from the table, and below it were seen a number of bones and sacred relics that had been brought from the cathedral.

Enlightened as Harold was, he was not altogether free from the superstitions of the age. For a moment he shuddered slightly and grew paler than before, then he drew himself up to his full height, and looked calmly into the exulting face of William.

"I call you all to witness," the duke said in a loud voice, "that Harold, Earl of Wessex, has taken a solemn oath upon the holy relics to be my faithful feudatory."

The shout that answered him was by no means universal, for there were many among the Norman nobles who were shocked at the base trick that the duke had played upon a guest for whom he had professed the warmest friendship. The Saxon thanes could scarce contain their expressions of indignation, but Harold as he sat down among them made a gesture commanding silence.

"We sail for England to-morrow night," he said in low tones. "The duke told me so as we came hither. The two ships will be in readiness for us to embark in the morning. I did not understand then the price I was to pay. Restrain yourselves now; when we are free men we can talk this over."

An hour later they returned to the palace, where there was a brief and formal interview between Harold and the duke. Both dissembled their real feelings. The duke said that he regretted that the King of England's wishes forced his guest to start so suddenly, and that he much regretted his departure. Harold thanked him for the hospitality he had shown him, but neither made any allusion whatever to the scene that had taken place in the courtyard. Wulf rode over to say good-bye to Guy and his father. The latter was walking up and down the hall with a gloomy face.

"I blush for what has taken place to-day, Wulf," he said. "Tell the earl that had we known what was going to occur there are few indeed who would have attended at the ceremony, and that I for one shall hold him in no way dishonoured if he breaks the vow that has thus been dishonourably extorted from him. It was a trick and a base one, and I would tell Duke William so to his face. What will men think of Norman faith when guests are thus tricked to their disadvantage?"

For an hour Wulf remained talking with the baron and his family.

"I hope to see you again, Wulf," De Burg said, as the lad rose to take leave. "Guy regards you as a brother, and though assuredly no Saxon will set foot on Norman soil after to-day's doings, we may yet meet again."

"I shall come over to England to see you, Wulf, if you come not here," Guy said. "I begin to think that I shall get over this, although I may never be really strong again. We shall often think and talk of you, Agnes and I; and I should like, of all things, to come and stay in your Saxon home."

"No one would be so welcome, Guy. If we are never to be brothers-in-arms as we once talked of, we shall surely be brothers in heart, whether absent or present."

A few more words and Wulf took leave of them all and rode back to Rouen. In the morning the duke accompanied Harold to the river bank and there took a courteous farewell of him. It is not probable that he thought for a moment that Harold would observe the oath, but he saw that its breach would be almost as useful to him as its fulfilment, for it would enable him to denounce his rival as a perjured and faithless man, and to represent any expedition against England as being a sort of crusade to punish one who had broken the most solemn vows made on the holy relics. Harold himself preserved his usual calmness of demeanour, and stood talking quietly to the duke while the latter's presents of hawks and hounds were taken on board the ship, and the Saxons, silent and sullen, had passed over the gangway. Then an apparently affectionate embrace was exchanged between the two rivals. Harold crossed on to the ship, the great sails were hoisted, and the two vessels proceeded down the river.

CHAPTER VIII. — TROUBLE WITH WALES.

Harold took his place on the poop as the vessel started, and remained looking fixedly at the duke, until the latter with the group of barons turned and entered the town.

"Farewell, William of Normandy," he said; "false friend and dishonoured host. How shall we meet next time, I wonder, and where?"

Hitherto the presence of the Norman attendants had prevented any private converse between Harold and his followers, but having the poop to themselves they now broke out into angry exclamations against the duke.

"It was an unworthy and unknightly trick," Harold said calmly; "but let us not talk of it now; it will be for the English people to decide the question some day, and for English bishops to determine whether I am bound by a vow thus extorted. Better at all events that I should be held for all time to have been false and perjured, than that the English people should fall under the Norman yoke. But maybe there will be no occasion for the oath ever to come in question, William of Normandy or I may die before the king, and then there will be an end of it. Let us talk of other things. Thank God we are free men again, and our faces are set towards England, where, from what I hear, we may have to meet open foes instead of false friends, and may have to teach the Welsh, once and for all, that they and their king cannot with impunity continually rise in rebellion against England.

"Well, Wulf, you are the only one among us who has brought back aught from Normandy, at least you and Beorn, for you have your horses and chains, and the promise of the duke to grant you a boon. But these are small things. You have gained great credit, and have shown yourself a gallant fighter, and have further promises from the duke."

"I care not for his promises," Wulf said hotly. "I hold him to be a dishonoured noble, and I would take naught from his hands."

"You are young yet, Wulf," Harold smiled, "and the duke's promise, made before his nobles, will be held binding by him if ever the time should come for you to claim it. Do not refuse benefits, lad, because you do not like the hands that grant them. You rendered him a service, and need feel no shame at receiving the reward for it. As soon as we return I shall take steps to raise you and Beorn to the full dignity of thanes, with all rights and privileges. My brother and my friends here can all testify to the service you rendered to us, for much as I may have to complain of the ending of my visit, it has at least been vastly better than our lot would have been had we remained in the hands of Conrad of Ponthieu. You are both very young to be placed in the position of rulers of your people, and in ordinary cases you would not have been sworn to thane's services for some years to come; but, as Earl of Wessex, I see good reason for departing from the rule on this occasion, and I think that my thanes here will all be of that opinion." There was a warm expression of approval from the Saxons. "Then as soon as we set foot on English soil we will hold a court, and invest you with your full rank."

They started from the mouth of the Seine, and as there was no nearer port than that from which they had sailed, Harold directed the masters of the ships to make for Bosham.

"It is like to be a fairer voyage than the last," he said, as with a light breeze blowing behind them they sailed out from the mouth of the Seine. "It will be longer, but assuredly more pleasant."

No incident whatever marked the voyage. The Saxons gave a shout of joy when they first made out the outline of the hills of the Isle of Wight, some twelve hours after leaving the mouth of the river; but it was not until eight hours afterwards that they entered the harbour of Bosham. As soon as the two Norman vessels were seen sailing up the quiet sheet of water, everywhere fringed with forest, boats put out to meet them, to ascertain the reason of their coming and to inquire for news of Harold and his companions. As soon as his figure was made out standing on the poop, one of the boats rowed off with the news, and by the time the vessels dropped anchor off Bosham the whole of the inhabitants had gathered on the shore, with loud shouts of joy and welcome.

As soon as they landed Harold and his companions proceeded at once to the church, where a solemn service of thanksgiving was held for their preservation from the dangers of the sea and for their safe return to England. As soon as the service was over Harold sent off two horsemen to bear to the king the news of his return, and to state that he himself would ride to London on the following day. Then the earl bestowed handsome presents upon the masters and crews of the ships that had brought them over, and gave into their charge hawks and hounds, rich armour, and other presents for the Duke of Normandy, and jewelled cups and other gifts to the principal barons of his court.

The gifts were indeed of royal magnificence; but Harold's wealth was vast, and, as he said to his brother, "We will at least show these Normans, that in point of generosity an English earl is not to be outdone by a Norman duke." As soon as these matters were attended to Harold held a court in the great hall of Bosham, and there received the oaths of fealty from Wulf and Beorn, and confirmed to them the possessions held by their fathers, and invested them with the gold chains worn by thanes as the sign of their rank. He afterwards bestowed a purse of gold upon Osgod, equal in value to the one he had received from the Duke of Normandy.

"Should aught ever happen to your master," he said, "come you to me and you shall be one of my own men, and shall not lack advancement in my service."

"In faith, Master Wulf," Osgod said after the ceremony, "my father warned me that the trade of a soldier was but a poor one, and that a good handicraftsman could gain far more money. He will open his eyes when I jingle these purses before him, for I might have hammered armour for years before I gained as much as I have done in the three months since I left England. I have enough to buy a farm and settle down did it so please me, and I have clothes enough to last me well-nigh a lifetime, and rings enough to set up a goldsmith's shop. For scarce one of the duke's barons and knights but followed his example, and gave me a present for my share in that little fight with the Bretons."

"As for the clothes, they will always be useful, Osgod; but were I you I would get a stout leathern bag and put the purses and rings into it, and bury them in some place known only to yourself, and where none are ever likely to light upon them. You have no occasion for money now, and we may hope that ere long all occasion for fighting will be over, and then, as you say, you can buy a farm and marry."

"I am going always to remain your man," Osgod said in an aggrieved tone.

"Certainly, Osgod, I should wish for nothing else. You will always be my friend, and shall have any post on the estates or in the house that you may prefer. There will be no occasion for you to farm your land yourself, you can let it, receiving the value of half the produce, and so taking rank as a landowner, for which you yourself may care nothing, but which will enable your wife to hold her head higher."

"I am not thinking of wives, my lord."

"Nonsense, Osgod, I want not to be called my lord."

"But you are a thane now and must be called so," Osgod said sternly; "and it would be ill-becoming indeed if I your man did not so address you. But I will take your advice about the gold, and when I get down to Steyning will bury it deeply under the roots of a tree. It will be safer there than if I buried it in my father's forge, for London is ever the centre of troubles, and might be sacked and burnt down should there ever be war between Mercia or Northumbria and Wessex."

"Heaven forbid that we should have more civil wars, Osgod."

"Amen to that, but there is never any saying. Assuredly Edwin and Morcar love not our earl, and as to Tostig, though he is his brother, he is hot-headed and passionate enough to play any part. And then there are the Normans, and there is no doubt the duke will have to be reckoned with. Altogether methinks my money will be safer under an oak-tree down at Steyning than at Westminster."

"You are right enough there, Osgod; by all means carry out your ideas. But there is the bell for supper, and I must go."

The next morning the party started at daybreak, and late that night arrived at Westminster. There were great rejoicings in London and throughout the south of England when it was known that the great earl had returned from Normandy. Much uneasiness had been felt at his long absence, and although accounts had come from time to time of the honour with which he had been treated by Duke William, many felt that his prolonged stay was an enforced one, and that he was a prisoner rather than a guest of the duke.

The king himself was as rejoiced as his subjects at Harold's return. Although in the early years of his reign he had been bitterly opposed to the powerful family of Earl Godwin, to whom he owed his throne, he had of late years learnt to appreciate the wisdom of Harold; and although still Norman in his tastes as in his language, he had become much more English at heart, and bitterly regretted the promise that he had years before rashly given to the Duke of Normandy.

Harold too had relieved him of all the cares of government, which he hated, and had enabled him to give his whole time and thought to religious exercises, and to the rearing of the splendid abbey which was his chief pleasure and pride. In his absence Edward had been obliged to attend to state business. He was worried with the jealousies and demands of the Earl of Mercia, with the constant complaints of the Northumbrians against their harsh and imperious master Tostig, and by the fact that the Welsh were taking advantage of the absence of Harold to cause fresh troubles. It was just Christmas when Harold returned, and the snow fell heavily on the night of his arrival at Westminster.

"It was lucky it did not come a few hours earlier, Beorn," Wulf said, as he looked out of the casement. "We had a long and heavy ride yesterday, and we could not have done it in one day had the snow been on the ground. I suppose there will be a number of court festivities over Harold's return. We have had enough of that sort of thing in Normandy, and I hope that Harold will let us return at once to our estates."

"Speak for yourself, Wulf; for myself I love the court, and now that I am a thane I shall enjoy it all the more."

"And I all the less," Wulf said. "Fifteen months ago we were but pages and could at least have some fun, now we shall have to bear ourselves as men, and the ladies of the court will be laughing at us and calling us the little thanes, and there will be no getting away and going round to the smithy to watch Osgod's father and men forging weapons. It will be all very stupid."

In a short time an attendant summoned them to breakfast, and here they sat down with the other thanes, Harold's wing of the palace being distinct from that of the king. The earl sat at the head of the table, and talked in undertones to his brother Gurth and two or three of his principal thanes. The personal retainers of the nobles stood behind their seats and served them with food, while Harold's pages waited on him and those sitting next to him.

"We were a merrier party in the pages' room," Beorn whispered to Wulf, for but few words were spoken as the meal went on.

"I think there is something in the air," Wulf said, "the earl looks more serious than usual. Generally the meals are cheerful enough."

As soon as it was finished Harold said, "The king will receive you all in half an hour, he desires to express to you his pleasure at your return home. After that I beg that you will again gather here, as I have occasion to speak to you."

The court was a more formal one than usual, the king's Norman functionaries were all present as were several ecclesiastics. Among them the Bishop of London, behind whom stood Wulf's old adversary, Walter Fitz-Urse. Earl Harold introduced his companions in captivity, the king receiving them very graciously.

"I am glad to see that you have all returned safely," he said. "The earl tells me that you have all borne yourselves well in the battles you have fought under the banner of my friend and ally Duke William of Normandy, and that you have proved to his countrymen that the English are in no whit inferior to themselves in courage. The earl specially recommended to me his newly-made thanes, Wulf of Steyning and Beorn of Fareham, who did him the greatest service by effecting their escape from the castle of Beaurain, and at great risk bearing the news of his imprisonment to Duke William. Wulf of Steyning, he tells me, gained the highest approval of the duke and his knights by a deed of bravery when their camp was surprised by the Bretons. The earl has informed me that in consideration of these services he has advanced them to the rank of thanes, and confirmed them in their father's possessions, and as service rendered to him is service rendered to me, I thus bestow upon them a token of my approval;" and beckoning to the young thanes to advance, he took two heavy gold bracelets from his arm, and himself fastened them on those of the kneeling lads.

When the ceremony was over, Harold's party returned to the room where they had breakfasted. It was an hour before the earl joined them.

"I have been in council with the king," he said, "and have thus been forced to keep you waiting. We heard when abroad that the Welsh were again becoming troublesome, but I find that matters are much worse than I had supposed. Griffith has broken out into open rebellion; he has ravaged all the borders, has entered the diocese of Wulfstan, the new Bishop of Worcester, and carried his arms beyond the Severn, laying waste part of my own earldom of Hereford. Edwin, who has just succeeded his father in the earldom of Worcester, is young and new to his government, and, moreover, his father was an ally of Griffith's. In any case, he needs far larger forces than those at his command to undertake a war with the Welsh. This time we must finish with them; treaties are of no avail they are ever broken on the first opportunity, and a blow must be dealt that will render them powerless for harm for generations to come.

"Therefore the king has commissioned me forthwith to act in the matter, not only as Lord of Hereford but as Earl of the West Saxons. Winter is upon us, and it will be impossible to undertake a regular campaign. Still a blow must be struck, and that quickly and heavily in order to stop the depredation and ruin they are spreading in the west counties. The preparations must be secret and the blow sudden. There is no time for calling out levies, that must be done in the spring. I must act only with mounted men. I have already sent off a messenger to Bosham to bid my housecarls mount and ride to Salisbury. They will number two hundred. I pray you all to leave at once for your estates, or to send an order by a swift messenger for your housecarls to ride to Salisbury, whither I myself shall proceed in three days. Will each of you give me the tale of the number of armed men who can take horse at an hour's notice."

Each of those present gave the number of housecarls in his service, and they all expressed their willingness to ride themselves, in order to get them ready the more speedily. The total mounted to three hundred and fifty men.

"That with my own two hundred will be well-nigh sufficient," Harold said; "but I will send off messengers at once to some of the thanes of Dorset and Somerset to join us at Gloucester with their men, so that we shall be fully a thousand strong, which will be ample for my purpose. I need not impress upon you all to preserve an absolute silence as to the object for which you are calling out your men. News spreads fast, and an incautious word might ruin our enterprise. There is no occasion for you all to accompany your men. Those of you who have been with me in Normandy will doubtless desire to stay for a while with your wives and families, and you may do equally good service by making preparations there for a more serious campaign in the spring. I beg these to send with their housecarls a trusted officer, and bid him place himself and his men under my orders."

The meeting at once broke up.

"I suppose you young warriors will bring your own men to Salisbury?" Harold said, as Wulf and Beorn came up to take their leave of him.

"Certainly, my lord," Beorn said. "We have neither family nor relations to keep us at home, and even if we had it would not suffice to keep us from following your banner."

"It will be a warfare like that in which you have been engaged across the sea," Harold said. "The Bretons you there fought with are kinsfolk of the Welsh, speaking the same language, and being alike in customs and in fighting. They trust to surprises, and to their speed of foot and knowledge of their wild country, rather than to hard fighting in the open plain. They have few towns to capture, and it is therefore hard to execute reprisals upon them. Like the Bretons they are brave, and fight savagely until the last, neither giving nor asking for quarter. They believe that their country, which is so wild and hilly as to be a great natural fortress, is unconquerable, and certainly neither Saxon nor Dane has ever succeeded in getting any foothold there. But when the spring comes I hope to teach them that even their wild hills are no defence, and that their habits of savage plundering must be abandoned or we will exterminate them altogether. But I have no thought of undertaking such a campaign now. Of course you will take that tall follower of yours with you, Wulf."

"I fear that he would not stay behind even if I ordered him to do so," Wulf laughed. "He will be overjoyed when I tell him there is a prospect of fighting again, and all the more if it is against kinsmen of the Bretons, against whom he feels a special grudge."

"The feeling would be more natural the other way," Harold said smiling, "seeing that he inflicted upon them far greater damage than he received. You will find fresh horses awaiting you. None of those that carried us from Bosham yesterday are fit for another such journey to-day."

Wulf had told Osgod the first thing in the morning that he could return to his family for a few days, only coming to the palace to serve his meals, and he now hurried away to the armourer's shop, where he found that but little work was going on, the men being absorbed in listening to Osgod's account of his adventures. Ulred and the men rose and saluted respectfully as Wulf entered.

"I am sorry to disturb you, Ulred," he said, "but I have come to fetch Osgod away again. That is if he would prefer riding with me to remaining quiet with you at home."

"If you are going, master, assuredly I am going with you," Osgod said. "I am dry with talking already, and father must wait for the rest of my story until I come back again. Are we going down to Steyning, my lord?"

"There first and afterwards elsewhere, but that is all I can tell you now. The horses are ready, and there is not a moment to lose. We must get as far on our way as possible before nightfall, for the matter is an urgent one."

"I am ready," Osgod said, girding on his sword and putting his cap on his head. "Good-bye, father. Tell mother I shall be back when I am back, and that is all I can say about it."

They reached Steyning at two o'clock on the following afternoon, and messengers were instantly sent round to the farms, bidding the men who were bound as housecarls to appear on horseback and armed, with two days' food in their wallets, an hour before daybreak next morning. Then a messenger was despatched with a letter to the prior of Bramber, telling him of Wulf's safe return, and begging him to excuse his coming over to see him, as he had ridden nigh a hundred and fifty miles in three days, and was forced to set out again at daybreak the next morning. As Wulf had hoped, the letter was answered by the prior in person, and to him Wulf related that evening the incidents of their stay in Normandy.

The prior shook his head.

"I have feared ever since I heard that Harold had fallen into the clutches of the duke, that he would never get off scot free, but would either have to pay a heavy ransom or make some concessions that would be even worse for England. It is a bad business, Wulf, a bad business. The church has ever been ready to grant absolution from oaths extracted by violence, but this affair of the relics makes it more serious, and you may be sure that William will make the most of the advantage he has gained. Harold is absolutely powerless to fulfil his oath. Neither he nor the king, nor any other man, can force a foreign monarch upon free England. And did Harold declare for the Duke of Normandy, powerful and beloved as he is, he would be driven into exile instantly. If he himself is elected king by the people, as there is no doubt whatever will be the case, he must needs obey their voice, and will have no choice between being King of England or an exile. Still it is unfortunate. He will be branded as a perjurer. William's influence may even induce the pope to excommunicate him, and although the ban would go for but little here, it would serve as an excuse for the other great earls to refuse to submit to his authority. Now tell me, how is it that you have to ride again so suddenly when but just arrived?"

"I can tell you, father, though I can tell no one else. Harold has ordered us to bring out our housecarls, and with them he means to deal a blow against the Welsh, who have been devastating our western counties. The expedition is to be secret and sudden, although against what point and in what manner the blow is to be struck Harold has kept his own counsel."

"The Welsh are ever a thorn in our side," the prior said, "and treaties with them are useless. I trust that Harold will succeed in thoroughly reducing them to obedience, for whenever there is trouble in the kingdom they take advantage of it, and are ready to form alliances with any ambitious earl who hoists the standard of revolt. And so you say Harold has already made you full thane? I am well pleased to hear it, if for no other reason than that it is good for people when they are ruled over by their own lord and not by a stranger; though I say nothing against Egbert, Harold's steward. Still no man can rule like the master himself."

At the first dawn of day Wulf mounted, and rode away from the palace followed by Osgod. He was clad now in the ringed armour, a suit of which he had had made of lighter material than usual. Only on the shoulders and over the chest was the leather of the usual thickness, elsewhere it was thin and extremely soft, and the rings did not overlap each other as much as usual. The weight, therefore, was much less than that ordinarily worn by thanes, although it differed but little from it in appearance. The helmet, also, was of stout leather, thickly covered with metal rings, and the flap fell down over the neck and ears, having a bar coming down in front to protect the nose.

Osgod's suit was thicker and heavier, and was similar to that of the forty men who were drawn up in two lines under the soldier whom Harold had sent down to train them. They were a stout set of young fellows, well mounted and armed, and as they broke into a cry of "Welcome to our thane," Wulf felt proud to command such a body.

"Thanks, my friends," he said heartily. "I am glad to see that not one is missing from your number, and feel sure that you will do credit to my banner."

They rode that day to Fareham, where they received a hearty welcome from Beorn, and starting in the morning with his troop of thirty men, reached Salisbury late that evening. They were met at the entrance to the town by one of Harold's officers, who conducted them to a large barn, where straw had been thickly strewn for the men to sleep on. The horses were fastened outside.

"Earl Harold arrived an hour since," the officer said, "and bade me tell you that he is lodged at the reeve's, where he expects you."

They found on arriving at the house that many of the thanes had already come in, and that some six hundred horsemen were bestowed in the town. On a great sideboard were pies, cold joints of meat, wine and ale, and each thane as he arrived helped himself to such food as he desired, and then joined the party gathered round Harold.

"We shall pick up another hundred or two as we march along tomorrow," Harold was saying when the two young thanes joined the group, "and shall have a good nine hundred men by the time we reach Gloucester, where I expect to find four or five hundred more awaiting us. I hear that our coming has made a great stir here in Salisbury, the citizens do not know what to make of so large a body of housecarls arriving in their midst. The reeve tells me that they were in some fear of being eaten out of house and home until they heard that we were to march on in the morning; after that they did their best for us, and have arranged that every man shall have his fill of meat and ale tonight, and again before starting."

Travelling as fast and as far as the horses could carry them, the force reached Gloucester. Here they received an even warmer welcome than had greeted them elsewhere, for the citizens had been greatly alarmed at the Welsh forays, and as soon as they knew that the great earl himself was with the troops they had no doubt that he had come to give them protection and to punish their enemies. The contingents from Somerset and Dorset had already arrived, and without the delay of a single day the troops again started.

The housecarls, although mounted, were not trained to fight on horseback. Their steeds were valuable only as enabling them to move with greater celerity across the country than they could do on foot, and to bring them fresh and in fighting condition to the scene of action. Once there they dismounted, and a portion being told off to look after the horses, the main body advanced on foot against the enemy.

There was yet a long ride before them. Following the Severn on its western side so as to avoid the passage of the Avon, they rode to Worcester, and then up through Dudley and Shrewsbury.

It would have been shorter to have passed through Hereford and Ludlow, but Harold feared that they might there come upon some marauding party of the Welsh, and any of these who escaped might carry the news across the border, when the fleet-footed mountaineers would quickly have conveyed it to the Welsh king at his castle at Rhuddlaw. Rhuddlaw, now a small village, is situated in Denbighshire, and was an important military position, situated as it was at no great distance from the sea, and commanding the Vale of Clwyd, the most important avenue into Wales from the north. From Shrewsbury they pushed forward as rapidly as possible to Rhuddlaw; but quickly as they had journeyed, the news of their coming was borne more rapidly. Griffith received the news an hour before their arrival, and mounting, rode down to the Avon and embarked on board ship.

Great was the disappointment of the earl and his followers when they found that the object of their long march across England had failed, and that the capture of the Welsh king, which would have put an end to the trouble, had been missed so narrowly. The castle was at once set on fire, the Welsh ships on the Avon were also given to the flames, and the very same day Harold led his troops away and by easy marches took them back to Gloucester. Here they halted. The housecarls from the south, who had never been in contact with the Welsh, were inclined to murmur among themselves at having been led back without striking a blow, but the contingents from the western counties, who had had experience of this wild warfare, told them that they might consider themselves fortunate.

"You know not what a war with these savages is," an old housecarl who had fought them again and again said to a listening group of Wulf's men. "You might as well fight with the evil spirits of the air as with them. Fight! there is no fighting in it, save when they have with them Danes from the North, or Norwegians. With these to bear the brunt of the battle the Welsh will fight valiantly in their fashion, but alone they know that they cannot withstand us for a moment. I have been after them a score of times, and it is a night-mare. You go up hills and through forests, you plunge into morasses, you scramble up precipices; you are wet, you are hungry, you are worn out, but never do you catch sight of one of them.

"Now and then, as you wind along the face of a hill, rocks will come thundering down; in the woods and swamps you hear their mocking yells and laughter. At the end of the day you drop down where you halt, and then just as you fall off to sleep there is a wild yell, and in a moment they are swarming among you, slashing and ripping with their long knives, crawling on the ground and springing upon you, getting among the horses and hamstringing or cutting them open. By the time those of you that are alive have got together they have gone, and all is so quiet that were it not for the scattered bodies you might believe that it was all a dream. Two or three times before morning the attack will be repeated, until you are forced to keep under arms in military array. As soon as it is light you recommence your march, and so it goes on day after day, until at last, worn-out and spent, and less in strength by half than when you started, you gather under the shelter of the walls of one of the border towns.

"I should have been glad indeed if we had caught their king, for if he had been held hostage in London we might have had peace; but well content am I that Harold has abstained from entering upon a campaign which, terrible as it is even in summer, would be beyond endurance of the strongest in winter."

"Well, for my part," Osgod, who was one of the listeners, remarked, "I would rather go on by myself and take the chance of getting a good blow at some of these wild men than ride all the way back to Steyning to be laughed at by the women there, as brave soldiers who have marched across England and back and never unsheathed their swords. Nor will I believe that Earl Harold can intend so to make a laughing-stock of us. The Bretons were just as active as are these Welshmen, but he brought them to reason there, and I warrant me he will do the same here. At any rate, he seems in no hurry to move. We have been here nigh a week already, and why should he keep us here if we are not to be employed?"

It was not very long before it became known that Harold had no intention of marching away and leaving the Welsh unpunished, and that in the spring a campaign on a great scale was to be undertaken against them. The thanes of all the western counties were ordered to hold themselves in readiness to join with their levies in the spring. The Somerset and Devon men were to gather at Bristol, and thence to be conveyed by ships to the southern coast of Wales; the troops at Gloucester were to march west, and Tostig was to bring down a body of Northumbrian horse, and to enter Wales from Chester. The housecarls, to their surprise, were ordered to lay aside their ringed armour and heavy helmets, in place of which leather jerkins and caps were served out to them; their heavy axes were to be left behind, and they were to trust to the sword alone. They were to abandon the tactics in which they had been trained of fighting shoulder to shoulder, with shield overlapping shield, and were to exercise themselves in running and climbing, in skirmishing with an imaginary foe, and rapidly gathering in close formation to resist anticipated attack. Harold himself gave them these instructions.

"You will have no foe to meet breast to breast," he said; "if we are to conquer and to root out these hornets it must be by showing ourselves even more active than they are. Speed and activity go for everything in a war like this, while our own methods of fighting are absolutely useless. Unless we make an end of this matter you may be called away from your homes once a year to repel these attacks, while if you conquer now there will be no Welsh foray again during your lifetime. Therefore it is worth while to make a great effort, and for once to lay aside our own method of fighting. Your commanders will see that all the exercises are well carried out, and will report to me regarding those who show most zeal and energy. Extra pay will be given to all, and I shall know how to reward those who are reported to me as most deserving of it."

The troops set to work with great energy, and soon recognized the advantage they gained by laying aside their heavy arms and armour. Swimming, running, and climbing were practised incessantly, and when May arrived, and with it the time for the commencement of the campaign, all felt confident of their ability to cope with the Welsh in their own methods of warfare.

CHAPTER IX. — IN THE WELSH VALLEYS.

Wulf and Beorn did not form part of the expedition which was to embark with Harold from Bristol, and to enter Wales by one of its southern valleys. It was necessary that the gathering of the levies at Gloucester should be strengthened by having as a nucleus three hundred trained soldiers. The levies were lightly armed, and accustomed to fight in the same irregular manner as their Welsh adversaries, whom they held in considerable dread, for the fierce hillmen had again and again proved themselves more than a match for the peaceable natives on the English side of the border. The addition then of three hundred housecarls was required to give them confidence. These had indeed abandoned for the time their armour, heavy weapons, and solid formation, but they could still were it necessary gather in a line, behind which the levies could rally, and which would be impregnable to the undisciplined attacks of the Welsh.

The young thanes were somewhat disappointed at finding that they were not to accompany the earl, but, as he told them, it was a mark of his confidence that he should post them with the force where the fighting was likely to be more severe and the risk greater than with that he himself led.

"I shall penetrate into the heart of Wales," he said. "I shall have horsemen with me, a strong force of trained soldiers and the levies, and the enemy will, I feel sure, be unable to oppose us successfully; but it is likely enough that when the Welsh find that my force from the south and Tostig's from the north cannot be withstood, they will pour out on their eastern frontier, and try to light such a flame in Worcester, Hereford, and Gloucester, that we should be obliged to abandon our work, and hurry back to stem the tide of their invasion.

It is necessary therefore that from this side also there should be a forward movement. My brother, Gurth, will command here. I have strongly recommended you to him. Your experience in the Breton war will be of assistance to you, and I have told him that you can be far better trusted than many older than yourselves in carrying out expeditions among their hills and valleys.

"I do not anticipate there will be any pitched battles; the Welsh know that they cannot withstand our trained soldiers. It will be a war of skirmishes, of detached fighting, of surprises, long marches, and great fatigues. Every valley in the country is to be harried with fire and sword. They are to be made to feel that even in their mountains they are not safe from us, and as they never take prisoners nor give quarter in the forays on our side of the border, so we will hunt them down like wolves in their own forests. The work must be done so thoroughly that for a hundred years at least the lesson will not be forgotten."

In the last week of May Gurth moved forward, marching first to Hereford as a more central point of attack, and then crossing the border and entering Wales. The troops carried no heavy baggage. Meat they expected to find; flour was carried on two hundred packhorses. The force was about 4000 strong. The housecarls marched in a body, keeping solid order. Behind them came the pack animals, each led separately, so that they could the more easily make their way through forests or over broken ground. They marched in lines, forty abreast. The light-armed levies, led by their respective thanes, moved as they chose on the flanks of the trained troops or followed in the rear.

When they halted on the first evening after crossing the frontier they lighted their fires and bivouacked. Wulf and Beorn walked together through the camp.

"In spite of the fact that they are all dressed somewhat alike in leather jerkins, it is easy to see which are the trained soldiers," Wulf said. "The housecarls are as merry over the food they have brought with them as if they were going upon a march of pleasure through the hills, while the border levies evidently regard the business as a serious one."

"That is no wonder," Beorn replied, "seeing how for years they have suffered at the hands of the Welsh. Look at those hills, Wulf, I can count a dozen beacons alight. Of course, they have heard of the preparations for attack, and they are flashing the news from hill to hill of the advance of our force. It will not be long before they gather to oppose us."

"It is like enough they may attack us to-night, Beorn. They may have had spies at Hereford, and will have known two days ago of our coming. They may reckon that we should anticipate no attack until farther among their hills, and that we shall in consequence be careless, as in truth we seem to be. I think it would be well to offer Gurth our housecarls to stand sentry to-night."

"He might laugh at us," Beorn said doubtfully.

"Well, let him laugh; he will laugh good-humouredly anyhow, for he is of a kindly and light-hearted disposition. At any rate there cannot be any harm in proposing it, and after the surprise we got from the Bretons we cannot be too cautious."

They walked to the fire where Gurth was sitting with four or five of his friends, all of whom had furnished bodies of housecarls. The border thanes had by his orders each remained with his own following, so that at all times they should be in readiness to give orders and lead them in case of surprise.

"Where have you been, young thanes?" Gurth asked. "You slipped away as soon as our meal was finished, as if you were afraid of the wine-cup."

"We care not much for drinking," Beorn said, "and have been going through the force to see how it was disposed. We have come to offer that our men shall to-night furnish guards for the camp."

"There is no occasion for it," Gurth said, "the Welshmen will not attack us until we are entangled among their hills."

"It depends upon how well they are led, my Lord Gurth," Wulf said. "If they are well led they may attack us to-night, for they must know of our approach, and will think it probable that we shall, being so near our own border, be at first careless. The Bretons gave us just such a lesson, and inflicted heavy loss upon the Norman army."

"Well, post your men as you like," Gurth said; "though it seems to me that it would be better for them to husband their strength for to-morrow's march."

"They shall have half a night's sleep each," Wulf said.

"If I had not known how stoutly you fought, and how your courage saved the Norman camp, I should have said you were over-cautious," Gurth laughed. "However I will not refuse your offer, young thanes, though methinks there is no chance whatever of the Welsh disturbing us here."

Having obtained the permission, Beorn and Wulf returned to the fires of their men.

"We are to have the honour of furnishing the guards to-night, Osgod. Tell the men that Gurth relies upon our watchfulness. We don't want a repetition of the surprise we had from the Bretons. It will be but a short night's watch. 'Tis nine now, and by four it will be broad daylight. Beorn's men and ours will march a hundred yards out from the camp. Half can lie down to sleep at once, the other half we can post as sentries and relieve them at half-past twelve. An attack if it comes will come from the front, therefore we will post the men twenty or thirty yards apart along there, and for some distance round the flanks. One of us will remain with the party that lies down, so as to be in readiness to lead them at once against any point attacked, the other will move round and round to see that the sentries are vigilant."

"That is good news to me," Osgod said. "Methinks that affair in the Breton wood has shaken my courage, for I have been looking at those trees in front of us, and wondering whether the Welsh are gathering there, and thinking how it would be with all these raw levies if they came down upon us to-night It went hard for a bit with the Normans, tried soldiers though they were, but I would not trust these levies to stand for a moment, for they hold the Welsh in mighty respect."

The men cheerfully took their arms and fell in. They considered it a compliment that they had been chosen to furnish the first guard. Beorn's men, with a portion of Wulf's, were to furnish the first line of sentries. The two young thanes, accompanied by Osgod, went round with them and posted them, after giving them strict injunctions to be watchful and vigilant.

"These savages," Beorn said, "will creep up through the grass as noiselessly as cats, so you must keep your ears as well as your eyes well open; and if you hear but the breaking of a twig challenge at once. Then, if they rise, shout the alarm at the top of your voice, and do the whole of you run back to us here if the cry comes from the front, if from either flank hurry to that spot, and we shall do the same from here; but be careful not to rouse the camp by a false alarm, for if you do, instead of gaining credit we shall become the jest of the whole force."

When the sentries were placed, Beorn, with the leader of his band, began to go the rounds, while Wulf and Osgod returned to their party.

"You can sleep, master, while I watch beside you," Osgod said. "I could not sleep if I lay down, for I have got the yells of those Bretons in my ears, and could not close an eye."

"Very well, Osgod; in that case I may as well take a nap."

He was soon sound asleep, and remained so until Osgod touched him. He sat up in a moment.

"By the stars it is past midnight, my lord, and it is time for us to relieve Beorn's party." The men were at once called to their feet, and the relief effected.

"If an attack comes," Wulf said, as with Osgod he proceeded to walk backwards and forwards along the line of sentries, "I fancy it will be just before daybreak. Many of them may come from long distances, and their leader would wait until the last moment in order to gather as large a force together as possible. Besides, men sleep heaviest at that time, and they would reckon that hour as best for a surprise." As they walked they frequently paused to listen intently, and though once or twice they thought they heard distant sounds, these might be caused by the passage of a wild animal through the bushes. The sentries were all vigilant. It was the first time that the Sussex lads had been in face of an enemy, and the stillness of the night, the sombre forest in front of them, and the possibility of a savage and unknown foe lurking there, kept them thoroughly on the alert. Once or twice Wulf and Osgod went forward to examine some bush that had seemed to the imagination of a sentry to have moved, but in each case the alarm was groundless.

"It must be nearly three o'clock now, Osgod," Wulf said at last. "Another half hour will decide it. I shall be glad when the morning comes, for this work is trying, and I keep on fancying I hear noises."

"I fancy so too," Osgod said. "It seems to me like a sort of whisper or rustling of leaves."

"That is just what it seems to me, Osgod. Let us stay where we are. We are just in the centre of the line now."

"There are certainly sounds, my lord. I thought it was fancy before, but I am sure now."

"I hear something," Wulf said. "It comes from the front. Run round to the right and bring the sentries from that flank and post them in the intervals of those in front, while I do the same on the left."

They had but just returned, when they heard a sharp sound like the cracking of a stick a short distance in front. A dozen of the sentries at once challenged. In an instant a number of figures sprang to their feet at a distance of some fifty yards in front of them. Then a wild yell was raised, and swarms of men came rushing towards them, while a volley of arrows and javelins whizzed through the air.

"Fall back on the others, men!" Wulf shouted at the top of his voice, and the line of sentries rushed back to Beorn's party, who leapt to their feet at the sound of the Welsh war-cry. They had scarce formed in line when the enemy were upon them. They received them with a volley of javelins, and then shield to shield they withstood the attack They were fighting in their own way now, and numerous as the Welsh were, they were unable, as they ran up in scattered order, to break through the line.

"Steady, men, steady!" Wulf shouted out from his post in the middle of the line. "Our friends will soon be up. Show a stout front. Do not give way a foot."

In vain the Welshmen, with wild yells, strove to beat back the Saxon line. Their very numbers were a hindrance to them. Those in front pressed forward, so that those behind were unable to use their javelins or arrows. Many creeping between the legs of the fighters of the front rank leapt with a cat-like spring upon the Saxons, and strove to rip them with their knives, but the light wicker-work shields covered with leather, which had taken the place of the solid and heavy ones generally carried by the housecarls, stood Wulf's followers in good stead; and although many of the shields were penetrated by the knives of the Welsh, they in most cases effectually screened the bodies of the soldiers.

The lightly-armed Welsh, on the other hand, were hewn down by the long swords of the Saxons in the front rank, while the javelins of those behind them flew with terrible effect among their assailants. There was, however, no pause in the fury of the attacks of the Welsh, until, with a great shout, the main body of the Saxons came up, and pressed forward in line with the little body who had hitherto borne the brunt of the battle, while on their flank the thane's levies poured in volley after volley of darts and arrows. The fight ceased as suddenly as it began. The sound of a deep-toned horn rose in the air, whereupon the Welsh instantly abandoned the struggle, and before the Saxons had time to realize that the fighting was over, they had disappeared in the forest.

"By St. Peter, young thanes!" Earl Gurth exclaimed as he came up to Wulf's band, who were panting from their exertions, "you have saved us from a grievous mishap this night. I take shame unto myself that I treated your suggestion so lightly; for, by the saints, we should have fared badly indeed had this wild foe taken us asleep. The thanks of the whole force are due to you, and I will take care that my brother Harold knows how narrow an escape we have had, and in telling the tale I shall not spare either myself or the older thanes, who were disposed to mock your proposal to keep guard over the camp, as showing an amount of caution altogether unnecessary. The attack has been a lesson to me that I shall not forget, and henceforth I shall select you and your force for any special service requiring watchfulness and valour."

In going among their men Wulf and Beorn found that but six had fallen, for the most part under the shower of javelins with which the Welsh had heralded their attack. Many of the others had received wounds more or less severe, but few of them were so badly hurt as to render it necessary to leave them behind. Gurth called the thanes at once to a council. Fresh wood was thrown on to his fire, and some twenty of the thanes took their places round it. Wulf and Beorn were specially asked by Gurth to attend. The attack of the Welsh had shown that they were by no means dismayed at the extent of the preparations for the invasion of their mountains, and that the advance must be conducted with the greatest caution and prudence.

"It is well," Gurth said, "that in the absence of Griffith they have many leaders, and will therefore fight without any general plan. Did their whole force fall upon one or other of our columns it might go very hard with it; but we may be sure that each chief will desire to keep his followers by him, in order to defend his own valleys. Nevertheless, they have shown to-night that they can gather rapidly and in considerable force, and we shall have to root them out piecemeal, and shall not be able to scatter our force too widely. I am told that the valley at whose mouth we now are contains a large number of villages, and to this we must confine ourselves until we have done the work there. I trust that they will oppose us stoutly. In that case we shall have the less trouble with them when we come to undertake the more difficult task of pursuing them among their hills."

The next morning the advance began, and they had proceeded but a short distance when the Welsh again poured down upon them. This time the force was prepared for the attack, and although the Welsh fought obstinately, they were driven back without much difficulty. As soon as the attack ceased Gurth gave the order for pursuit, and the housecarls held their course straight up the valley at full speed, while the levies swarmed up the hillsides to prevent the Welsh from rallying and attacking in flank. The troops now felt the benefit of the abandonment of their heavy armour and weapons, and pressed so hotly upon the flying Welsh that they entered the first village with them. For a time the natives turned and fought desperately in defence of their homes, but they were unable to withstand the skill and discipline of the Saxon troops, and the measure that they had so frequently dealt out to the Saxon villagers now fell on them. No quarter was given. Every man, woman, and child was slaughtered, and the houses given to the flames. Village after village was captured and burnt, but the resistance became fainter and fainter, and the last three villages at the head of the valley were found to be entirely deserted. Then, just as the sun set, the force bivouacked for the night, the horns calling in the scattered levies, who gradually rejoined them.

The next morning the force was broken up into five or six columns, each having a proportion of the regular soldiers and a body of the levies. These penetrated side valleys and climbed the hills. In many cases they encountered resistance, stones being rolled down upon them, and the Welsh defending strong barricades of felled trees. But everywhere the Saxons were successful, and day after day continued the work, until at the end of five days they were able to move where they would without encountering any resistance. The force now marched forward from the head of the valley, crossed a range of hills, and descended into another valley. They had now grown more confident in themselves, and while a third of the force proceeded to lay waste the valley, the rest, broken up into small columns, ascended the hills on either side, carrying fire and sword into every hamlet they came upon.

Several of the fortalices of the Welsh chiefs, perched on almost inaccessible eminences, gave great trouble, and were only taken after serious loss. One day Beorn and Wulf, with their own following and two hundred and fifty light-armed levies, were despatched by Gurth to Porthwyn, a stronghold belonging to a powerful chief named Llewellyn ap Rhys.

"It is, from all I hear," he said, "a very strong place, and will require all our force to capture it. Indeed it is reported to be so strong that it may be necessary to leave it unmolested until we form a junction with Harold, and can besiege it regularly. It would not do to make an unsuccessful attack, for that would raise the spirits of the Welsh. All that I wish of you is to obtain a view of the castle from all sides if possible, to bring me back an exact account of its defences, and to give me your opinion as to our chances of capturing it if we decide to lay siege to it."

Porthwyn was forty miles distant, and Beorn and Wulf determined to march some thirty of these, and then to push forward at daybreak so as to obtain a view of the fortress in the early morning. They took with them a Welsh boy as a guide. He had been spared in the last village captured, and had been told that his life depended upon his guiding them faithfully. The places of ten men who had fallen during the various fights had been filled up by an equal number of Gurth's own housecarls. The seventy soldiers kept with their leaders and the guide, the levies spreading out on either side.

Two of the irregulars who spoke a little Welsh accompanied the young thanes to question the guide if necessary. The march was a heavy one. At times they passed through thick forests in the valleys and on the lower hillsides, at times crossed over bare hills, on whose summits the ground was frequently so boggy that the men had to march with the greatest caution. The guide, a sullen lad with matted hair, whose only attire was a sheep-skin, was several times questioned sharply as to whether he was certain of the way. He answered in monosyllables, saying that he knew every foot of the road, and indeed he never hesitated for a moment.

"I suppose he is right," Wulf said, "although I thought it lay more to the west than we are going, but we have wound about so among these forests and hills that I am quite confused. There is one comfort, Beorn, if the guide proves treacherous and we lose ourselves altogether, we have but to set our faces to the rising sun and we shall find ourselves back on the border, for I am sure that we could not retrace our steps to Gurth's camp."

The sun was just setting when they found themselves on a bare plateau on the crest of a range of hills higher than any they had before crossed.

"Ask him how far we are from Porthwyn," Wulf said to the interpreter.

"He says twelve miles, my lord."

"Then when we get across this flat, which looks full two miles wide, we will camp in the first valley we come to."

As they advanced the ground became more and more boggy, and the troops had to move carefully, stepping from one tussock of coarse grass to another, the intervals being filled with black slimy mud.

"Ask him if this gets deeper," Beorn said angrily, "for if it does so we are like to be all swallowed up. I believe he must be leading us wrong."

Osgod had charge of the boy, and was walking close beside him. As the question was put by the interpreter the boy muttered that he knew the way. The man turned to translate his answer to Beorn, when there was a sudden shout. At the moment that Osgod was making a long step from one tuft to another the boy stooped and caught his foot, and with a roar of surprise and fury Osgod fell head-foremost into the morass. At the same moment the lad darted away with a yell of defiance, leaping from tuft to tuft with the agility of a hare. Several of the men started after him, but unaccustomed to the treacherous bog four or five were immersed in it to their waist before they had gone a dozen paces.

"Shoot! shoot!" Beorn shouted, and a dozen javelins were thrown, but the boy was almost beyond distance, and his rapid and irregular movements rendered it well-nigh impossible to take aim with any accuracy. Most of the javelins flew wide of him, and he was soon beyond reach. Osgod was well-nigh smothered before he could be rescued, and some of the other men were only hauled out with the greatest difficulty. Three or four of the most active men were sent forward, but presently returned with the news that the bog became worse.

"The sun has already set," Wulf said, "and if darkness catches us here our plight will be a bad one. Let us retrace our steps at once, Beorn."

It was with great difficulty that they made their way back to firm ground. By the time they did so darkness had fallen.

"This is a bad business altogether, Beorn," Wulf said. "In the first place we have lost our guide; in the second place we have no idea where we are, for we may for aught we know have been going in the wrong direction all the time; and, besides this, the boy will raise the country against us, and in the morning we may be attacked by an overwhelming force."

"What do you think we had better do, Wulf?"

"Well, I should say we had better, in the first place, retrace our steps to the valley, there we will light fires and cook the meat we have brought with us. Then I should say we had best march for some hours. It matters not in what direction so that we get as far as possible from here."

As Beorn could suggest nothing better, Wulf's counsel was carried out. Supper was cooked and eaten in the forest, and after two hours for rest, for the march had been a very fatiguing one, they started. The night was moonless, and in the shadow of the trees the darkness was intense. The housecarls kept together, moving as closely as possible to each other. The levies were ordered to follow them.

After proceeding for two hours, Wulf said, "Let us halt and see if we are all together." The housecarls halted, but when he went to the rear Wulf could see no signs of the irregulars.

"Let no man speak or move," he said, "I want to listen."

But no sound broke the stillness of the wood.

"How foolish of Oswald and Edred," he said to Beorn.

"We told them to follow with their levies close behind us, and they must have allowed them to fall to the rear. However, they can't be far behind."

They waited for half an hour, but the silence continued unbroken.

"Do you shout, Osgod," Wulf said; "they ought to hear miles away on a still night like this."

Osgod—who had scarcely spoken since his fall, so furious was he at having been outwitted by a boy, and having not only allowed him to escape, but being himself rolled in the mire—raised his voice in a tremendous shout. All listened intently, but no answering sound came back.

"They must have gone altogether wrong," Wulf said. "You know that we crossed a streamlet that ran into this brook soon after we started. They must have followed that up, thinking we had done so, and have gone up some other valley. What is to be done, Beorn?"

"We crossed that streamlet half an hour after starting," Beorn said, "and as we have spent half an hour here they must have by this time marched up it two-hours' journey, and if we retrace our steps to that point they will have got an hour and a half farther away; besides, they may have gone back when they missed us. There is no saying which way to look for them. I think we had better go on as before. In the morning we shall be able to see the nature of the country, but to look for people who may be miles and miles away, when one cannot see one's own hand, would be but lost time and labour, and methinks we shall have need to husband all our strength before we get out of the scrape into which we have fallen. If the two thanes had obeyed orders and kept closer this would not have happened. They have lost us by their own carelessness, and must manage as they can. We shall have all our work to do to look out for ourselves. Seventy men lost in the heart of these savage hills, which by to-morrow morning will swarm with Welsh, have but a poor chance of ever seeing the English border again."

"It is not so bad as that, Beorn. I do not say that we are not in an unpleasant position, but at any rate we are a great deal better off than we were when we were driving headlong on to the coast of Normandy, or when there were but three of us in the midst of the Bretons. They have to find us in the first place, and it will need a good many of them to overcome us when they do. I fancy that we are very near the head of this valley, the ground is rising rapidly. I propose that we push on now till the trees cease, and lie down there till morning breaks, and then cross the next hill so as to find shelter in some other valley before the sun is fairly up. From the top of the hill we may get a general view of the country, and shall have some idea as to the course to take. We must first of all try to find a native who can tell us which is the direction of Porthwyn and how far it lies away. Our orders are to reconnoitre it and that must be done before there is any question of return. Even if I were absolutely alone, I would carry out that order."

Beorn was silent for a minute, and then said doubtfully, "Perhaps you are right, Wulf; but when Gurth gave us the order he gave us more than three hundred men to carry it out, and we have now but seventy."

By this time they were on their way up the valley, followed by their men.

"The fact that two hundred and fifty men have left us really makes the matter easier than it would otherwise have been," Wulf said. "Of course our guide carried the news of our coming straight to Porthwyn, and it is like enough that fires are at present blazing on the hills. The larger division is more likely to be seen than ours, and to be attacked, and we shall have all the more chance of getting up unobserved. I sincerely trust that the thanes, when they discover that they have lost us, will at once lead their men back to Gurth's camp. In that case they may escape before the Welsh can assemble and attack them; and as it would naturally be supposed that as soon as we had lost our guide we retreated in a body, the Welsh will imagine that there is no occasion for further vigilance."

"You are always too full of arguments for me, Wulf," Beorn laughed; "and if you have made up your mind to go on, it is not of the least use my saying anything against it; so have your own way."

At last the forest became less dense, and when they reached its edge they lay down. Wulf slept for two or three hours, and then roused himself and waited for the first sign of dawn. It was a heavy responsibility, for though Beorn was of equal rank with himself he always gave way to his opinion. He thought over whether it would not be better that Beorn should march with all speed with the force to the east, and that he himself with Osgod and perhaps two other men should make their way to Porthwyn; already the Welsh might be out all over the mountains, and it was the larger body that would be likely to be discovered and attacked. The Welsh would know that on such a dark night, and in a strange country, they could not have got a very long distance from the bog where the guide had escaped from them, and the valley at whose head he now was would be the first place to be searched. However, he did not like severing himself from the men who had marched under his banner from Steyning, and he finally determined that the whole should stay together. It was about half-past two when he roused the band, and they at once started up the bare hillside.

"As it gets lighter," he said, "scatter and proceed singly. We shall be far less likely to be noticed by anyone at a distance than if we march together in a solid body. We must travel as fast as possible, so as to get under shelter again before the sun is really up."

The men were all by this time well accustomed to climbing and hardened by exercise, and at a rapid pace they breasted the hill, although it was in some places exceedingly steep. By the time they reached its crest there was light enough to permit of a view of the country round. In all directions hills rose around them, bare and brown, and the growing light in the sky showed that the east lay behind them. After waiting for a minute or two to recover breath, they proceeded at a brisk trot. They met with no bogs of importance, and after running for a mile the ground began to slope downwards again, and they saw below them a wooded valley, similar to that which they had left. By this time the hilltops were all lit up by the rising sun. The spot where they stood, however, was still in shadow, and in scattered order they ran rapidly down the hillside until they reached the cover of the trees.

CHAPTER X. — PORTHWYN.

There was a short halt to enable the band to quench their thirst at a little rivulet that trickled down the centre of the valley; then they prepared to continue their march, Wulf impressing upon them the necessity for moving as silently as possible.

"If we come upon a village of any size," he said, "we must avoid it. The main point is to capture a native, and find out exactly where we are."

After walking for an hour they came suddenly upon a hut. It stood in a cleared patch of ground; a small herd of goats were browsing round, and some smoke curled up from a hole in the roof. Wulf halted his men.

"Beorn, you and I and Osgod and one of the interpreters had best go in alone; there are not likely to be more than one or two men within, and it will be well at any rate that our numbers should not be known."

Before advancing, however, he told the band to surround the clearing. "Let no one escape," he said; "it would cost us our lives did one get away to tell of our being here. See, too, that you bring down two or three of the goats. Our meat is nearly exhausted, and it is well to replenish our store."

After waiting until the men were in their places, Wulf ran forward across the open ground with his three companions. There was no door to the hut, and on entering it they saw that its only occupant was a decrepit old woman. She gave a cry of dismay at the entrance of the strangers.

"Tell her not to be alarmed," Wulf said to the interpreter.

"We do not desire to do her any harm. Now ask her if she lives here by herself," he went on, when the interpreter had spoken to the old woman.

"She lives here with her two sons," the man said; "they are away. There were beacon-fires on the hills last evening, and they went out. She does not know when they will return."

"Ask her how far it is to Porthwyn."

The answer was most satisfactory. "It is but three miles away, my lord. It lies in the valley of which this is a branch."

"That is good news indeed, Beorn," Wulf said. "The boy led us in the right direction, perhaps because he thought that if he did not do so we should perceive it and tax him with treachery. But it is more likely that he wished to lead us so close that he could, when he escaped, carry the news of our being in the neighbourhood, in time for the Welshmen to surround and cut us off before we could return. As she says that the beacon-fires were lighted in the evening he can have lost no time, and the country must be aroused. I wish we had the whole force here."

"What shall we do with this old crone?" Beorn said. "It would never do to risk her giving an alarm, and though she looks feeble she might be able to get down to Porthwyn."

"We will tie her securely, Beorn; we can't hurt the poor old creature. Her sons are no doubt out with the Welsh bands hunting for us; but they will return here sooner or later, so that no harm will come to her."

By his orders Osgod securely bound the old woman with a rope he found in the hut, and then leaving her they went outside and called upon the men to close in. Eight of the goats were killed, and were then cut up and divided among the men. After a consultation Wulf and Beorn agreed that instead of following the valley down, where they might meet with other huts, or even a good-sized village, they had best keep along on the hillside, just inside the line of trees, as in that way they would come out high up on the side of the main valley, and probably obtain a good view of the fortalice.

In single file they made their way among the trees, and in an hour the valley that they were in opened considerably, and through the trees they saw a large village at their feet. A quarter of a mile farther and they stood on the side of a wide valley. There were numerous flocks and herds to be seen grazing in it, and four or five villages could be made out; their attention, however, was chiefly directed to the object of their journey. Some three hundred feet below the spot where they stood a rock jutted out from the hillside, and extended some five or six hundred feet into the valley. Its sides were perpendicular save where it stood out from the hill. Here a strong wall some forty feet high ran across it; two square towers stood at the angles, but there was no gateway visible. The wall was continued right round the top of the rock, which was crossed by two other walls each defended by flanking towers. The castle itself stood at the extremity of the rock, and was a strong and massive-looking building. The men were all ordered to lie down as soon as the castle was visible between the trees, and among these Wulf and Beorn followed by Osgod moved cautiously, until they reached a spot whence they could obtain through the foliage a full view of the building.

"It is a formidable place," said Beorn. "The chief who first planted himself here knew what he was doing. Yes. I should fancy from the look of it the castle at the end was built first, then gradually the walls were added until the whole rock was inclosed. This bit nearest to us is evidently an addition during the last few years. You can see that by the colour of the stone. You see the other two walls have gateways in them while this has none. I should say until this was built the entrance to the castle was along the neck, but they must have got some other way now, and so shut it up altogether. How on earth can they get in?"

"Certainly not at the sides," Wulf said, "for they are as near perpendicular as possible. It must be at the other end of the rock, which we can't see. It may slope a little more gradually there, and they may have cut a zigzag road up. Suppose we climb the hill behind us, till we get high enough to see over the trees and get a complete view of the valley. There is no fear of our being noticed. We are a good five hundred feet above it now, and even if anyone did see us up there they would take us for two herdsmen. Of course we will leave our shields and weapons behind us."

On attaining a spot from which a clear view of the whole valley could be obtained, Wulf said:

"There, Beorn, do you see the hill juts out into the plain on the right, half a mile from the castle, and is wooded to its foot. I think if we were to make our way down there we should be able to obtain a view of the face of the rock below the castle without leaving the shelter of the trees." Beorn agreed that it was worth trying, and they returned to the men, rearmed themselves, and spoke to Osgod.

"We are going to reconnoitre, Osgod, and may be an hour away. As we shall not leave the forest there is no danger, and even were we seen we can climb the hill again as fast as any Welshman can follow us. Do you keep an eye on the castle, but do not stir until we return even if you hear shouts. I have no doubt that we shall be able to rejoin you, and it is most important that even if they do make us out they should have no reason for supposing that there is any force behind us." After half an hour's walking Beorn and Wulf found themselves at the edge of the wood in the valley.

"There is the road, you see," Wulf exclaimed. "It goes straight up that gradual slope to the bottom of the rock, then it makes two zigzags to the edge of that point that juts out a little, whence there is a bridge thrown across a gap to the point where there is a turret. I can't see it beyond that. I should think they must have driven a tunnel from there right up into the castle, for you see there are fifty feet of perpendicular rock above that turret. In case of attack, of course, they would cut away the bridge, and it would be next to impossible to throw another across. They could overwhelm any force attempting it with stones from above, besides sweeping the zigzag road below."

Beorn agreed that the place was absolutely impregnable on that side, and that it could only be attacked from the hillside, and by carrying the walls in succession.

"Well, there is nothing more to see," Wulf said, "so we may as well return. You see there is a large village nestling down there just at the foot of the rock. We could not see it from where we were before.

"Well, Osgod, have you seen anything going on in the castle?"

"No, my lord, everything has been very quiet It seems to me that there are very few men about for such a strong place."

"No doubt most of them are out in pursuit of us, Osgod; we know that the country was roused by the beacons, and that there must be a big force somewhere in the hills. I only hope they wont find Oswald and Edred, or I fear it will go hard with them. The levies fight well when they have the housecarls with them, but by themselves and in a strange country I am afraid they would lose heart. Now, Beorn, I am going down to the wall on this side. We can see that there is no sentry on it, and I want to find out if there is any other defence besides what we can see. It is very important to know that, as we agreed that this is the side from which the attack must be made."

Descending among the trees Wulf cautiously approached the wall. He found on nearing it that a perpendicular cut some thirty feet wide and twenty feet deep had been made across the rock. It stretched from the foot of one flanking tower to the foot of the other, the wall between them being some ten feet from its edge. Having ascertained this he returned to Beorn. Having told him what he had seen, he sat looking at the castle.

"What are you thinking of, Wulf?" Beorn asked. "I suppose we had better stop where we are till nightfall and then make eastward."

"I am thinking, in the first place, that it would cost a great number of lives to take that place by assault."

"That it would," Beorn agreed. "We have seen no place of anything like equal strength in Wales, or indeed anywhere else."

"There is no doubt about that," Wulf agreed. "If well defended it ought to hold out for weeks, for when we have taken that wall in front of us only a third of the work has been done. In the next place, I am thinking that Llewellyn and the greater part of his garrison are away in the hills."

Beorn nodded.

"And that being so, it seems to me that the best plan will be to take it ourselves."

Beorn looked at his friend to see if he were serious, but there was no smile on Wulf's face.

"Do you really mean it, Wulf?"

"Yes I mean it, certainly. What is to prevent our taking it? There may never be such a good opportunity again. We have not seen a dozen men on the walls, and I don't suppose there are fifty there altogether. But even if there are a hundred, they will have no chance with our men if we are once among them. You see the gates through those inner walls are open, and once over this first one the place will be all open to us."

"That is true enough, but how in the world are we to climb that wall?"

"That is what I am puzzling over, Beorn. You see there is no time to lose, for Llewellyn and his men may be back to-night. If they find Oswald's party this morning they will return at once, if they don't they may not be back till the morning. But we cannot count on that, what has to be done must be done at once."

He sat thinking a little longer. "We must cut down a couple of trees and make a ladder, Beorn. The pine-trees grew very close together where we passed through them a quarter of a mile before we got here, and were very slender for their height. We have no axes or we could fell a couple of them in a few minutes; but even if we had them, we should not dare use them, for the chances are that the villagers are forbidden to cut down trees anywhere near the castle, and the sound might bring people up from below to see who was chopping. I was thinking of burning two of them down, but in this dry weather the flames might run up them, and we should get a blaze that would bring all the villagers up here." He beckoned to Osgod, and when he came up told him that Beorn and he had agreed to try and take the place.

"That is good," Osgod said joyfully. "I have been thinking of it, but I did not see how you were to climb that wall."

"We must cut down two young pine-trees, but we must not chop them down."

"It would take a long time with our knives," Osgod said doubtfully. "It is easy enough to cut through a pole three inches thick, but when it comes to nine or ten it is a different matter."

"Then we must cut down small ones and tie them together. Bring twenty men at once with you, Osgod, let the rest lie quiet, the less movement there is the better."

As soon as the men were ready Wulf led them back to the point where the pine-trees grew, then he selected eight of the tallest and slightest. They were about three inches through at the foot, and were, he judged, at least an inch and a half at twenty feet from the ground. Two men were set to work at each tree, and in less than half an hour the eight trees were on the ground. The branches were then lopped off, and four of the stems were cut across five-and-twenty feet from the foot. The thin ends were then placed together so as to overlap five feet. There was no difficulty about lashings, as thongs were cut off the bottom of the men's leather jerkins. The joint was made stronger by a light pole fifteen feet long being firmly lashed across the junction. Thus the two poles for the ladder forty-five feet long were ready for use. It needed only to lash cross-pieces for steps, and in little over an hour from the time that work was begun the ladder was complete. From the other young trees two ladders, each twenty-five feet long, had been constructed in the meantime, and the whole were then raised and carried back to the place where the band was lying.

"Now, men," Wulf said, "we are going to take this castle at once. I should wait until nightfall were it not that I fear the return of the Welsh, but as they may come back at any time there is not a minute to be lost. Now let each understand his work. The short ladders are to enable us to cross a cut twenty feet deep they have made through the rock; when we get over this we can plant the long ladder against the wall. As soon as we gain the top every man must lie down and crawl along over those who have preceded him. If we are seen before a few of us are on the top of the wall we shall fail, because they will have time to give the alarm, and shut the inner gates.

"So far we have seen no one go in or out of the courts between these walls, and have every hope that we shall find no one there. I expect they are places where the cattle are kept in case of siege. Our great danger is in the chance of our being noticed by men on other parts of the walls or on the castle. However, as far as we can see their attention is entirely directed the other way, for they are no doubt on the look-out for news from their chief or for his return. My intention is that all shall gain the top of the wall before a movement is made, but if an alarm is given, those who have got to the top are at once to follow us down the staircase into the courtyard and run at full speed to the gate. Not a moment's halt is to be made there; we must run on to the next gate and there defend ourselves until the rest come to our aid. They will be taken so completely by surprise that, even if we are but four or five, we can hold the gate until the rest come up, and each man, as soon as he gains the top of the ladder, must run on at full speed to our aid. Cut down all with arms in their hands, but do not hurt women or children. Tell off six men, Osgod, to carry the ladder and place it against the wall, and to be the first to follow us. Let the others follow in the order in which they stand in rank."

They made their way down through the trees. As soon as they reached the cut one short ladder was lowered, and the other was handed down and placed against the opposite side of the cut. The end of the long ladder was then lowered, and it was swung over and the upper end placed against the wall. Six men then ascended the short ladder, and raised the long one until it stood on the rock at the foot of the castle-wall.

"Now, Beorn, do you mount first and I will follow you."

"You should go first," Beorn said, "but I will do as you tell me."

As soon as Beorn was half-way up Wulf began to follow him, saying to Osgod and the men, "Keep the same distance apart. Do not let more than two be on the ladder at once whatever happens inside, if it were to break it would be fatal to us all." As soon as he gained the top Wulf threw himself down by the side of Beorn, and lay there watching the men on the other walls and on the summit of the castle. Osgod and four men had joined them when Wulf noticed a sudden stir and heard a shout. He leapt to his feet.

"Follow quickly, but be careful of the ladder," he called to those below; then he dashed along the wall to the top of the staircase, and closely followed by the others ran down and on through the gate in the next wall. Here some five or six men were asleep in its shade, while some women were standing in front of some low huts which bordered the yard on either side. They gazed in astonishment for a moment at the seven men who appeared so suddenly from the outer yard, and then set up a shrill cry of alarm. Without heeding them Wulf ran on to the next gateway. Just as he reached it a number of men came running up from the other side. "Osgod, do you and Alfred cover our rear while we keep these men in front at bay."

The five men held the gate without difficulty against the Welsh who first arrived, for these, at the shout of one of their comrades that men were climbing the wall, had run down only with their knives, and could do nothing against the Saxon shields and long swords. Presently, others with spears and axes ran up, but the two young thanes and their three followers still kept them back, for in the narrow gateway they could not be attacked by more than their own number. Amid the yells of the Welsh Wulf could hear nothing of what was passing behind them, and he was delighted when he heard the voice of Osgod in his ear.

"There are eight here now, Wulf; we have finished with the Welshmen in the courtyard, so you are clear behind. Our men are coming down from the wall fast. In five minutes we shall have the whole band here. Now let me have a turn;" and he stepped forward and took the place of one of the Saxons who staggered back with a javelin in his shoulder.

Every moment added to the number of the Saxons.

"Let me know when they are all up," Wulf said to one of those behind him, as he cut down a Welshman who sprang at him with uplifted knife. The attack was growing weaker, as their assailants saw that instead of five men they had now to face a considerable number, and Wulf had difficulty in restraining his men.

"Keep back!" he shouted; "we must wait until we are all up, and then drive them headlong before us and follow them into the castle. If they have once time to shut the doors there we shall have a troublesome task." As he spoke he yielded his place in the front rank to one of his followers, and turned to see how matters stood behind. "Are they all up?" he asked.

"The last man told me that there were six more to come, my lord."

"Then we need wait no longer. Now, Beorn, all is ready— charge!" and with a rush the Saxons swept through the gate, carrying the Welsh before them and hewing down the front ranks. In an instant the defenders turned and fled, but the Saxons pressed hard on their heels. Some of the Welsh ran up the staircases to the walls, and many of the Saxons would have followed them, but at Wulf's "To the castle, to the castle, we can deal with them afterwards!" they followed him at once. On the steps up to the gateway of the castle a desperate struggle was going on among the Welsh themselves.

Seeing the Saxons pressing on the rear of the fugitives, those within the castle strove to shut the door, but strove in vain, as the terror-stricken men outside tried to force their way in. The two young thanes, with Osgod and many of their followers, cut their way through the struggling mass and reached the door. Those trying to shut it had already seen the hopelessness of the endeavour, and had fled into the hall beyond, in which a number of terrified women were wailing and shrieking. As Wulf burst in he shouted to the Welsh, "Throw down your arms and surrender, and your lives shall be spared" but his words were not understood, and as the Welsh never gave quarter themselves they had no thought of quarter being offered to them.

The women ceased screaming and broke into a death chant, many of them seizing weapons from the walls, and joining the men in a last desperate effort to drive back the Saxons.

For a moment those who had entered had difficulty in resisting the desperate attack, but as others poured in they advanced, and although Wulf continued to shout, "Spare all who throw down their arms," his orders were of no avail, for the Welsh continued to fight desperately until the last fell under the Saxon swords, most of the women, who fought with even greater fury than the men, sharing their fate. As soon as the struggle was over Wulf ordered Osgod to take eight or ten men, to find the entrance to the tunnel leading down to the road on the face of the cliff, and to guard it against any attack from without. Then, through his interpreters, he called to the Welshmen on the walls that their lives should be spared if they would lay down their arms. He was answered by derisive shouts and a shower of javelins.

"We should lose a good many men in storming those two narrow staircases, Beorn. There are but twenty or thirty of them, but that is enough to defend such steep approaches. Let us take twenty men up to the top of the castle, from there they can hurl javelins down at them, and they will soon see that resistance is useless."

They ascended the stairs, but paused at the end of the room over the hall which had been the scene of the conflict. An aged woman, whose dress showed her high rank, was seated on a settle; beside her was a white-headed harper, while two little children, a boy and a girl, stood at her knee and looked fearlessly at the intruders.

Wulf despatched one of the men down to the hall to bring up the interpreter. As soon as he arrived Wulf doffed his helmet and stepped forward.

"Ask who this lady is and who are these children."

At a gesture from the old lady the harper answered:

"This is my mistress, Gweneth, the mother of Prince Llewellyn ap Rhys; these are his children. In his name she bids you defiance. You have taken his castle, but he will know how to avenge her and his children."

"I have no desire or intention of acting with any disrespect, still less of injuring either your mistress or the children of Llewellyn," Wulf replied, when this was translated to him. "My friend and I are Saxon thanes, who have been forced to leave our homes and to embark on this war in order to put a stop to the ravages committed across the border—the burning of towns and villages, and the massacre of men, women, and children by your countrymen. Llewellyn ap Rhys has brought this misfortune upon himself, and did we render him motherless and childless, it would be but the fate that he and his followers have inflicted upon many an Englishman. But we do not make war upon women or children. Prisoners, of course, you must be, but be assured of honourable treatment. None shall enter this room save with your permission, and you can have your female attendants to serve you as usual."

While the interpreter was repeating his speech Wulf and Beorn left the room, and with the men ascended to the top of the castle, where they were joined by the interpreter, who addressed the Welsh on the walls. These replied with shouts of defiance, and a volley of javelins was poured down upon them. Three or four were struck, the rest, seeing that all hope was gone, rapidly gathered in a body at the head of the staircase leading from the wall.

"They are going to run down," Beorn exclaimed, and leaning over the parapet shouted to the Saxons in the courtyard below to stand on their guard.

A minute later the Welsh rushed down, each intent on killing at least one foe before he died. The Saxons' weapons and discipline were, however, too much for them; but they fought until the last, not one of them throwing down his weapon or asking for quarter.

"They are brave men. I would that we were not forced to slay them; but it is their choosing and not ours, Beorn, and if they would but leave us alone I am sure that nobody would wish to interfere with these wild countrymen."

"What is the next thing to be done, Wulf?"

"I should say let us turn all the women and children, save the old lady's attendants, out of the castle, they would only be a trouble to us. Then we must examine the store of provisions, plant sentries and cut away that bridge, or, at any rate, cut away so much of it that a blow or two with an axe will suffice to send it down. We must not forget to haul up our ladders. Llewellyn and his men may be back at any moment. Let us go down together to that turret we saw on the face of the rock."

Orders were at once given, and the women and children collected and told to leave the castle. They were allowed to carry away with them some eight or ten men who were found to be still living. They went for the most part in silence, but some of the elder women poured out voluble curses on the Saxons. Beorn and Wulf had already gone down to the turret. There was a very strong gateway in the courtyard, beyond this a tunnel sloping steeply down, eight feet high and four feet wide, had been cut in the solid rock. Following it they emerged upon a platform, principally occupied by the turret. The path led through a strong gateway under this on to the wooden bridge. Here Osgod with his ten men had taken their station.

"The women and children and a few wounded will be coming down directly, Osgod. As soon as they have passed do you set to work with your men and pull up the planking of the bridge, all save a single plank; loosen that, so that you can if necessary at once cast it down after the rest. If you see the Welshmen pouring up the road, throw it over at once without waiting for further orders, then close the gate and take your station in the turret."

"We are all getting very hungry, master. We have eaten nothing this morning, and fighting sharpens the appetite."

"I had forgotten all about it, Osgod. I will see that food is cooked at once, and will send down a portion for you and your men, and some tankards of whatever liquor we can find in the cellars. We are going to make an examination of them at once."

Returning to the courtyard, they told off a body of men to search the cellars and granaries, and were glad to find that there was an ample store of grain to last for months, together with large quantities of ale and a few casks of wine.

"So far all is well," Beorn said, "but would it not be prudent to send off at once to Gurth, to let him know that though we are masters of the castle at present, we may in a few hours be surrounded by a swarm of angry Welshmen?"

"That certainly is most desirable," Wulf agreed. "The question is, who are we to send? It would be a terribly dangerous enterprise. Even now there are a score of men from the village watching our movements from the wood above. At any rate we must wait until nightfall."

Four sentries were posted on the wall by which they had ascended, as after making a circuit of the place, this was they agreed the only point at which a surprise was possible, unless there existed some secret passage into the castle. They had just finished their inspection of the walls, when there was a shout from their look-out at the top of the castle.

"A great number of men are coming down the valley," he cried to the thanes in the courtyard below, and they at once mounted to the battlements. A mile away great numbers of men could be seen running at the top of their speed. There was neither order nor formation. Among them were a few horsemen riding in a knot together, and round these a number of the footmen were running in a close mass; but by far the greater proportion straggled across the valley, some being a considerable distance behind the rest.

"They are like a swarm of bees," Beorn said.

"Yes, and are just as angry. Of course, the news of what has happened here was sent off to them at once, and has brought them back again. I trust that it reached them before they came upon Oswald's party."

"They must have been on their return," Beorn said. "It was but two hours ago that we won the castle. Had a swift messenger started the moment the news reached the village, and had he known exactly the position where he would find Llewellyn, he could not have taken the news to him and brought them back here had they been some eight miles away. It must be farther than that to the spot where we lost Oswald, and as the thanes would surely be making their way either back to camp or eastward to the border, they must have been many miles from here an hour since. We know that the Welsh levies were summoned in the evening, and probably reached the spot where we were deserted by the guide, before daybreak, and took up the search at once. Therefore I think, Wulf, there can be no doubt that the messenger from here must have met them as they were returning; but whether they had overtaken and destroyed Oswald's command, or had failed in their search for them, we cannot tell."

Wulf shook his head. "I fear the former is most likely. The Welsh here must know every foot of their mountains, so that by scattering through the valleys they could scarcely fail to come upon the traces of Oswald's passage, and they would pursue him as hotly as wolves chase a deer. My only hope is that Oswald may have established himself at daybreak this morning in some strong position, and fortified himself there, in hopes that we might rejoin him, and that Llewellyn had not begun the attack upon it when the news reached him of the capture of his castle. How many, think you, are there in that approaching throng?"

"Some four or five thousand I should say."

"Yes, quite five thousand, Beorn."

At the call of the watchmen the men had, of their own accord, all mounted to the walls.

"We had better divide our commands," Beorn said. "Your force is double mine. For the present I will undertake the defence of the rear walls if you will take the front. Of course till an attack actually commences it will not be necessary to keep more than a strong guard on duty."

"Certainly not," Wulf agreed. "The danger will be far greater at night than by day, and we must give the men as much rest as possible. But I think that you with your men and half of mine ought to take the command in front, while I with the rest defend the rear."

"Not at all, Wulf, this is your affair altogether. I should never have thought of trying to take the castle. It was your idea, and has been carried out by you altogether. You are much fuller of plans than I am. I will do my best to second you, but you must continue to be the head in the matter."

"Very well, Beorn. I refuse to be considered in command, but we will apportion our forces as you suggest. We will take care that at any rate the Welsh shall not capture the castle as rapidly as we did, and so will put four men always on duty at each of the gates in the interior walls, so that if by any chance they manage to effect an entrance into one of the yards they will be able to get no farther until our whole force can assemble to oppose them."

CHAPTER XI. — THE SECRET PASSAGE.

Beorn called his men together and distributed them along the rear wall, while Wulf made a fresh examination of the front. He had before noticed that great piles of stone in blocks from fifty to a hundred pounds in weight were piled along by the parapet, in readiness to hurl down upon any foe attempting to ascend the road, while in the courtyard below was an immense reserve of these missiles. He placed twenty of his men here, and posted the other ten as sentries on the side walls, and then went down through the passage to Osgod. The bridge was entirely demolished as he had directed, with the exception of a single plank, which could be thrown over in a moment. Osgod had closed the gate, and had fastened a rope from the top of the turret to the plank, so that this could be hauled up, without those engaged in the operation being exposed to missiles from the other side of the chasm.

"One feels almost ashamed at being so safe," Osgod said, as Wulf joined him on the turret. "It does not give one the chance of a fight."

"You have had one good fight to-day, Osgod, and can do without another. I should be glad if we did not have to strike a blow till we see Gurth's banner coming down the valley."

"We have done very well," Osgod agreed; "and I should be quite contented if I had but come across that rascal who nearly smothered me in the bog."

"You need not bear malice against him, Osgod; for if he had not deserted us and led Llewellyn's force away to the spot where he left us, we should not be masters of the place as at present, and it would have been a terrible business had we been obliged to take this stronghold by storm."

"That is true enough, master; except by hunger or by a surprise, such as we carried out, I don't see how the place is to be taken if stoutly defended. There is no reason why the Welsh should have been in such a hurry to return, for they must know as well as we do that there is but little chance of their getting in again. They have come to a halt now down there, and half of them have thrown themselves on the ground like a pack of tired hounds."

"I have no fear whatever of an open attack, Osgod. They can see for themselves that the bridge is destroyed, and I do not think they will dream of coming up that road, which, as they know, we can sweep with stones from above. If they attack openly at all, it will be by the wall we scaled. If they make twenty ladders such as we had they may think they might gain a footing, especially as their archers high among the trees would be able to fire down on the defenders of the wall. But what I am really afraid of is that there may be some secret passage."

"Do you think so?" Osgod said, startled. "Where could it come from?"

"Well, Osgod, you see they have cut this winding road up the rock and have made the tunnel hence to the courtyard, so the chiefs have had abundance of labour at their disposal. They would naturally wish to provide a means of escape if the castle were besieged, and like to fall by force or famine; moreover it would enable them to send out messengers or receive messages from without. A passage four feet high and two feet wide would suffice. They may have driven such a passage from some place in the wood behind and it may come up somewhere in the courtyard, perhaps in one of the little huts along the side. Of course the entrance would be covered here by a stone, and would be hidden among the bushes at the other end. Still I do not think that this is likely, for a hostile force would almost certainly take up its post in that wood, and attack the place in the rear. If there is such a passage I think that it must open somewhere on the face of the rock, on one side or the other. It looks to us almost perpendicular, but there may be inequalities by which active men might ascend at some point or other. For a considerable distance we could see there were tufts of shrubs growing here and there, and one of these may conceal a small opening. From this point a staircase may have been driven up into the castle."

"That would be very awkward, master, if it were so."

"It would indeed. To-night all the force except the sentries shall gather in the castle, where ten men by turns shall keep guard, one or two being placed in the lower chambers. In this way we shall be safe; for before more than three or four can enter we should be all on foot, and as they can but come up in single file, could repulse them without difficulty. Tomorrow we will lower men down with ropes from the walls, and examine every clump of bushes growing on the face of the rock If we find any signs of a path or entrance we shall have no difficulty in discovering where it enters into the castle, and can effectually block it up. I shall then feel much more comfortable than I do at present."

"I was looking forward to a good night's sleep," Osgod grumbled, "but your idea, master, has quite done away with that. If I went off I should dream that I had one of those Welsh wolves at my throat. However, it is a good thing that you thought of it."

"I think, my lord," one of the soldiers said, "there are a number of our men among the Welsh. I can make out helmets and shields, and I think many are clad in leather jerkins."

Wulf looked attentively.

"Yes, there are certainly shields and helmets," he said. "I fear there is no doubt they have overtaken Oswald's levies."

"And have made them prisoners?"

Wulf shook his head. "They never take prisoners, you know. I fear they have slain them all and possessed themselves of their arms and clothes. In no other way can there be Saxon shields and helmets among them."

"By St. Nicholas!" Osgod exclaimed, "it is too bad that we should be standing here doing nothing. Why doesn't Llewellyn attack us instead of keeping his men gaping there at the castle?"

"Because at present he can do nothing, and is not fool enough to throw away hundreds of lives; besides, he must know that his mother and children are in our hands."

Presently a white flag was raised among the Welsh. Wulf had expected this, and had ordered a white cloth to be held in readiness to raise in reply. As soon as this flew out to the wind three men were seen to advance with the flag towards the foot of the road up to the castle. Wulf at once sent for the two interpreters to join him.

"Shall you let them come up, master?" Osgod asked. "They are as treacherous as snakes. See how that boy led us astray in the bog."

"You cannot get that boy out of your head, Osgod," Wulf laughed. "There is no conceivable way by which three men could recapture this castle. There is nothing for them to learn. They know its strength and everything connected with it, and they can see for themselves that we have destroyed the bridge. I shall be glad to hear what they have to say. Llewellyn himself is, most likely, one of the number."

The little party mounted the road until they stood on the platform from which the bridge started. One of them was a tall figure, dressed in armour, and with long black hair flowing down from under his helmet over his shoulders. Wulf at once, from the descriptions he had heard of the chief's appearance, recognized him as Llewellyn ap Rhys.

"I would speak with the commander of the Saxons who have, in my absence, taken my castle by treachery."

"I am the commander," Wulf said.

The Welshman's fingers clenched, and he glanced furiously at the young Saxon. By a great effort, however, he restrained his passion, and said courteously: "I am Llewellyn ap Rhys. To whom have I the pleasure of speaking?"

"I am Wulf of Steyning, prince. I don't know altogether that I have taken your castle by treachery, indeed I claim to have won it by fair fighting. You went out with your force to attack me among the hills, and during your absence I attacked and captured your castle. I will do your garrison credit to say they fought bravely in spite of the surprise. I would gladly have given them quarter, but they refused my offers, and, save a few wounded, whom I allowed the women to carry off, died to a man fighting bravely. No women were hurt or insulted, save those who took up arms and fought among the men, and it was no fault of ours that they were killed. Methinks that in your incursions into England you have not always shown the same mercy."

Llewellyn was silent for a minute. He had indeed never shown any pity in his forays, but had never expected that his castle and family would be in the hands of the Saxons.

"I learn," he said at last, "from the women, that my mother and my children are alive in your hands, and I thank you for the honorable treatment I hear that they have received."

"They are safe and well," Wulf replied. "We Saxons do not massacre women and children in cold blood. They will be honourably treated until I can hand them over to the care of Earl Gurth, who will doubtless send them to England as hostages."

"I shall try to win back my castle," Llewellyn said. "May I be sure that whatever happens they will be safe?"

"You may. Even were you forcing your way into the castle I will guarantee that no hair of their heads shall be injured. And now, prince, it is my turn to question. I see Saxon helmets and shields among your followers. Whence come they?"

A cloud passed over Llewellyn's face. He had not reckoned on their being observed from the castle. Concealment was now out of question, and he said boldly: "I defeated a party of your countrymen this morning. They came with hostile intent into my territory, and they have been destroyed." Although he had expected the answer, Wulf was shocked at the confirmation of his fears. Llewellyn, indeed, had fallen on Oswald's levies and annihilated them soon after daybreak. Having no idea that a party had separated from them during the night, he was returning exulting in the idea that he had destroyed the whole of the invaders, when the news had reached him of the capture of his castle. Wulf was silent. "It is the fortune of war," he said gravely. "It is not to me that you have to reckon for the deed, but with Earl Gurth, for whom I hold this castle."

Llewellyn made no reply, but with a wave of his hand turned and went down the hill again.

"I am even more than before convinced, Osgod, that there is a secret passage. I was watching him closely when the interpreter told him that I should hand his mother and children over to Gurth. He pressed his lips together, and his face lighted up with exultation for a moment."

"What do you think he came here for, master?"

"He came here to assure himself if possible that their lives would not be sacrificed in the event of his attacking."

"It is a pity you told him they would be safe," Osgod said.

"But they will be safe, and even if we are surprised and slain I would not that Llewellyn should say that it was only the suddenness of his attack that saved their lives. I will place two of our best men at their door with orders that come what may they are to prevent anyone from entering. But I don't think it will come to that. Should the passage enter into the castle, as, if it exists, I have no doubt it does, we shall be prepared to deal with them, if it opens elsewhere we shall have all our force save a few sentries assembled, and though all the walls fall into their hands, we ought to be able to hold it successfully till Gurth arrives to our rescue."

Wulf returned to the castle, and then joined Beorn at his post on the wall facing the wood. He communicated to him his ideas as to the probable existence of a secret passage.

"We must provide a mode of retreat for your men on guard here, Beorn, in case the Welsh enter by either of these yards instead of by the castle. These flanking towers at the angles of the walls cut off all passage. We will construct bridges with two or three planks across these towers, so that your sentries can retreat from the rear wall to the next, and again on to the inner wall. The doors between the courtyards shall be closed, so that should they enter either of these outer courts they will be delayed, and your men will have plenty of time to join us in the defence of the last wall. However, I am convinced the castle itself will be the scene of action. Five sentries will be enough to place on this wall. I will put two on each of the cross walls, so that if your men give the alarm it will be passed along speedily. I shall remove the last plank of the bridge at nightfall, and have Osgod and four men in the turret and two on the wall above them. We shall therefore have fifty-five men in the castle, and that should be ample. They can keep watch and watch, so there will be over twenty-five men under arms, and ready to throw themselves upon the Welsh wherever they may enter."

These arrangements were carried out. At ten o'clock all lights were extinguished, save a torch burning in each room on the ground floor. The floors and walls had been carefully examined and sounded, but nothing suspicious had been discovered. Four men were told off to each room except the great hall, where twenty were gathered in reserve. Half were to keep watch, but all were to lie down. The orders to those who were to keep awake were strict If they heard a noise or saw a stone move they were to keep silent, until two or three men had stepped out, then they were to give the alarm, leap up, and throw themselves upon them.

"Were the alarm given," he said, "before they fairly issued out the stone might be moved back again, and it would give us immense trouble before we could demolish it or find the secret of the spring. Therefore, let them get a footing first."

From time to time either Beorn or Wulf got up and went noiselessly round to the different rooms to see that the watch was vigilant. As had been arranged, each of those on guard raised a hand as they entered a room, so as to show that they were awake. Wulf did not expect that any attempt would be made before midnight. After that hour he sat in a corner of the dais, leaning as if asleep, but with his eyes wandering round the room watching every stone, and his ears listening for the faintest sound. He had no feeling of sleepiness whatever, his senses being all strung up to the highest pitch.

From time to time he held up a hand, and ten others were at once elevated, showing that the watchers were as vigilant as himself. It was, he thought, about one o'clock when he heard a faint creaking sound. It did not seem to him to be in the hall itself, but in a room adjoining it, the doors having all been left open. He rose to his feet, touched Beorn, who lay a pace or two away, and stole noiselessly out, grasping his sword in his hand. He stopped before he got to the open door of the next room and listened. All seemed perfectly quiet. He stood motionless, until a minute later there was a sudden shout, followed almost instantly by a clash of arms.

With a shout to his followers Wulf ran into the room. The four Saxons were on their feet, and were attacking three men, who, as he entered, were joined by a fourth from behind. He and Beorn threw themselves into the fray just as one of the Saxons fell with his head cloven by a sweeping blow from the tall figure opposed to him. One after another in rapid succession the Welsh poured in from a narrow opening, but the Saxons rushed up in overwhelming numbers. There was a brief fierce fight, and the Welsh were slain or overpowered. The men who last emerged turned to fly, but meeting those crowding up from behind were unable to do so. Others ran in only to be cut down as soon as they appeared; a sound of fierce shouting and angry struggle came through the opening. When no more showed themselves, Wulf called for torches, and a dozen were soon at hand. Seizing one he passed through the narrow opening. A winding staircase met his view. With Beorn and some Saxons following close behind him, he descended for a considerable distance, then he found himself in a low and narrow passage, and following this for twenty yards stepped out into the open air.

"We need do no more to-night, Beorn," he said. "We will see where this comes out and block it up in the morning, though they are not likely to try again. We can sleep now without fear of interruption."

His first step was to examine the bodies of the fallen Welshmen. He had recognized in the tall man with whom he had crossed swords Llewellyn ap Rhys, and found him lying beneath four of his followers, who had stood over him and defended him to the last. He was glad to find that the Welsh prince still lived, and directed that he should be at once carried to a room and that every attention should be shown him. None of the other fourteen Welshmen who had fallen showed any signs of life.

Ordering their bodies to be carried out into the courtyard, Wulf placed four men on guard at the upper opening of the secret passage. They were to be relieved every hour. He then went out and saw to the relief of the sentries on the walls, and called down to Osgod that the attack had been made and repulsed. He then went back and slept soundly till daybreak. On going to the walls he learned that there had been a great commotion down in the valley. Fierce shouts, loud wailing cries, and a confused sound of running and talking had been heard. At daybreak the Welsh were still there, and their fires had been lighted: one party were seen to march away as soon as it was light, but others arrived, and their numbers appeared about the same as on the previous evening. There was no general movement, but it could be seen that they gathered in clusters, and listened to men who addressed them with animated gestures.

"They don't know what to do," Wulf said to Osgod, whom he had joined in the turret. "They believe their chief to be dead; they know that his mother and children are prisoners in our hands; they can have little hope of capturing this place, which they believe to be impregnable to open attack. At present they must be without a leader, and yet they must be so animated by a spirit of hate and revenge, and by the desire to wipe out their humiliation by retaking this place, that they will not stir from in front of it."

As he spoke a messenger came from Beorn, saying that the Welsh were pouring arrows and javelins from the hill upon his sentries on the walls, and that these were unable to show a head above the parapet. In one of the sheds a large quantity of hides had been found, and taking a party laden with them Wulf proceeded to the wall at the rear. Here he directed the ladders that were still lying there to be cut up into lengths of eight feet. These were fixed at intervals upon the parapet, and a cord fastened along the top, the men engaged in the operations being protected by the shields of their comrades from the rain of missiles from the trees. Hides were thrown over the ropes, and these hid those on the wall from the view of the enemy, while they themselves could peep out from time to time between the hides to see that no preparations were being made for an attack.

The secret passage was next investigated; it was found that the opening was about half-way down the rock, and that the assailants must have climbed up by a path that a goat could scarce traverse. Wulf set a party to work to carry down stones from the courtyard, and to block up the passage solidly for ten feet from the opening, a sentry being posted on the wall above. After the erection of the shelter of hides the Welsh only sent an occasional javelin from the trees, but by the loud yells that were from time to time raised, there was no doubt they were still there in force.

"It is evident that they are going to besiege us, Beorn," Wulf said when they sat down to breakfast together. "The question is, are we to remain here until rumour carries the report of our capture of the place to Gurth, or shall we despatch messengers to him?"

"As you yourself said yesterday, the messengers could never get away, Wulf. I would give a year's revenue if we could do so, for it may be a long time before news comes to Gurth's ears. He may possibly hear of the annihilation of Oswald's force, for any Welsh woman taken captive might mention that in triumph, but they would certainly say nothing of such a grievous blow to the Welsh cause as the capture of Porthwyn and the death of Llewellyn in an attempt to recapture it. Gurth, therefore, naturally supposing that we had been involved in Oswald's disaster, may abandon all idea of moving against this place until the greater part of the country was reduced to obedience."

"I see, Beorn, that the difficulty of a messenger getting through would be indeed enormous; the Welsh must know that we are but a small band, and that our first aim would be to communicate with Gurth. You may be sure, therefore, that they will keep a vigilant guard all round the place at night to see that no messenger makes his way out. Our two interpreters do not know anything like enough Welsh to pass as natives, none of our people know a word of the language, it would be sending anyone to almost certain death. I think we must be content to depend upon ourselves. Gurth is sure to learn the news sooner or later, for it will make a great stir all through the country. I have just seen Llewellyn, he is very sorely wounded. I think it would be a good thing to let the Welsh know that he is in our hands, it will render them more chary of attacking us. We might hang out a flag of truce, and when they come up in reply tell them that he is alive but sorely wounded, and that they may send up a leech, who would better attend to his wounds than we can do."

This was accordingly done. Two Welshmen of rank came up to the broken bridge and were informed that their prince was sorely wounded, and that a leech would be allowed to enter to attend upon him. An hour later a man with a boy carrying a large basket came up the hill and crossed the plank into the turret. The basket, which contained various herbs and medicaments, was taken from the boy, who was then sent back again, while the leech was taken up to the room where Llewellyn was lying, in the care of his mother and her maids.

Three days passed without any change. The force in the valley was seen to be considerably diminished, no hostile demonstration had taken place; but twenty men always remained in the courtyard in the rear, in readiness to run up to the wall in case the sentries gave an alarm.

On the fourth morning, just as day was breaking, a man ran into the castle with the news that the Welsh were attacking the wall. Beorn and Wulf sprung to their feet, and with every man except those on duty as sentries ran off to the scene of attack. That it was a serious assault was evident by the wild yells and shouts that were heard.

Wulf ran up the stairs to the wall. A storm of missiles was striking against the hides; many of them failed to penetrate, but others did so, and several of the men were lying wounded under shelter of the parapet, while the rest were hurling down javelins between the openings of the hides.

"What are they doing?" he asked the sub-officer in command of the party.

"They are preparing to scale the wall, my lord; they have numbers of ladders."

Wulf was about to look out between the hides, but the officer exclaimed, "Do not so risk your life, my lord; you can see down without danger;" and he pushed out the lower side of one of the skins from the wall, so that Wulf could look down without being seen by the Welsh archers. The fosse in the rock and the narrow platform at the foot of the wall were alike crowded with foes, who were planting a number of ladders side by side. These were strongly constructed, and were each wide enough for two men to mount abreast. Eight or ten of these ladders were already planted against the wall, and the enemy were climbing up them. Wulf turned, and waving his sword shouted to the men running into the courtyard from the walls and castle to hasten up. Already a dozen had joined him, and scarce had these placed themselves along the battlements when the heads of the Welshmen appeared above it.

For a minute or two it seemed that these would overmaster the defence. Several succeeded in crossing the parapet, but they were either cut down or cast headlong into the courtyard. By this time the whole of the Saxons, save the guard in the turret by the bridge, were on the wall, and were able to form a close line along the parapet against which the ladders were placed. The Welsh fought with an utter disregard of life; as fast as those at the top were cut down or hurled backwards others took their place. So closely did they swarm up the ladders that several of these broke with their weight, killing many of those clustered below as well as those on the rungs. But for an hour there was no pause. It was well for the defenders that they had the protection of the line of hides, and were therefore screened from the arrows of the bowmen on the hill; but these soon ceased to shoot, as many of their comrades were hit by their missiles, while they were unable to see whether the arrows had any effect whatever upon the hidden defenders. At length the leaders of the assailants saw that the task could not be achieved, and gave the signal by the blowing of cow-horns that the attack should cease; but so furious were their followers that many disregarded the summons, and continued their efforts to gain a footing upon the wall, or at least to kill one of its defenders, for some time after the main body had withdrawn. As soon as the last of these was killed the garrison hurled the ladders backwards and then gave a shout of triumph, which was answered by renewed yells of defiance by the Welsh.

"It has been a hard fight, Wulf," Beorn said, as he removed his helmet.

"It has indeed. It was a well-planned attack, and was nearly successful. We ought to have had a stronger guard there; but I did not think that they would venture to attack at daylight, nor that they could have so quickly run forward and placed their ladders. Had we been but a minute later in arriving here they would have gained this wall and the courtyard. They would, indeed, have got no farther, but their success would have so excited them that we should have had to fight night and day. What has been our loss?"

Five of the men were killed; many of the others had received severe wounds on the head and shoulders from the knives of their assailants, and had it not been for the protection afforded by the leathern helmets and jerkins the number of killed would have been very much larger.

"I would as lief fight with a troop of wild cats," exclaimed Osgod—who, as soon as he saw that there was no movement down on the plain, had run up with half his little garrison to join in the defence of the wall,—as he tried to staunch a deep wound that extended from his ear to his chin. "Over and over again I saw a shock head come up above the wall, and before I had time to take a fair blow at it the man would hurl himself over upon me like a wild animal. Three times was I knocked down, and I am no chicken either; if it had not been for my comrades on each side it would have gone hard with me. I was able to return the service several times, but had the Welsh been imps they could not have been more active or more fierce. There must be a hundred lying slain along here or in the courtyard. I do not wonder that Oswald's men were all killed by them, though after our previous fights I held them in but small respect."

"It is a different thing, Osgod," Beorn said. "In the field we have always had the advantage from our order and our discipline; but here it was man against man. We had the advantage of position and they of numbers; but discipline went for nothing on either side, and I doubt if we should have done as well as they did had we been the assailants."

"I am ready to own that," Osgod agreed. "I like to fight with my feet on firm ground, and should make but a poor figure balanced on the top of a ladder."

When the tumult in the wood had died away Wulf raised a white flag, and ordered one of the men who spoke Welsh to shout to the enemy that they might approach without molestation and remove their wounded and dead from the foot of the wall, and also said that the Saxon leaders desired to speak to an officer of rank.

Two of these came out from the trees. "Hitherto," the interpreter cried with a loud voice, "my lords, the noble thanes, Beorn of Fareham and Wulf of Steyning, have given the most honourable treatment to your chief, Llewellyn ap Rhys, wounded and a prisoner in their hands, and to his family. Nor have they altered that treatment while you were attacking our walls; but they bid me warn you and all others in arms against the authority of our sovereign lord the king, that henceforth they will hold them as hostages, and that their lives will be forfeited if any fresh attack be made upon the castle."

Three days passed without any further acts of hostility by the Welsh. At the end of that time Llewellyn was sufficiently recovered to sit up supported by pillows on his couch. He had already heard of the defeat, with terrible slaughter, of the attempt of his countrymen to recapture the castle, and of the warning that had been given the Welsh that if the attack was renewed the lives of himself and his family would be forfeited. Beorn and Wulf paid him a visit as soon as they heard that he was in a condition to talk to them.

"Prince," Wulf said through his interpreter, "it is, you must see, hopeless for your followers to attempt to recapture this castle. The bridge is destroyed, the secret passage by which you entered blocked up, and we can resist any attack upon the rear wall. We have shown you and yours a mercy such as you would certainly not have extended to English men and women under similar circumstances, and grieved as we should be to be obliged to proceed to extremities with prisoners, yet were the castle again attacked, and were we to see that there was a prospect of its being recaptured, we should not hesitate to slay you, as it would be treachery to the king to allow so formidable an enemy as yourself to regain his freedom.

"Your cause is hopeless. Harold, Tostig, and Gurth are carrying fire and sword through your valleys, and your people will have to choose between submission and death. Why should so hopeless a struggle continue? Gurth will be here shortly, and then the fate that has befallen the districts already subdued will light upon yours. Surely it will be better for yourself and your people that this should be averted. This can only be done by your sending orders to your followers to scatter to their homes and to lay down their arms. We will at once in that case send a messenger to the earl to tell him that the district has submitted. I must request that in order the message shall reach him you shall bid two officers of rank accompany our messenger to Gurth's camp; we giving them our undertaking that they shall be allowed to leave it unmolested."

"Your offer tallies with my own intentions," Llewellyn said. "Had I been free I would have resisted to the last, but as a prisoner, and with my mother and children in your hands, I am powerless. My harper tells me that fully four hundred of my followers fell in the attack, and with my stronghold in your power, my tribesmen without a leader, and your armies desolating the land, I see that further resistance here would but add to the misfortunes of my people. I am ready, therefore, to send down my harper and doctor to bid four of my chiefs come up here, under your safe conduct. I shall lay the matter before them, and tell them that I being a prisoner can no longer give them orders, but shall point out to them that in my opinion further resistance can but bring terrible disasters upon the district. This, on their return, they will lay before their men, and if, as I trust, these will agree to scatter to their homes, they will furnish the escort you desire for your messenger."

Two hours later three of the chiefs summoned arrived, the fourth having fallen in the assault. They had a private interview with Llewellyn and then left. A great meeting was held down in the valley, and in the afternoon the three chiefs and six others came up to the castle and formally made their submission before Beorn and Wulf, and besought them to send a messenger to the earl praying him to forgive past offences and to have mercy on the people. An hour later two of the Saxons bearing a letter from Beorn and Wulf to Gurth started under an escort provided by the chiefs.

CHAPTER XII. — EDITH.

Two days after the departure of the messengers from the castle the look-out gave notice that he perceived a large body of horsemen and footmen coming down the valley, and half an hour later the banner of Gurth could be made out. The garrison at once set to work to replace the planking of the bridge, and this was accomplished by the time that the Saxon earl, accompanied by several thanes, and followed by a strong body of troops, reached the platform at the other end. As he did so Beorn and Wulf crossed the bridge to meet him.

"You have done well indeed, thanes!" Gurth exclaimed. "You have made a conquest to be proud of; for as we rode along this place seemed to us well-nigh impregnable. But your messengers have told me how you captured it, and how stoutly you have since defended it. It was a daring thought, indeed, to attempt the assault of such a place with a handful of men. You have rendered a splendid service to the king; for with the capture of this fortress, and of Llewellyn himself and his children, there is no fear that there will be trouble in this part of Wales for years to come. We, too, are specially indebted to you, for had we been forced to besiege this place it could only have been taken with a vast loss of life, and it might well have resisted all our efforts. That seventy men should have taken it, even if weakly defended, is wonderful indeed."

"It is to Wulf, my lord, that the credit is chiefly due," Beorn said. "It was he who proposed and planned the attack; and though I have done my best to support him, I have but acted as his second in command. He is quicker-witted than I am, and far more fitted to lead."

Wulf was about to speak, when Gurth stopped him with a gesture of the hand.

"At any rate, Beorn," he said, "you possess qualities that are by no means common. That you are a brave soldier I know well, but so I trust are all my thanes; still, it is not every one who has the wit to perceive that another has sharper wits than himself, still fewer who would have the generosity to stand aside and to give the major share in an exploit like this to another. What you may lose in credit by your avowal you will at least gain in the esteem of us all. Now, commandant," he said to Wulf with a smile, "show us the way into this capture of yours."

Before entering the castle itself Gurth made a detour of the walls, and upon seeing them was still more surprised than before at the manner in which the capture had been effected.

"You see, thanes," he said, "the matter hinged on the possession of these gates through the cross walls. That the rear walls should have been taken by surprise was a daring action, but it would have availed nothing had the garrison had time to close even the second of these gates; for though, as it seems, no more numerous than our men, they could have easily held it until reinforced from the village below, and would then have turned the tables on their assailants. The capture was due to the quickness and boldness with which Wulf and Beorn, with the few men who had obtained a footing on the wall when the alarm was given, rushed forward and held the inner gateway until the rest came up."

Gurth paused for a time on the wall above the point where the secret passage came out on the face of the rock, and having asked many questions as to how it was that they were so well prepared for Llewellyn and his followers when they made the attack, he commended Wulf very strongly for his conduct in this matter.

"Others might have taken the castle as you did, young thane," he said, "but assuredly most would have lost it again, for having set guards on the walls they would have given themselves up to feasting and sleep, without a thought that there might possibly exist a secret passage through this rock, which looks as if nothing short of a winged army could scale it. What say you, thanes?"

The Saxons cordially agreed with the earl. They were stout fighters, but better in the field than in council, and it was in no small degree to the Danish blood in their veins that the sons of Godwin owed the vigour and intellect that had raised the family to so lofty a position among their countrymen. On concluding his inspection of the walls Gurth entered the castle, and after first examining the entrance to the secret passage, sat down with the thanes to a banquet, the preparation of which had been begun as soon as their coming was perceived. After that Gurth paid a visit to Llewellyn.

"Your fate is not in my hands, prince," he said to him, "but in that of my brother Harold. As, however, you have used your influence to persuade your people to submit, I shall do my best to induce him to take a favourable view of your case."

The next day the main body of Gurth's force arrived, and encamped in the valley. Llewellyn's chiefs all came in and made their submission, but the people for the most part took to the hills. As, day after day, news came of the terrible retaliation dealt out by the troops of Harold and Tostig they lost heart altogether, and sent in messengers craving to be allowed to come in and lay down their arms. Gurth at once accepted their submission, and hundreds returned to their homes. In other parts of Wales the feeling that resistance was vain rapidly extended. Their most fertile valleys had all been turned into deserts, and even on their own hills and among their own forests, where they had hitherto deemed themselves safe from attack, they were pursued and hunted down by the now lightly-armed Saxons. From all parts, therefore, offers to submit were sent in, and as a proof of their submission and regret for past behaviour, they seized Griffith their king, killed him, and sent his head to Harold, who thereupon granted them terms, and ordered his forces to withdraw beyond the border.

The campaign had lasted less than three months, but so terrible had been the blow dealt to the Welsh that a hundred years passed before they again ventured to renew their incursions into England. Llewellyn was pardoned, but great breaches were made in the walls of the fortress facing the hill, and these he was forbidden ever to repair. His children were taken to England, to be brought up there, and to serve as hostages for his future good behaviour. Harold, when he learnt the particulars of the capture and defence of Porthwyn, expressed his approval in the warmest terms.

"You have performed the greatest and most important feat of the war, Wulf," he said. "Yes, it is right that you should give every credit Beorn for his share in the matter; but I know you both well, and am assured that Beorn would never have conceived and carried out the attack, and that had he done so successfully, he and his men would all have been slain by Llewellyn that night. Beorn is a good youth; he is brave and kind-hearted; he is no fool, and will make and excellent thane; will become a favourite at court, and be always loyal and staunch. But I shall look to see you more than this. You have a head quick to plan, readiness and decision in danger, and, as you have shown, a genius for war. Study the writings of the Romans, the greatest masters of war the world has ever seen, make yourself acquainted with the methods of Caesar and other great commanders, and do not neglect to ponder on their laws and customs.

"When matters are settled here, travel to the various courts of Europe and acquaint yourself with the ways of peoples who are far more advanced than we in civilization, and you may come to stand some day among the most trusted councillors of the king, and as one of the best leaders of his troops. I see that the success you have attained while as yet so young has not puffed you up in any way. Always remember, Wulf, that though success may be envied, those who are successful may yet be liked if only they themselves do not seem conscious of success. I should say you had best not make a long stay at court, but betake you, shortly, to your estate. It is a good school, and one who can rule his own people wisely has a sound preparation for posts of larger responsibility. You will always find in the prior of Bramber a wise adviser, who will direct your studies, and will aid you where your Latinity falls short.

"It will be time enough in another five years for you to go abroad; but, of course, I do not wish you to remain all that time away from court. It is never good to be forgotten; therefore, come up two or three times a year. I trust that there will be no fresh wars or troubles to hinder your studies or interfere with your life; but remember that there is always danger from Normandy, therefore always keep on foot your force of housecarls; and if, as I think, your estates can afford it, add to their number, so that if trouble does come you will be able to again play a prominent part in it."

Wulf's contingent marched with the rest of the troops from the east as far as Reading, and there struck off by the nearest road to Steyning. He and Beorn accompanied Harold to London, and after staying there for a short time, and taking part in the fetes with which the conquest of the Welsh was celebrated, Wulf returned to Steyning and took up the life he had previously led there. Before starting he asked Harold's advice as to whether he should fortify Steyning after the manner of the Norman castles.

"By no means, Wulf. Such castles are useful only against quarrelsome neighbours. Wars are decided by great battles, and if these are lost a castle does but bring ruin upon its possessor, for it must sooner or later be taken. The man who, when a cause is lost, returns quietly to his home and goes about his usual work may escape unnoticed, while one who shuts himself up in a castle is certain to suffer at last from the vengeance of the conquerors. Resistance maintained in forests and swamps, as was done by the Bretons and Welsh, may weary out a foe, but a conqueror can wish for nothing better than that the defeated may assemble themselves in towns and castles, where he can slowly, perhaps, but surely destroy them piecemeal."

The time passed quickly and pleasantly at Steyning. Wulf studied hard for three or four hours a day, looked after his tenants, hunted and hawked, doubled the number of his company of housecarls, and often rode over to the priory of an evening. He now took his place naturally among the thanes in that part of the country, the reputation he had gained in the two wars giving him a standing among them, to which, from his youth, he would not otherwise have been entitled. In accordance with Harold's advice he went three times during the year up to court, where he generally met Beorn, who spent the greater part of his time there.

"How you can like all this formality and ceremony is more than I can imagine, Beorn."

"I don't care either for the formality or the ceremony, but I like the amusement and the gaiety, and should ask with much more reason how can you like to spend your time studying parchments and reading the doings of those old Romans, when you might be enjoying yourself here. The matter is altogether beyond me."

"I like it for itself, and I like it because it may some day be of great service to me."

"You see you are ambitious, Wulf, and I am not. I don't want to be a great commander or a state-councillor, and if I did want it ever so much I know I should never be one or the other. I am content to be a thane, as my father was before me, and seek no greater change than that of a stay for a month at court. That brightens one up more than anything; and one cannot be all one's life hunting in the woods and seeing after the tenants. By the way, I had a quarrel the other day with your old Norman enemy, Fitz-Urse. Your name was mentioned, and he chose to sneer offensively. I told him that you had done more already than he would ever do if he lived to be an old man. We came to high words, and next day met in the forest and there settled it. He ran me through the arm, and I slashed his cheek. As quarrelling is strictly forbidden he made some excuse and went over to France, while I went down home till my arm was well again. I fancy we hurt each other about equally, but the scar on my arm won't show, while I fancy, from what the leech who dressed his wound told me, the scar is likely to spoil his beauty for life."

"I am sorry you quarrelled with him about me, Beorn. It would have been better to have said nothing, though I thank you for your championship."

"Nonsense, Wulf. I know very well you would not hear anyone speak ill of me without taking up the cudgels for me."

Wulf could not deny this. "Certainly not, Beorn; still it is a pity to make an enemy, and Fitz-Urse has shown in my case that he is not one who forgives."

The Welsh campaign had terminated at the end of August, and it was a month later that Wulf had returned to Steyning. Just a year afterwards he received a message from Harold to come up to London, and to order his housecarls to hold themselves in readiness to start immediately on receiving an order from him. Somewhat surprised, for no news had reached him of any trouble that could call for the employment of an armed force, Wulf rode for London alone, bidding Osgod follow with the housecarls as soon as he heard from him. When he reached the palace he heard news that explained the cause of his summons. Northumbria had risen in rebellion against Earl Tostig. He was accused of tyranny and oppression, and had been continually away from his earldom, leaving it to be governed in his absence by a thane.

The country north of the Humber had for a long period of years been independent, appointing their own rulers, who owed no allegiance whatever to the kings of the West Saxons. Although now incorporated in the kingdom of England the Northumbrians regretted their lost independence, and this all the more, that the population were for the most part Danish, and viewed with an intense feeling of jealousy the preponderance gained by the West Saxons. Tostig at the time the revolt declared itself was hunting with the king—who had a great affection for him—in the forests of Wiltshire, and had not arrived in town when Wulf reached the capital. It was not until the afternoon that Wulf had an interview with Harold. The earl had just come from a council and was alone.

"Thank you for coming up so speedily," he said as he shook the young thane by the hand. "You have heard the news, I suppose?"

"I have heard that Northumberland has risen in rebellion."

"Yes, that was the news that arrived four days since."

"Is it serious?"

"Yes, very serious; the rebellion grows each day. It is headed by several of the greatest landowners in the north, both Danish and Saxon, and the worst part of the news is that the trouble has, as I hear, been stirred up by Edwin of Mercia and his brother. It is the old rivalry between the House of Leofric and ours. They are jealous of our influence with the king, and would gladly rend England into two kingdoms again. We hear to-day that the Northumbrian nobles have summoned a Gemot to meet, which amounts in fact to a rebellion, not only against Tostig but against the king."

"If Mercia joins Northumbria it would be a more serious business than that in Wales."

"I think not that it will be so," Harold said. "Edwin has been always conspiring. He stirred up the Welsh, he has encouraged the Norwegians, he has intrigued in Northumbria. He and his brother have ever been a source of trouble, and yet he has never openly rebelled; he sets others to do the fighting for him, prepared if they are successful to reap the fruits of their victory. There is, of course, still hope that moderate councils may prevail, but I fear that the Northumbrians will consider that they have gone too far to turn back. At present, at any rate, no steps will be taken. As long as no armed forces are set in motion there are hopes that matters may be arranged, but the approach of an army would set all Northumbria on fire. The Gemot is summoned to meet this day week—that is on the third of October—and we shall wait to hear what steps they take. Messengers have already been sent to a large number of thanes to be prepared for service. I would that all kept a force of housecarls as you do. I am going down to-night to my house near Hampton. Do you come down with me, Wulf. Edith will be glad to see you."

Wulf had in the days of his pageship several times accompanied Harold to Hampton, and knew well the lady, who was known to the Saxons as Edith of the Swan-neck. She was by birth far inferior in position to Harold. The relation between them was similar to that known throughout the middle ages as left-hand marriages. These were marriages contracted between men of high rank and ladies of inferior position, and while they lasted were regarded as being lawful; but they could be, and frequently were, broken off, when for politic or other reasons the prince or noble had to seek another alliance. The lady was of great beauty and talent, and exercised a large influence over Harold. This was always employed for good, and she was much beloved by the Saxons.

The alliance had been formed while Harold was quite a young man, and he and Edith were fondly attached to each other. His rise, however, to the position of the foremost man in England, and the prospect of his accession to the throne, rendered it probable that ere long he would be obliged to marry one who would strengthen his position, and would from her high birth be fitted to share the crown with him. William of Normandy was perfectly well aware of the relation in which Edith stood to Harold, and had not regarded her as any obstacle to the earl's marriage with his daughter; and even Harold himself had not attempted to give it as a reason for declining the offer of the hand of the Norman princess.

As they rode down to Hampton the earl said, "I dare say you are somewhat surprised at my leaving the court at this crisis, Wulf, but in truth I want to keep my hands free. Tostig, you know, is rash and impetuous. I love him well, but am not blind to his faults; and I fear that the people of Northumbria have some just cause for complaint against him. He is constantly away from his earldom. He was absent for months when he went to Rome, and he spends a great part of his time either at the court here or with the king at his hunting-lodges. The Northumbrians are a proud people, and it is small wonder that they object to be governed by an absent earl. Tostig is furious at what he terms the insolence of the Northumbrians, and I would fain avoid all questions of dispute with him. It is not improbable that the king and his councillors may be called upon to hear the complaints of the Northumbrians, and to decide between them and Tostig. This will be bitter enough for my brother. He may return at any moment, and I greatly wish to avoid all argument with him before the matter is discussed in council."

The house at Hampton was a large one, and here Edith lived in considerable state. Grooms ran up and took the horses as Harold and Wulf dismounted. Six retainers in jerkins embroidered with the earl's cognizance appeared at the doors. As they entered the house, Edith came out from an inner room and fondly embraced Harold.

"Who is this you have with you, Harold?"

"What, have you forgotten Wulf of Steyning, who has, as I told you, turned out a great fighter, and was the captor of the castle of Porthwyn, and of its owner, Llewellyn ap Rhys?"

"I did not know you again, Wulf," Edith said holding out her hand to him, "but now that I hear who you are I recognize you. Why, it is four years since I saw you, and you were then a mischievous little page. Harold has often spoken to me about you, and your adventures in Normandy and Wales. I did not expect to see you, Harold," she went on turning to the earl, "after what you told me in the letter you sent me yesterday, about the troubles in the north. I feared that you would be kept at court."

"Tostig and the king are still away," he said, "and he will return so furious at this revolt against his authority, that, thinking as I do that he is in no small degree at fault—for I have frequently remonstrated with him at spending so large a portion of his time away from his earldom,—I thought it best to get away."

"It is strange how Tostig differs from the rest of you," Edith said. "You and Leofwyn, and Gurth are all gentle and courteous, while Tostig is fierce and impetuous."

"Tostig has his faults," Harold said; "but we love each other dearly, and from the time we were boys together we have never had a dispute. It will be hard indeed upon me if I am called upon to side against him. We have learnt, Edith, that Edwin and Morcar have been intriguing with the Northumbrians. These Mercian earls are ever bringing troubles upon the country, and I fear they will give even greater trouble in the future. If they stir up disturbances, as they have done, against the king, who is king by the will of the people, and also by right of birth, what will it be when—" and he stopped.

"When you shall mount the throne, my Harold," Edith said proudly. "Oh, that this feud between Leofric's house and Godwin's were at an end. It bodes ill for England."

"It is natural," Harold said gently. "It is as gall and wormwood to the earls of Mercia to see the ascendancy of the West Saxons, and still more would it be so were I, Godwin's son, without a drop of royal blood in my veins, to come to be their king."

"The feud must be closed," Edith said firmly, though Wulf noticed that her face paled. "I have told you so before, Harold, and there is but one way."

"It shall never be closed in that way, Edith; rather would I lie in my grave."

"You have not to think of yourself, Harold, still less of me. It is of England you have to think—this England that will assuredly choose you as its king, and who will have a right to expect that you will make any or every sacrifice for its sake."

"Any but that," Harold said.

She smiled faintly and shook her head. Wulf did not understand the conversation, but there was a look of earnest resolve in her face that deeply impressed him. He had moved a short distance away, and now turned and looked out of the window, while they exchanged a few more words, having been, as he saw, altogether oblivious of his presence in the earnestness with which they both spoke.

For a week Harold remained at Hampton. Wulf saw that he was much troubled in his mind, and concluded that the messengers who came and went every day were the bearers of bad tidings. It was seldom that he was away from the side of Edith. When they were together she was always bright, but once or twice when Wulf found her alone her features bore an expression of deep sadness.

"We must ride for London, Wulf," Harold said one morning after reading a letter brought by a royal messenger. "The king has laid his orders on me to proceed at once to town, and indeed the news is well-nigh as bad as can be. The Gemot has voted the deposition of Tostig, has even had the insolence to declare him an outlaw, and has elected Morcar in his place. It has also issued decrees declaring all partisans of Tostig outlaws, and confiscating their estates. Two of Tostig's Danish housecarls were slain on the first day of their meeting. Two hundred of Tostig's personal followers have since been massacred; his treasury has been broken open, and all its contents carried off. The election of Morcar shows but too plainly the designs of the earls of Mercia. They wish to divide England into two portions, and to reign supreme north of the Wellan. This will give them full half of England, and would assuredly, even did we not oppose them now, lead to a terrible war. The more terrible as William of Normandy will be watching from across the channel, ready to take instant advantage of our dissensions. God avert a war like this. Every sacrifice must be made rather than that the men of the north and south of England should fly at each other's throats."

The earl scarcely spoke a word during the ride to London, but rode absorbed in his thoughts with a sad and anxious countenance.

Day after day the news became more serious. Morcar accepted the earldom of Northumbria, hurried to York, and placing himself at the head of the Northumbrian forces, marched south, being joined on the way by the men of Lincoln, Nottingham, and Derby, in all of which shires the Danish element was very strong. At Northampton, which had formed part of the government of Tostig, Morcar was joined by his brother Edwin at the head of the forces of Mercia, together with a large body of Welsh. They found the people of Northampton less favourable to their cause than they had expected, and in revenge harried the whole country, killing and burning, and carrying off the cattle as booty and the men as slaves.

Harold bore the brunt of the trouble alone, for, regardless of the fact that half the kingdom was in a flame, King Edward and Tostig continued their hunting expeditions in Wiltshire, in spite of the urgent messages sent by Harold entreating them to return. In the meantime, still hoping that peace might in some way be preserved, Harold sent messages to all the thanes of importance in Wessex, ordering them to prepare to march to London with the whole of their retainers and levies, as soon as they received orders to get in motion. But while he still tarried in Wiltshire the king acceded to Harold's request that he might be empowered to go to Northampton to treat in Edward's name with the rebels.

As soon as he received this permission Harold hastened to Northampton, accompanied by only half a dozen of his thanes, among whom was Wulf. He was received with respect by the rebels, but when their leaders assembled, and in the king's name he called upon them to lay down their arms, to cease from ravaging, and to lay any complaints they might have to make against Tostig before the king or the National Gemot, he met with a flat refusal. They would not listen to any proposition that involved the possibility of the return of Tostig, and boldly said that if the king wished to retain Northumbria as part of his realm he must confirm the sentence of their Gemot upon Tostig, and must recognize their election of Morcar to the earldom.

In all this Harold perceived clearly enough that, although it was the Northumbrian leaders who were speaking, they were acting entirely under the influence of Edwin and Morcar. All that he could obtain was that some of the northern thanes should accompany him to lay their demands before the king himself. Edward, upon hearing, by a swift messenger sent by Harold, of the failure of his attempt to induce the Northumbrians to lay down their arms, reluctantly abandoned the pleasures of the chase, and proceeded to Bretford, near Salisbury, where there was a royal house, and summoned a Witenagemot. As, however, the occasion was urgent, it was attended only by the king's chief councillors, and by the thanes of that part of Wessex.

Between Tostig and Harold the quarrel that the latter had feared had already broken out. Harold was anxious above all things for peace, and although the blow to his own interests and to those of his family, by the transfer of Northumbria from his brother to one of the Mercian earls, was a most serious one, he preferred that even this should take place to embarking in a war that would involve the whole of England. Tostig was so furious at finding that Harold was not willing to push matters to the last extremity in his favour, that he accused him of being the secret instigator of the Northumbrian revolt. The absurdity of such an accusation was evident. It was as much to Harold's interest as to that of Tostig that the great northern earldom should remain in the hands of his family; but an angry man does not reason, and Tostig's fury was roused to the highest point by the outspoken utterances of many of the members of the Witenagemot. These boldly accused him of cruelty and avarice, and declared that many of his acts of severity were caused by his determination, under a show of justice, to possess himself of the wealth of those he condemned. Tostig then rose and declared before the assembly that the whole rising was the work of Harold.

The latter simply denied the charge on oath, and his word was accepted as sufficient. The Witan then turned to the question as to how the revolt was to be dealt with. The king was vehemently in favour of putting it down by force of arms. Tostig was of all the Saxons his favourite friend, and he considered the insult offered to him as dealt against himself. So determined was he, that he sent out orders for the whole of the forces of Wessex to march and join the royal standard. In vain Harold and Edward's wisest councillors endeavoured to dissuade him from a step that would deluge the country in blood, and might lead to terrible disaster. In vain they pointed out that while all the thanes would willingly put their forces at his disposal to resist a foreign foe, or even to repel an invasion from the north, they would not risk life and fortune in an endeavour to force a governor upon a people who hated him, and, as most thought, with good reason.

The king was immovable; but Harold and his councillors took steps quietly to inform the thanes that the Witan was opposed to the order, and that for the present no harm would be done by disregarding the royal mandate. The king, in his anger and mortification at finding himself unable to march against the rebels with an overwhelming force, fell ill, and the control of affairs passed into Harold's hands; and the king, whose fits of passion, though extreme while they lasted, were but short-lived gave him full power to deal with the matter as he thought best.

Harold had done all that he could for Tostig when he went to Northampton, but had failed. There was no alternative now between a great war, followed probably by a complete split of the kingdom, or acquiescence in the demands of the men of the North. He did not hesitate, but in the name of the king confirmed the decisions arrived at by the Gemot of York—recognized Morcar as Earl of Northumbria, and granted a complete amnesty for all offences committed during the rising, on condition only that a general Witenagemot should be held at Oxford. At this meeting Northern and Southern England were again solemnly reconciled, as they had been forty-seven years before at an assembly held at the same place.

CHAPTER XIII. — HAROLD, THE KING.

The day before the great Witenagemot was to assemble, Wulf, as he came out from the house where Harold had taken up his abode, was approached by a man, who by his attire appeared to be a retainer of a thane; his face seemed familiar to him, as he placed a letter in his hand. Wulf was now very much in the confidence of Harold. It was a relief to the earl in the midst of his trials and heavy responsibilities to open his mind freely to one of whose faith and loyalty he was well assured, and he therefore was far more communicative to the young thane than to the older councillors by whom he was surrounded. Wulf opened the letter. It contained only the words: "I am here; the bearer of this will lead you to me. Edith."

Looking more closely at the man he recognized him at once as one of the servitors at Hampton, though his dress bore no signs of any cognizance. Greatly surprised to hear of Edith's presence in Oxford unknown to Harold, he at once followed the servant, who conducted him to a house on the outskirts of the town. Wulf was ushered into a room, and the servant then left him. A moment later Edith entered.

"My message must have surprised you, Wulf," she said, as he knelt on one knee to kiss the hand she held out to him.

"It did indeed, lady, for it was but yesterday that the earl received a letter from you written at Hampton. He said to me as he opened it, 'Would I were in peace at Hampton, free from all these troubles and intrigues.'"

"I have come down in a horse-litter," she said, "and save the two retainers who accompanied me none knew of my intentions. I know, Wulf, that you have the confidence of the earl and that you love him and would do your best for him."

"I would lay down my life for him, lady. Even did I not love and honour him as I do, I would die for him, for he is the hope of England,

and he alone can guide the country through its troubles, both from within and without. The life of a single man is as nought in the scale."

"Nor the happiness of a single woman," she added. "Now, Wulf, I want to know from you exactly how matters stand here. My lord, when he writes to me always does so cheerfully, ever making the best of things; but it is most important that I should know his real mind. It is for that that I have travelled here. This Witenagemot that assembles to-morrow—what will come of it?"

"The earl thinks it will doubtless pass the resolution reconciling the North and South, and declaring that there shall be oblivion for the past, and that all things shall go back to their former footing save as to the change of earls."

"It is easy to vote that," she said quietly; "but will it be held to? It depends not upon Northumbrians nor Saxons, but upon Edwin and Morcar. They have made a great step forward towards their end; they have united under their government the northern half of England, and have wrested Northumbria from Godwin's family. After making this great step, will they rest and abstain from taking the next? Northumbria and Mercia united are as strong as Wessex and East Anglia. Will they be content to remain under a West Saxon king? Above all, will they submit to the rule of one of Godwin's sons? I feel sure that they will not. What thinks the earl?"

"He thinks as you do, lady, although he considers that for the time the danger is averted. He himself said to me yesterday, 'If these Mercian earls are ready to defy the head of the royal line of England, think you that they will ever recognize the sway of a member of my father's house?'"

"And what said you, Wulf?"

"I said that I did not doubt the ill-will of the Mercian earls, but that I doubted whether Mercia would follow them if they strove to break up the kingdom. 'Mercia is following them now,' he said; 'and has with Northumbria stood in arms for some weeks past. There has ever been jealousy of the supremacy of the West Saxons since the days when the kingdom was united in one. These brothers will intrigue as their father did before them. They will bring down the Welsh from their hills to aid them, for though these people will not for generations try their strength alone against us, they would gladly take advantage of it should such an opportunity for revenge occur. Even now, when the blood is scarce dry on their hearthstones, there is a large force of them under Edwin's banner.'"

"It is a grievous look-out for England," Edith said. "It would seem that nothing can bring about peace and unity save the end of this terrible feud between the families of Godwin and Leofric."

"That would indeed be a blessing for the country," Wulf agreed; "but of all things that seems to me most hopeless."

"They must be reconciled!" Edith said, rising from her seat. "What is a woman's love or a woman's life that they should stand in the way of the peace of England? See you not, Wulf, there is but one way in which the feud can be healed? Were it not for me Harold could marry the sister of these earls, and if she were Queen of England the feud would be at an end. A daughter of the house of Leofric, and a son of the house of Godwin, would command the support of Mercia and Wessex alike, and as brothers of the queen, Edwin and Morcar might well be content to be friends with her husband and his brothers. I only stand in the way of this. I have already urged this upon Harold, but he will not hear of it. Until now the Mercian brothers might be a trouble, but they were not strong enough to be a danger to the kingdom. Now that they hold half of it in their hands this marriage has become a necessity. I must stand aside. What is my happiness and my life that I should be an obstacle alike to my lord's glory and the peace of England? Go to Harold; tell him that I am here, and pray that he will come to me. Give your message to him briefly; say naught of what I have said to you, though his heart will tell him at once what has brought me here."

Silent, and confounded by the immensity of the sacrifice she proposed, for he knew how deep and tender was her love for Harold, Wulf knelt on both knees and reverently placed her hand to his lips, and then without a word left the house, half blinded with tears, signing to the servant, who was waiting without, to follow him. When he reached Harold's house he found that the earl was with his brother Gurth and several of his councillors. He did not hesitate, however, but entering the room, said, "My Lord Harold, I pray to have speech of you for a minute upon an affair of urgent importance."

Somewhat surprised the earl followed him out.

"What is it, Wulf?" he asked as they entered Harold's private closet. "You look pale and strange, lad."

"I have a message to give you, my lord. The Lady Edith is here, and prays that you will go to her at once."

The earl started as if struck with a blow. "Edith here!" he exclaimed, and then with a troubled face he took several short turns up and down the room.

"Where is she?" he said at last in a low voice.

"Her servant is without, my lord, and will conduct you to her."

"Tell Gurth and the others I am called away for an hour on urgent business," he said. "Say nothing of Edith being here." Then he went out.

The man who was waiting doffed his hat, and at once led the way to the house where Edith was staying. She moved swiftly towards him as he entered the room and fell on his neck. Not a word was spoken for a minute or two, then he said:

"Why have you come, Edith? But I need not ask, I know. I will not have it, I will not have it! I have told you so before. Why is our happiness to be sacrificed? I have given my work and my life to England, but I will not give my happiness too, nor will I sacrifice yours."

"You would not be worthy of the trust England reposes in you, Harold," she said quietly, "were you not ready to give all. As to my happiness, it is at an end, for I should deem myself as a guilty wretch, as the cause of countless woes to Englishmen, did I remain as I am. I have been happy, dear, most happy, many long years. To my last day it will be a joy and a pride, that nothing can take away, that I have been loved by the greatest of Englishmen, and my sacrifice will seem light to me under the feeling that it has purchased the happiness of England."

"But is my happiness to go for nothing?" Harold exclaimed passionately.

"You too, Harold, will have the knowledge that you have sacrificed yourself, that as you have often risked your life, so have you for England's sake given up your love. I have seen that it must be so for years. As Earl of Wessex I might always have stood by your side, but as soon as I saw that the people of England looked to you as their future monarch, I knew that I could not share your throne. A king's heart is not his own, as is that of a private man. As he must lead his people in battle, and if needs be give his life for them, so must he give his hand where it will most advantage them."

"I cannot do it," Harold said. "I will not sacrifice you even for England. I will remain Earl of Wessex, and Edwin may reign as king if he so chooses."

"That cannot be, Harold. If the people of England call you to the throne, it is your duty to accept the summons. You know that none other could guide them as you can, for already for years you have been their ruler. They love you, they trust in you, and it were a shame indeed if the love we bear each other should stand in the way of what is above all things needful for the good of England. You know well enough that when the national council meets to choose a king the South will declare for you. But if Edwin and Morcar influence Mercia and the North to declare for another, what remains but a breaking up of the kingdom, with perhaps a great war?"

"I cannot do it, and I will not," Harold said, stopping in his walk and standing before her. "My life, my work, all save you I will give up for England—but you I will not."

Edith turned even paler than before. "You will not give me up, Harold, but you cannot hold me. I can bear my life in seclusion and retirement, and can even be happy in the thought of our past love, of your greatness, and in the peace of England, which, I should have the consolation of knowing, was due to the sacrifice that we had both made, but I could not live happy, even with your love and your companionship, knowing that I have brought woes upon England. Nor will I live so. Death will break the knot if you will not do so, and I could die with a smile on my lips, knowing that I was dying for your good and England's. If you will not break the bond death shall do so, and ere to-morrow's sun rises, either by your sacrifice or by my own hand, you will be free. Marry for the good of England. Here is the ring by which you pledged your troth to me," and she took it from her finger and dropped it in the fire that blazed on the hearth. "There is the end of it, but not the end of our love. I shall think of you, and pray for you always, Harold. Oh, my dear lord and master, do not make it too hard for me!" and she threw herself on his neck in a passion of tears. For two or three minutes they stood locked in each other's close embrace, then she withdrew herself from his arms.

"Farewell," she said. "You have left my side many a time for battle, and we parted bravely though we knew we might never meet again. Let us part so now. We have each our battles to fight, but God will comfort us both, for our sacrifice will have brought peace to England. Farewell, my dear lord, farewell!" She touched his hand lightly and then tottered from the room, falling senseless as soon as she had closed the door behind her.

Harold sank into a chair and covered his face with his hands, while his breast heaved with short sobs. So he sat for some time; then he stood up.

"She is stronger and braver than I," he murmured; "but she is right. Only by this sacrifice can England be saved, but even so I could not have made it; but I know her so well that I feel she would carry out her threat without hesitation." Then he went out of the house, but instead of returning to the town took his way to the lonely path by the river, and there for hours paced up and down. At last his mind was made up, the sacrifice must be accepted. As she had said, their happiness must not stand in the way of that of all England. He walked with a firm step back to Oxford, and went straight to the house where Edwin and Morcar had taken up their quarters.

"Tell Earl Edwin that Harold would speak with him," he said to the retainer at the door. The man returned in a minute, and led the way to the room where Edwin and his brother were standing awaiting him. They had had several interviews since they arrived at Oxford, and supposed that he had come to arrange some detail as to the assembly on the following day.

"Edwin," Harold said abruptly, "methinks that for the good of our country it would be well that our houses should be united. Why should the sons of Leofric and Godwin regard each other as rivals? We are earls of the English people, and we cannot deny that the unfriendly feeling between us has brought trouble on the country. Why should there not be an end of this?"

Greatly surprised at this frank address, Edwin and Morcar both hastened to say that for their part they had no quarrel whatever with any of the house of Godwin, save with Tostig.

"Tostig will soon be beyond the sea, and will no longer be a source of trouble. There is, it seems to me, but one way by which we can unite and bind our interests into one. I have come to you to ask for the hand of your sister Ealdgyth in marriage."

The two earls looked at each other in surprise. The proposition was altogether unexpected, but they at once saw its advantages. They knew as well as others that the choice of the nation at Edward's death was likely to fall upon Harold, and it would add both to their dignity and security that they should be brothers-in-law of the king. Such an alliance would do away with the danger, that once seated on the throne Harold might become reconciled with Tostig, and endeavour to replace him in the earldom of Northumbria. This danger would be dissipated by the marriage.

"You would perhaps like to consult together before giving an answer," Harold said courteously.

"By no means," Edwin said warmly. "Such an alliance is, as you say, in all respects to be desired. Ealdgyth could wish for no nobler husband. We should rejoice in obtaining such a spouse for her, and the union would assuredly unite our families, do away with the unfriendly feeling of which you spoke, and be of vast advantage to the realm in general. We need no word of consultation, but accept your offer, and will with pleasure give Ealdgyth in marriage to you. But is there not an obstacle?"

"The obstacle is at an end," Harold said gravely. "Of her own free will and wish, and in order that there should be peace and union in England, the Lady Edith has broken the tie that bound us."

The brothers, seeing that the subject was a painful one, wisely said no more, but turned the conversation to the meeting on the following day, and assured Harold that they hoped the decision would now be unanimous, and then after a short time skilfully brought it round again to the subject of the marriage. By nightfall the news was known throughout the city, and was received with universal joy. The union seemed to all men a guarantee for peace in England. The two great rival houses would now be bound by common interests, and the feud that had several times been near breaking out into civil war was extinguished.

The moment he returned to his house Harold called Wulf.

"Wulf, go at once to the Lady Edith. Tell her that though it has taken all the brightness out of my life, and has made all my future dark, I have done her bidding, and have sacrificed myself for England. Tell her that I will write to her to-night, and send the letter to Hampton, where, I trust, it will find her."

Wulf at once carried the message. He found Edith sitting with eyes swollen with weeping, and yet with a calm and composed expression on her face.

"I knew that my lord would do as I prayed him," she said; "he has ever thought first of England and then of himself. Tell him that I start in an hour for Hampton, and shall there stay till I get his letter; there I will answer it. Tell him I thank him from my heart, and that, much as I loved and honoured him before, I shall to the end of my life love and honour him yet more for having thus sacrificed himself for England. Tell him that you found me calm and confident that he would grant my prayer, and that with all my heart I wish him happiness."

Her lips quivered and her voice broke, and Wulf hurried away without saying another word, for he felt that he himself was at the point of bursting into tears. Harold was anxiously awaiting his return, and after listening to the message turned abruptly and entered his private closet, with a wave of the hand signifying that Wulf would not be further required.

The next day the Witenagemot met. It was solemnly decreed that all old scores should be wiped out; that Northern and Southern England were again to be reconciled, as they had been forty-seven years before in an assembly held by Canute in Oxford. It was decreed unanimously that the laws of Canute should be renewed, and should have force in all parts of the kingdom.

Until this decision was arrived at by the assembly Tostig had remained with the king, but he now went into exile, and crossed the sea to Flanders, where he had at an earlier period of his life, when Godwin's whole family were in disgrace, taken refuge. He was accompanied by his wife and many personal adherents. He left filled with rage and bitterness, especially against Harold, who ought, he considered, to have supported him to the utmost, and who should have been ready to put the whole forces of Wessex in the field to replace him in the earldom.

By the time that Harold returned to London Edith had left his abode at Hampton. He would have gladly handed it over to her and maintained it as before, but she would not hear of this, though she had accepted from him an income which would enable her to live comfortably in seclusion.

"I only do this," she said in her letter to him, "because I know that it would grieve you if I refused; but I entreat you, Harold, make no inquiries whither I have gone. I do not say that we can never meet again, but years must pass over before we do so. You must not think of me as always grieving. I have done what I am sure is right, and this will give me comfort, and enable me to bear your absence; but you know that, even if I never see you again, you will dwell in my heart as long as I live, its sole lord and master. I have so many happy memories to look back upon that I should be sorely to blame did I repine, and although I may not share the throne that will ere long be yours, nor the love which Englishmen will give their king, I shall be none the less proud of you, and shall be sure that there will be always in your heart a kind thought of me. Forbear, I pray you earnestly, to cause any search to be made for me. Doubtless you might discover me if you chose, but it would only renew my pain. In time we may be able to meet calmly and affectionately, as two old friends, but till then it were best that we stood altogether apart."

Harold put down the letter with a sigh. But he had little time to lament over private troubles. The king was ill; he had not rallied from the state of prostration that succeeded his outburst of passion when he found himself powerless to put down the Northern insurrection by force, and to restore his favourite Tostig to his earldom. Day succeeded day, but he did not rally. In vain the monks most famous for their skill in medicine came from Canterbury and Glastonbury; in vain prayers were offered up in all the cathedrals, and especially in his own Abbey of Westminster, and soon the report spread among the people that Edward, the king, was sick unto death, and all felt that it was a misfortune for England.

Edward was in no sense of the word a great king. He was a monk rather than a monarch. The greatest object of his life had been to rear an abbey that in point of magnificence should rival the stateliest fane in England. To that his chief care was devoted, and for many years he was well content to leave the care of government to Harold. But after the monarchs who had immediately preceded him, his merits, if of a passive kind, were warmly appreciated by his subjects. His rule had been free from oppression, and he had always desired that justice should be done to all. In the earlier part of his reign he was Norman in tongue, in heart, and in education; but in the latter years of his life he had become far more English in his leanings, and there can be no doubt that he bitterly regretted the promise he had rashly given to William of Normandy that he should succeed him.

It was not only because the people respected and even loved the king that they were grieved to hear that his days were numbered, but because they saw that his death would bring trouble on the land. With him the line of the Oethelings would become extinct, save for the boy Edgar and his sisters. The boy had been born beyond the sea, and was as much a foreigner as Edward himself had been, and Edward's partiality for the Normans in the early years of his reign had so angered the English that Edgar's claims would on this account alone have been dismissed. Moreover, boys' hands were unfit to hold the sceptre of England in such troubled times. It was to Harold that all eyes turned. He had for years exercised at least joint authority with Edward; he was the foremost and most noble of Englishmen. He was skilled in war, and wise in counsel, and the charm of his manner, the strength and stateliness of his figure, and the singular beauty of his face rendered him the popular idol. And yet men felt that it was a new departure in English life and customs for one who had in his veins no drop of royal blood to be chosen as king. His sister was Edward's wife, he was Edward's friend and counsellor, but although the men of the South felt that he was in all ways fitted to be king, they saw too that Northumbria would assuredly stand aloof, and that the Mercian earls, brothers-in-law as they were to be to Harold, would yet feel jealous that one of their own rank was to be their sovereign.

The Witan, as the representative of the nation, had alone the right of choosing the sovereign; but though they had often passed over those who by birth stood nearest to the throne, they had never yet chosen one altogether outside the royal family. It was a necessary step—for young Edgar was not to be thought of—and yet men felt uneasy, now that the time had come, at so complete a departure from custom.

Rapidly the king grew worse, and prayers were uttered up for him in every church in England. The Christmas Witan met at Westminster, but little was done. The great minster was consecrated on December 18th, and the absence of its founder and builder was keenly missed at the ceremony.

The members of the Witan remained in attendance near the palace, hoping for some guidance from the dying king. He had no power to leave the throne to whom he wished, and yet his words could not but have great weight; but he lay almost unconscious, and for two days remained speechless. But on the 5th of January, the year being 1066, he suddenly awoke from sleep, in the full possession of his senses. Harold was standing on one side of his bed, Archbishop Stigand at the other. His wife sat at the foot of the bed, chaffing her husband's feet; Robert Wymarc, his personal attendant, stood by his head. The king on awakening prayed aloud, that if a vision he had had was truly from heaven he might have strength to declare it; if it were but the offspring of a disordered brain he prayed that he might not be able to tell it.

Then he sat up in bed, supported by Robert; some of his chosen friends were called in, and to them, with a strangely clear voice and with much energy, he told the vision. It was that some monks he had known in his youth had appeared to him, and told him that God had sent them to tell him that on account of the sins of the earls, the bishops, and the men in holy orders of every rank, God had put a curse upon England, and that within a year and a day of his death fiends should stalk through the whole land, and should harry it from one end to another with fire and sword.

The king's words filled his hearers with awe, Stigand alone deeming the story but the dream of a dying man. Then Edward gave orders as to his burial. He bade his friends not to grieve for him, but to rejoice in his approaching deliverance, and he asked for the prayers of all his people for his soul. At last those standing round called his mind to the great subject which was for the moment first in the heart of every Englishman. Who, when he was gone, they asked, would he wish to wear the royal crown of England? The king stretched out his hand to Harold and said, "To thee, Harold, my brother, I commit my kingdom." Then, after commending his wife and his Norman favourites to Harold's care and protection, he turned his thoughts from all earthly matters, received the last rites of the church, and soon afterwards passed away tranquilly.

Rapidly the news spread through London that the king was dead. The members of the Witan were still there, for the assembly had not separated, but knowing that the king was dying had waited for the event. The earls and great thanes of the South and West, of East Anglia and Wessex, were all there together, probably with many from Mercia. There was no time lost. In the afternoon they assembled. All knew on whom the choice would fall, for Harold had been for long regarded as the only possible successor to the throne, and the news that the dying king had, as far as he could, chosen him as his successor, doubtless went for much in the minds of many who had hitherto felt that it was a strange and unknown thing to accept as monarch of England one who was not a member of the royal house. There was no hesitation, no debate. By acclamation Harold was chosen king of the land, and two great nobles were selected to inform him that the choice of the Witan had fallen upon him.

They bore with them the two symbols of royalty, the crown and the axe, and bade him accept them as being chosen both by the voice of the Witan and by the king, whom he had so well and faithfully served. There was no hesitation on the part of Harold. He had already counted the cost and taken his resolution. He knew that he alone could hope to receive the general support of the great earls. Leofric and Gurth were his brothers, the Earls of Mercia and Northumbria had been mollified by the alliance arranged with their sister. The last male of the royal line was a lad of feeble character, and would be unable either to preserve peace at home or to unite the nation against a foreign invader. The oath he had sworn to William, although obtained partly by force partly by fraud, weighed upon him, but he was powerless to keep it. Did he decline the crown it would fall upon some other Englishman, and not upon the Norman. The vote of England had chosen him, and it was clearly his duty to accept. The die had been cast when Edith had bade him sacrifice her and himself for the good of England, and it was too late to turn back now. Gravely he accepted the dignity offered him.

Throughout London first, and then throughout the country, the news that the Witan had unanimously chosen him, and that he had accepted, was received with deep satisfaction. There was no time to be lost. The next day was Epiphany, the termination of the Christian festival, the last upon which the Witan could legally sit, and had the ceremony not taken place then it must have been delayed until another great feast of the church—another calling together of the Witan. All night the preparations for the two great ceremonials were carried on. At daybreak the body of the dead king was borne to the noble minster, that had been the chief object of his life to raise and beautify, and there before the great altar it was laid to rest with all the solemn pomp of the church. A few hours passed away and the symbols of mourning were removed. Then the great prelates of the church, the earls and the thanes of England, gathered for the coronation of the successor of the king whom they had just laid in his last resting-place. Eldred the primate of Northumberland performed the rites of consecration— for Stigand, primate of England, had been irregularly appointed, and was therefore deemed unfit for the high function. Before investing him with the royal robes Eldred, according to custom, demanded in a loud voice of the English people whether they were willing that Harold should be crowned their king, and a mighty shout of assent rang through the abbey. Then the earl swore first to preserve peace to the church and all Christian people; secondly, to prevent wrong and robbery to men of every rank; thirdly, to enforce justice and mercy in all his judgments as he would that God should have mercy on him. Then after a solemn prayer the prelate poured the oil of consecration upon Harold's head; he was vested in royal robes, and with symbols appertaining to the priesthood. A sword was girded to his side, that he might defend his realm, and smite his enemies and those of the church of God. Then the crown was placed on his head, the sceptre surmounted with the cross and the rod with the holy dove placed in his hands, and Harold stood before the people as the king chosen by themselves, named by his predecessor, and consecrated by the church. A great banquet followed the coronation, and then this day memorable in the history of England came to its close.

Wulf had been present at the two great events at the abbey and at the banquet, and knew, better than most of those present, that the gravity on Harold's face was not caused solely by the mighty responsibility that he had assumed, but by sad thoughts in his heart. Wulf on his return from the abbey had handed to Harold a small roll of parchment that had been slipped into his hand by a man, who at once disappeared in the crowd after handing it to him, with the words, "For the king". In the interval before the banquet he handed this to Harold, who had opened and glanced at it, and had then abruptly turned away. It contained but the words: "That God may bless my dear lord and king is the prayer of Edith."

"Do you know where she is?" Harold asked abruptly, turning upon Wulf.

"No, my lord."

"I have respected her wishes and made no inquiry," the king said. "Others think, doubtless, that I am rejoicing at having gained the object of my ambition, but as God knows, I would far rather have remained Earl of the West Saxons with her by my side than rule over England."

"I know it, my lord," Wulf said. "But who beside yourself could rule here?"

"No one," Harold answered; "and it is for England's sake and not my own that I have this day accepted the crown. If you can find out where she has betaken herself without making public inquiry I charge you to do so, and to tell her that on this day I have thought mostly of her. Tell me not where she is. What is done cannot be undone, but I would fain that, in the time that is to come, I may at least know where to send her a message should it be needful."

CHAPTER XIV. — WULF'S SUSPICIONS.

Beyond the fact that the name of the king had changed, the death of Edward and the accession of Harold made no sensible difference in the government of the southern half of England. Harold had practically reigned for years, and the fact that he was now able to give his orders direct instead of having nominally to consult Edward, had only the effect that the affairs of the state moved somewhat more promptly. Such of the Norman favourites of Edward as desired to leave were permitted to do so, and were honourably escorted to the coast, but many remained. The Norman prelates and abbots retained their dignities undisturbed, and several of the court officials of Edward held the same positions under Harold.

A fortnight after the coronation a party of Norman barons arrived, bearing a summons from Duke William to Harold to fulfil the oath he had sworn to be his man, and also to carry out his engagement to marry one of William's daughters. They were received with all honour, and Harold informed them that he would, without delay, reply to the duke's summons. A few days later three thanes of high rank started for Normandy with Harold's reply. Wulf accompanied them.

"I would that you should go with them, Wulf," Harold had said to him. "You are too young to be one of my embassy to Duke William, but it would be well that you should form one of the party. The duke knows you and has a liking for you, and possibly may speak more freely to you than to my official messengers. Moreover, you have many acquaintances and friends there, and may gather valuable news as to the feeling in Normandy and the probability of William's barons embarking in a desperate war for his advantage."

"I shall be glad to go, my lord."

"The duke knows well enough what my answer must be. He is aware that were I ready either to resign my kingship to him, or to agree to hold my crown as his vassal, the people of England would laugh to scorn my assumption so to dispose of them, and would assuredly renounce and slay me as a traitor who had broken the oath I swore at my coronation. It is a mere formal summons William makes, as one summons a city to surrender before undertaking its siege. It is but a move in the game. That he will, if he can, strike for the kingdom, I doubt not in any way, but it may well be that his barons will refuse to embark in a war beyond the seas, which is altogether beyond the military service they are bound to render. At any rate, we have breathing time. Vast preparations must be made before he can invade England, and until he is ready we shall have messengers passing to and fro. A few of my chief councillors, the earls and great thanes, refuse to believe that William will ever attempt by force of arms to grasp the crown of England, but for myself I have no doubt he will do so. I shall at once prepare for war; and the first step of all is to unite England from the northern border to the southern sea, so that we may oppose the Normans with our whole strength. This must be my personal work, other matters I must for a time intrust to the earls."

The train was not a large one. One ship bore the thanes and their attendants from Southampton to Rouen. They were received with all honour at their landing, conducted to a house that had been assigned to their use, and informed that they would be received by the duke on the following day. They had brought their horses with them, and as soon as they were housed Wulf mounted, and attended by Osgod rode to the castle of the De Burgs. Three years had past since he had last been there. He had from time to time received letters and greetings from Guy de Burg by the hands of Normans who visited the court, and knew that although he had gained in health and strength the predictions of the surgeons had been fulfilled, and that he would never be able to take part in knightly exercises or deeds of arms. The warden at the gate had sent in Wulf's name, and as he alighted a tall young man ran down the steps and embraced him.

"I am overjoyed to see you, Wulf," he exclaimed. "When we heard that Harold would send over an English embassy to answer the duke's demands, I hoped that you would be among the number. Harold would be likely to choose you, and I felt sure that you would come over to see me. I had a messenger waiting at Rouen to bring me tidings of the arrival of your ship, and it is scarcely an hour since he rode in with the news that, by inquiries among the servants as they landed, he had learned that you were indeed of the party. But I had hardly looked to see you until to-morrow morning, and had indeed intended to ride over on my palfrey at daybreak."

"I would not delay, Guy, for the answer we bear will not be to the duke's liking, and for aught I know he may pack us off again as soon as the interview is ended. Therefore, I thought it best to lose not a moment."

"I see you have brought your tall retainer with you, Wulf. I am glad to see the stout fellow again. But come in, they will chide me for keeping you so long at the entrance."

Wulf was warmly received by the baron and his wife. "You are just what I thought you would grow up, Wulf," the former said. "Indeed your figure was so set and square before, that there was little chance of great alteration. We have heard of you from time to time, and that you distinguished yourself greatly in the war against the Welsh, and stood high in the favour and affection of Harold. Guy has overshot you, you see, in point of height, though he is scarce half your breadth," and the baron looked with a suppressed sigh at the fragile young fellow, who stood with his hand on Wulf's shoulder.

"He looks better and stronger than I expected, my lord," Wulf said. "You must remember when I last saw him he could scarce walk across the room, and in my heart I scarce hoped to ever see him again."

"He gains strength very slowly," De Burg said wistfully; "but although he has to be careful of himself, he has no ailment."

"He could hardly gain strength while growing so fast," Wulf said; "but now that he has gained his full height he will, doubtless, gather strength, and as three years have done so much for him, another three years will I hope do far more. The Lady Agnes is well, I trust?"

"She is well, and will be here anon," the baroness said.

Guy laughed with something of his former heartiness. "She was here when the man brought news of your arrival, Wulf, but she fled away like a startled deer, and has, I suppose, gone to put on her best kirtle in your honour."

As he spoke Agnes entered the room. Considerable as was the change that three years had wrought in the young men, it was still greater in her case, for she had grown from a pretty young girl into a very lovely maiden, whose cheek flushed as she presented it for Wulf's salute.

"Would you have known her again, Wulf?" Guy asked with a smile.

"I should certainly have known her, though she has so greatly changed," Wulf replied. "I thought that you would be grown up and altered, but I scarcely looked for so great an alteration in her, though I might of course have known that it would be so."

"And now tell me, Wulf," the baron said, abruptly changing the conversation, "how go things in England—are people united in choosing Harold as their king?"

"The South, the East, and West are as one man," Wulf said. "Mercia, which comprises the midlands, has accepted the choice. Northumbria has as yet held itself aloof, although its earl has sworn allegiance and its primate has placed the crown on Harold's head; but in time, I am well assured, the North will also accept him. As I said when we spoke about it after Harold had been tricked into taking an oath to be William's man, he had no more power to pledge himself for England than I had. Englishmen are free to choose their own king, and as Harold has long been their ruler, their choice naturally fell on him.

"Harold is about to marry the sister of the Earls of Northumbria and Mercia, the widow of Griffith of Wales, and this will, I hope, bind these two powerful nobles to him. The only trouble is likely to come from Tostig, who is, as you know, at the court of Norway. But as he is hated in Northumbria, and the earl and his brother of Mercia both have personal enmity against him, he can gather no following there, while Anglia and Wessex are devoted to Harold. Still he and the King of Norway may cause trouble."

"The answer of Harold's ambassadors is, of course, a refusal?"

"Assuredly," Wulf said. "I do not know the exact import of the reply, as, although I have accompanied them, I am not a member of the embassy, being too young to be intrusted with so weighty a matter. But there can be but one answer. Harold is powerless to carry out his oath. He had the choice of becoming King of England, and thus defending our rights and freedom, or of refusing the crown, in which case he must have fled here, and could have given no aid whatever to William, as he himself would be regarded as the worst of traitors by the English. The duke must be perfectly well aware that a king of England could not, without the assent of the people, accept a foreign prince as his liege lord."

De Burg nodded.

"That is plainly so, Wulf; and although the duke professes intense indignation against Harold, he himself has, over and over again, broken his own oaths of allegiance to the King of France. Breaches of oaths go for little, except they serve as pretexts for war. It would have been the same thing if Harold had never taken the oath, except that his breach of it will be an aid to William in a war against him. We northmen came to France and conquered a province, simply by the right of the strongest. The duke has doubled his dominions by the same right. He deems himself now strong enough to conquer England; whether he is so remains to be seen. At present methinks that but few of us are disposed to follow him in such an enterprise, but there is never any saying how things will go at last. When war is in the air men's minds become heated. There will be dignities, estates, and titles to be won, and when many are ready to go, few like to hang back. More than once already William has embarked on a war against the wishes of the majority, but he has finally carried all with him, and it may be so again, especially if he can win over the pope to excommunicate Harold for the breach of an oath sworn on the relics."

"His excommunication will go for little in England," Wulf said sturdily. "Many of our prelates, and almost all our clergy are Englishmen, and hold in very small respect the claim of the pope to interfere in the affairs of England."

"And if Harold died who would be likely to succeed him?"

"I have never thought of that," Wulf said, "and I should think that few Englishmen have done so. If such a misfortune should happen, methinks that England would be rent in two, and that while Wessex and Anglia would choose one of his brothers, Mercia and the North would take Edwin or his brother Morcar as their king, but assuredly no foreign prince would be chosen."

"No, but with England divided the chance of conquest would be easier. You are about the king, Wulf. Keep a shrewd guard over him. I say not for a moment that the duke would countenance any attempt to do him harm, but there are many rough spirits who might think that they would gain his favour greatly did they clear his path of Harold, and who would feel all the less scruple in doing so, should the pope be induced to excommunicate him. Such things have happened again and again. Mind, I have no warrant for my speech. Methinks the honour of De Burg is too well known for anyone to venture to broach such a project before him, but so many kings and great princes have fallen by an assassin's knife to clear the way for the next heir or for an ambitious rival, that I cannot close my eyes to the fact that one in Harold's position might well be made the subject of such an attempt. The history of your own country will furnish you with examples of what I say."

"Thank you, my lord," Wulf said gravely. "The thought that an assassin's knife might be raised against Harold, who is of all men the most beloved in England, has never once entered my mind, but I see there may be indeed a danger of such an attempt being made. I do not greatly trust Morcar or his brother, and the danger may come from them, or, as you say, from one desirous of gaining favour with your duke. I will lay your warning to heart."

The conversation now turned on other topics, on the Welsh war and the life Wulf had been leading since they last met, and upon what had happened to the many acquaintances Wulf had made in Normandy. They talked until long past the usual hour for retiring to rest; Wulf slept at the chateau, and rode into Rouen at an early hour in the morning.

The audience next day was a public one. William was surrounded by his officers of state, and by a large number of his barons. The English envoys were ushered in, and the duke asked them in a loud voice what answer they brought to his just demands on the part of his sworn liegeman, Harold.

"The king of England bids us state, duke, that he holds an oath taken by a prisoner under force to be invalid, especially when taken in ignorance of the sanctity of the concealed relics; secondly, he says that he has been elected by the people of England, and that he has no power whatever to transfer the rights that they have conferred upon him, and which he has sworn to maintain, and that they would absolutely refuse to be bound by any act on his part contrary to the welfare of the kingdom, and to their rights as freemen; thirdly, as to your demand that he should carry out his promise to marry your daughter, he points out that the lady whose hand was promised to him has since that time died; and lastly, that although as Earl of Wessex he might transfer that engagement to another of your daughters, as king of England he is unable to do so, as the will of the people is that their king shall marry no foreign princess, but that the royal family shall be of unmixed English blood."

William frowned heavily. "You hear, my lords," he said, after a pause, to the Norman barons, "this English earl who was here as my guest refuses to carry out the engagements to which he swore upon the holy relics. I cannot, however, bring myself to believe that he will really persist in this foul perjury, and shall persevere in my endeavours to bring him to a sense of his duty, and to show him the foul dishonour that will rest upon him should he persist in this contempt alike of our holy church and his honour as a knight and a Christian, conduct that would bring upon him eternal infamy and the scorn and contempt of all the princes and nobles of Europe, and draw upon his head the wrath of the church." Then he abruptly turned on his heel and left the audience-chamber, while the English envoys returned to their house and made preparations for immediate departure.

A few minutes after his arrival there one of the duke's pages brought word to Wulf that the duke desired to speak to him in private. He at once went across to the palace. The duke received him cordially.

"I marked you were with the other thanes, and was glad to see one whom I count as my friend. Tell me frankly, what think the people of England of this monstrous act of perjury on the part of Harold?"

"To speak the truth, my lord duke," Wulf replied, "they trouble their heads in no way about it. They hold that the right of electing their king rests wholly with them, and that Harold's promise, to do what he had no more power to do than the lowest born of Englishmen, was but a waste of words. Harold himself feels the obligation far more than anyone else, and had there been any other Englishman who could have united the people as well as he could himself, he would gladly have stood aside; but there is none such, and he had no choice but to accept the decision of the Witan, and, for the sake of England, to lay aside his own scruples. The late king, too, nominated him as his successor, and although his voice had no legal weight, he is now regarded as almost a saint among the people. The fact, therefore, that he, full of piety and religion as he was, should have held that Harold's oath in no way prevented the people from choosing him, has gone very far to satisfy any scruples that might have been felt."

"Edward at one time named me as his successor," the duke said shortly.

"So I have heard, my lord duke; but as he grew in years and learned more of English feeling and character he became fully aware that the people would accept no foreign prince, and that only the man who had for thirteen years governed in his name could be their choice."

"And the great earls and thanes are likewise of that opinion?"

"Assuredly in Anglia and Wessex they are so. I know not the minds of Earls Morcar and Edwin, but they were at the Witan and stood by his side at the coronation, and doubtless felt that they could not rely upon their own people if they attempted any open opposition to Harold."

"And you will support this usurper against me, Wulf?"

"I shall fight, my lord duke, for the king chosen by the people of England. Should that choice some day fall on you I should be as faithful a follower of yours as I am now of Harold."

"Well answered, young thane. You have twice done me loyal service, and I at least do not forget my promises. As yet my mind is not made up as to my course, but should fate will it so, William of England will not forget the services rendered to William of Normandy."

A few minutes later Wulf rejoined his companions, and before nightfall the ship was far on her way down the river.

"Shall we go back to Steyning, my lord, when we return home?" Osgod asked as they stood by the bulwark together watching the passing shores.

"No, Osgod. I mean for a time to remain with the king. Baron de Burg yesterday hinted to me that he thought it possible that some of the duke's followers might endeavour to remove the obstacle between him and the throne of England. There are in every country desperate men, who are ready for any crime or deed of violence if they but think that its committal will bring them a reward. We have had English kings assassinated before now, and it has been the same in other countries. Moreover, there are many Normans who were forced to fly from England when Godwin's family returned from exile. These having a personal grudge against him would be willing to gratify it, and at the same time to earn a place in William's favour. Harold is so frank and unsuspicious that he will never think of taking precautions for his personal safety. You and I, then, must serve as his watch-dogs. It may be a difficult task, for we have no idea from what quarter that danger may come, and yet by chance we may discover some clue or other that will set us on the right track At any rate, if we are near him, and keep a watchful eye on any strangers approaching him, we may save him from a treacherous blow."

"Good, my lord. Methinks that Harold was wrong in not sending every Norman across the seas, and every man with whom I have spoken thinks the same. But at any rate we can, as you say, keep a sharp look-out, and although I cannot be always near his person, I shall go about and listen; and it will be hard if anything is on foot without my hearing some whisper of it. You will tell him no word of your suspicions, I suppose?"

"Certainly not. I have fears rather than suspicions, and Baron De Burg certainly spoke as if he regarded it as likely that such an attempt might be made, and he knows his own people better than I do. He expressly said that he had no special reason for giving me the warning, but he may have heard some angry remark or some covert threat against Harold; and although the duke would not, I feel sure, openly countenance his slaying, I think that the slayers might confidently look for a reward from his gratitude did they by their daggers open a way for him to the throne of England."

On the return of the embassy to London King Harold said to Wulf: "I have no further occasion for your services at present, Wulf, and I suppose you will return home and increase the number of your housecarls. It is not with undisciplined levies that the Normans, if they come, must be met. It is no question this time of Welsh mountaineers but of trained warriors, and should they land they must be met by men as firm and as obedient to orders as themselves. I am trying to impress this on all our thanes, but most of them are hard to move, and deem that all that is necessary on the day of battle is that men shall have strength and courage and arms."

"With your permission, my lord, I would rather abide near you, and leave the training of my men to the officer who taught those who fought by my side in Wales."

"I thought you did not care for the gaieties of the court?" Harold said, in some surprise.

"Nor do I, my lord. For its gaieties I care nothing, but in times like these there is much to be learned, and I would not bury myself in Steyning when there is so much of importance going on in London."

"Then stay, Wulf, I shall be glad to have you here. I have but little time to myself now, but it is a relief to put aside grave matters sometimes. I will appoint a room for you near my own chamber. You have heard no news of her, I suppose?"

"In truth, my lord, I know not how to set about the task, and it seems to me that my only chance is to run against one of her serving-men in the street."

"That is but a slight chance, Wulf; but even I, with all the power of England in my hands, am equally at a loss. I cannot send round to all the thanes of Wessex to ask if a strange lady has taken a house in their jurisdiction, nor to all the parish priests to ask if a new worshipper has come to their church. However, I believe that sooner or later she will herself advise me where she has hidden. It may be that your stay here will not be a long one, for I purpose journeying to the North."

"To Northumbria!" Wulf said in surprise.

"Yes; the people there refuse to recognize me, and I would win them by going among them rather than by force. My dear friend Bishop Wulfstan will accompany me. I shall take with me a body of my housecarls, partly as a guard, but more because I cannot now travel as a private person. It is very many years since an English king has visited Northumbria, and it is not strange that these northern men should object to be ruled by a stranger from the South. I shall take with me two or three of my thanes only, but shall be glad for you to ride with me. Young as you are, you have a quick eye and ready wit, and in case trouble should arise, I can rely upon you more than upon many men far older than yourself."

The palace of Westminster was not an imposing edifice. London had not yet become the capital of England, Oxford being the seat of government of most of the kings, so that the palace was built on a simple plan, and had been altered by Edward until the interior arrangements more nearly resembled those of a convent than of a palace. Below was the great banqueting-hall, and beyond this the chamber where the king heard complaints and administered justice. Leading from this were the king and queen's private chambers, where the one sat and read or received his chief councillors, and the other worked with her maids, and listened to the music of the harpers or the tales of war and love sung by bards.

Behind was the chapel. On the floor above a corridor ran from one end of the building to the doors which separated the royal sleeping-rooms from the rest. On either side of the corridor were small bed-chambers, where the officers of the household and guests at the court slept, their attendants lying in the corridor itself or in the kitchens, which with other offices were contained in a separate building. The room assigned to Wulf, and which Harold had ordered was henceforth to be retained for him, was that on the right hand of the corridor, next to the door leading to the royal apartments. Like the others it was a mere cell, with the straw pallet covered with sheep-skins, with some rugs for covering. This constituted the whole of the furniture. In the morning water was brought in brass ewers and basins, either by the pages or servants of the guests.

"Nothing could be better, my lord, than this," Osgod said. "I am a light sleeper, and lying across your door I am sure that no one could enter the king's apartments without my hearing those heavy doors move."

"There is but little chance, Osgod, of an attack being made on him in that fashion. Doubtless some of the royal servants sleep on the other side of the door. No, if any design be attempted against his life it will be when he is travelling, or when he is abroad amid a crowd."

"I saw Walter Fitz-Urse to-day, master, in the train of William of London."

"Then he must have returned within the last day or two, Osgod, for he has been absent for more than a year, and I know that when we sailed for Normandy he was still absent, for I inquired of one of the court officials if he had been here of late. What should bring him back again, I wonder. He has long been out of his pageship, and he can hope for no preferment in England while Harold is king. He has, I know, no great possessions in Normandy, for I asked Guy about him, and learned that his father was a knight of but small consideration, either as to his state or character, and that the boy owed his place as page to William of London, to the fact that he was a distant relation of the prelate.

"I would say harm of no man, but I should think he is as likely as another to be mixed up in such a plot as we are talking of. He is landless, hot-tempered, and ambitious. He owes no goodwill to Harold, for it was by his intervention that he was sent away in disgrace after that quarrel with me. At any rate, Osgod, since we have no one else to suspect, we will in the first place watch him, or rather have him looked after, for I see not how we ourselves can in any way keep near him. He knows me well, and has doubtless seen you with me, and having seen you once would not be likely to forget you."

"I think I can manage that," Osgod said confidently. "My father has a small apprentice who well-nigh worries his life out with tricks and trifling. I have more than once begged him off a beating, and methinks he will do anything for me. He is as full of cunning as an ape, and, I warrant me, would act his part marvellously. My father will be glad enough to get him out of the forge for a while, and when I tell him that it is in your service he will make no difficulty about it. He is fifteen years old, but so small for his age that he would pass for three years younger than he is."

"I think it is a very good plan, Osgod. You had best see your father in the morning, and if he consents to your having the boy, bring him down to the river-bank behind the abbey, where I will be awaiting you, and can there talk to him without observation. You are sure that he can be trusted to keep silence regarding what I tell him?"

"He can be trusted, my lord. In the first place he will enjoy playing his part, and in the second he will know well enough that I should nearly flay him alive with my stirrup-leather if he were to fail me, and that his life in the forge would be worse than ever."

The next morning Wulf strolled down to the river-bank after breaking his fast, and it was not long before Osgod joined him with the boy.

"Have you told him what he is required for, Osgod?" Wulf asked, as the boy, doffing his cap, stood before him with an air of extreme humility.

"I am not good at the telling of tales, as you know, my lord, and I thought it better that you should tell him just as much or as little as you chose."

"You don't like your work at the forge, Ulf?" for that Wulf had learned was the boy's name.

"I think that I like it better than it likes me," the boy replied. "When I get to do the fine work I shall like it, but at present it is 'fetch this tool, Ulf, or file that iron, or blow those bellows,' and if I do but smile I get a cuff."

"No, no, Ulf," Osgod said. "Of course, at present you are but a beginner, and at your age I too had to fetch and carry and be at the bidding of all the men; and it is not for smiling that you get cuffed, but for playing tricks and being away for hours when you are sent on a message to the next street, and doing your errands wrongly. My father tells me you will be a good workman some day. You will never be strong enough to wield a heavy hammer or to forge a battle-axe, but he says your fingers are quick and nimble, and that you will some day be able to do fine work such as clumsy hands could not compass. But that is not to the point now."

"You will be glad to be out of the forge for a bit, Ulf?" Wulf asked.

"That should I, but not always."

"It will not be for very long. I want a watch set upon a Norman in order to know where he goes, and whom he meets, and what he purposes. Osgod tells me that he thinks you could play the part rarely, and that you would be willing for his sake to do our bidding."

The boy looked up into Osgod's face with an expression of earnest affection.

"I would do anything for him," he said, "even if I were to be cut to pieces."

"Osgod is as much interested in the matter as I am, Ulf; and as he has assured me that you are to be trusted, I will tell you more as to the man, and my object in setting you to watch him."

"You can trust me, my lord," the boy said earnestly. "I will do your bidding whatever it is."

"You know, Ulf, that the Duke of Normandy desires the crown of England?"

"So I have heard men say, my lord."

"Were King Harold out of the way, his chances of obtaining it would be improved."

The boy nodded.

"I am sure that the duke himself would take no hand in bringing about Harold's death, but there are many of his people who might think that they would obtain a great reward were they to do so."

The boy nodded again.

"The man I wish you to watch is Walter Fitz-Urse, who is in the train of the bishop. I have no particular reason for suspecting him, beyond the fact that he has but just come over here, and this is scarcely a time a Norman would come to London; though as the bishop is a relation and patron of his he may have come merely to visit him. Still he has, as he thinks, a cause for enmity against the king. He is needy, and, as I know, somewhat unscrupulous. All this is little enough against a man; still it seems to me that his coming bodes danger to the king, and this being so I desire that he shall be watched, in order that I may find out what is his real object in coming over here. I want you to post yourself near the gate of the bishop's palace, and whenever he comes out to follow him save when he is in the train of the bishop—most of all if he sallies out alone or after dark.

"It will not do for you to be always dressed as an apprentice. Osgod will procure for you such clothes as you may require for disguises. One day you can be sitting there as a beggar asking alms, another as a girl from one of the villages with eggs or fowls. You understand that you will have to follow him, to mark where he goes in, and especially, should he be joined by anybody when out, to endeavour to overhear something of what they say to each other. Even a few words might suffice to show me whether my suspicions are true or not. Do you think you can do that? Osgod tells me that you are good at playing a part."

"I will do it, my lord, and that right gladly. It is a business after my own heart, and I will warrant that those who see me one day will not know me when they see me the next."

"Osgod will go with you now, and will stay near the bishop's palace until the man you are to watch comes out, and will point him out to you. In a day or two I may be going away with the king; when we return you will tell us what you have found out. Till we go, Osgod will meet you here each morning as the abbey bell rings out the hour of seven. You can tell him anything that you have learned, and then he will give you such further instructions as may seem needful; and remember you must be cautious, for Walter Fitz-Urse would not hesitate to use his dagger on you did he come upon you eavesdropping."

"I will give him leave to do so if he catches me," the boy said.

"Very well, then; Osgod will go with you to buy such clothes as may be necessary, and remember that you will be well rewarded for your work."

"I want no reward," the boy said, almost indignantly. "I am an apprentice, and as my master has bid me do whatever Osgod commands, he has a right to my services. But this is nothing. There is not one in London who would not do aught in his power for Harold, and who would scorn to take pay for it. As this is a matter in which his very life may be concerned, though I am but a boy, and a small one at that, there is nought that I would not do, even to the giving of my life, to spoil these Norman plots."

Osgod was about to chide the boy angrily for this freedom of speech, but Wulf checked him.

"You are right, lad; and I am sorry I spoke of a reward. I myself would have answered the same at your age, and would have died for Harold then as I would now. I should have bethought me that the feelings of Englishmen, gentle or simple, are the same towards the king, and I crave your pardon for treating your loyal service as a thing to be paid for with money."

The boy's eyes filled with tears; he dropped on one knee, and seizing Wulf's hand placed it to his lips, and then without a word sped away, halting a hundred yards off till Osgod should join him.

"You have made a good choice," Wulf said; "the boy is wholly trustworthy, and unless his face belies him he is as shrewd as he is faithful. My only fear in the matter is, that he may be over rash in his desire to carry out the trust we have given him. Warn him against that, and tell him that should he be discovered and killed it would upset all our plans."

CHAPTER XV. — A MEETING BY THE RIVER.

During the three days that elapsed between Ulf's being set upon the track of Walter Fitz-Urse and the departure of the king for the North, the boy had no news to report to Osgod. The young Norman had not left the bishop's palace alone. He had accompanied the prelate several times when he went abroad, and had gone out with some of his countrymen who still held office at the court. In one or other of the disguises Wulf had suggested, the boy had hung about the gate of the bishop's palace until late in the evening, but Walter Fitz-Urse had not come out after dark. On the day before starting, Wulf was with Osgod when the latter met the boy at the rendezvous.

After he heard Ulf's report Wulf said: "As we leave to-morrow this is the last report you will have to make to us. So far it would seem that there is nothing whatever to give grounds for suspicion, and if, after a few days, you find that the Norman still remains quietly at the bishop's, there will be no occasion for you to continue your watch until the time is approaching for the king's return."

"Yes, my lord. But I cannot say surely that he does not go out of an evening."

"Why, I thought you said that he certainly had not done so?"

"No, my lord; I said only that I had not seen him. He has certainly not gone out through the great gates in his Norman dress, but that it seems to me shows very little. As the bishop's guest he would pass out there, but there is another entrance behind that he might use did he wish to go out unobserved. Even at the main entrance I cannot tell but that, beneath the cowl and frock of one of the many monks who pass in and out, Walter Fitz-Urse may not be hidden. He would scarce go about such a business as we suspect in his dress as a Norman noble, which is viewed with little favour here in London, and would draw attention towards him, but would assume, as I do, some disguise in which he could go about unremarked—it might be that of a monk, it might be that of a lay servitor of the palace."

"You are right, Ulf; I had not thought of that. That is indeed a difficulty, and one that I do not see how you can get over. Are you sure that he has not passed out by the main gate?"

"I have marked his walk and carriage closely, my lord. He steps along with a long stride, and unless he be a better mummer than I judge him to be, I should know him whether in a monk's gown or a servitor's cloak. It is no easy thing to change a knight's stride into the shuffle of a sandalled monk, or the noiseless step of a well-trained servitor in a bishop's palace."

"You are a shrewd lad indeed, Ulf," Wulf said warmly; "and I feel that you will fathom this matter if there be aught at the bottom. But, as you say, you cannot watch more than one place."

"The other entrance is not altogether unwatched, my lord. The first day you gave me my orders I went to one of my cronies, who has shared with me in many an expedition when our master deemed that we were soundly asleep. Without, as you may be sure, giving any reason, I told him that I had come to believe that the Norman I pointed out to him was in the habit of going out in disguise, and that I was mightily curious to find whither he went and why, and therefore wanted him to watch, at the entrance behind the palace. I bade him mark the walk of the persons that went out, and their height, for the Norman is tall, and to follow any who might come out of lofty stature, and with a walk and carriage that seemed to accord ill with his appearance. So each evening, as soon as his house was closed and the lights extinguished, he has slipped out, as he knows how, and has watched till ten o'clock at the gate. It seemed to me that that would be late enough, and indeed the doors are closed at that hour."

"You have done well, Ulf; but has not the boy questioned you as to your reasons for thus setting a watch on the Norman?"

"I have told him nought beyond what I have said, my lord. He may guess shrewdly enough that I should not myself take so much trouble in the matter unless I had more reason than I have given; but we are closely banded together, and just as I should do, without asking the reasons, any such action did he propose it to me, so he carried out my wishes. I cannot feel as sure as if I had watched him myself that Fitz-Urse has not passed out in disguise unnoticed, but I have a strong belief that it is so. At any rate, my lord, you can go away with the assurance that all that is possible shall be done by us, and that even if he pass out once or twice undiscovered there is good hope that we shall at last detect him."

After again commending the boy, Wulf returned to the palace with Osgod.

"I feel half ashamed of having entertained a suspicion of Fitz-Urse on such slight grounds, Osgod."

"I think you have done quite right, my lord. You know how the fellow gave a false report to the bishop of that quarrel with you. At any rate, should nothing come of it, no harm will have been done. As to the boys, so far from regarding it as a trouble, I feel sure that they view it as an exciting pleasure, and are as keenly anxious to detect the Norman going out in a disguise as you yourself can be. When they get tired of it they will give it up."

Ulf, at any rate, was determined not to relax his watch during the absence of the king. The more he thought of it the more certain he felt that if Walter Fitz-Urse went out on any private business after nightfall he would use one or other of the entrances at the rear of the palace, and accordingly next day he arranged that one friend should watch the front entrance of an evening, while he himself took post behind. As soon as it was dark he lay down by the wall close to the entrance at which the servitors generally passed in and out. The moon was up but was still young, and the back of the palace lay in deep shadow; a projecting buttress screened him to a great extent from view, while by peeping round the corner he could watch those who came out and see them as they passed from the shadow of the building into the comparatively light space beyond.

Many came in and out. The evening was bitterly cold, and his teeth chattered as he lay, cautiously putting his head beyond the edge of the stonework every time he heard any one leaving the palace. The heavy bell had just struck eight, when a man wrapt up in a cloak passed out. He differed in no respect from many of those who had preceded him, save that he was somewhat taller. The hood of the cloak was drawn over his head. Ulf raised himself to his knees and gazed after the figure. The man was walking more slowly than the others had done, for most of them had hurried along as if in haste to get their errands finished and to be in shelter again from the keen wind.

"If that is Fitz-Urse, he is walking so as to avoid the appearance of haste in case anyone should be looking after him," Ulf muttered to himself. "At any rate I will follow him, he is more like the Norman than anyone I have yet seen, though he carries his head forwarder and his shoulders more rounded." As he watched him, the boy saw that as he increased the distance from the palace the man quickened his pace, and when he came into the moonlight was stepping rapidly along.

"That is my man," Ulf exclaimed. "He knows well enough that no one is likely to be standing at the door, and thinks he need no longer walk cautiously." Feeling sure that even if the man looked back he would not be able to see him in the shadow, he started forward at a run, paused before he reached the edge of the moonlight, and then, as soon as the figure entered a lane between some houses, ran forward at the top of his speed. The man was but a hundred yards in front of him when Ulf came to the entrance of the lane. Just as he turned into it the man stopped and looked round, and Ulf threw himself down by the side of a wall.

"That settles it," he said to himself. "No one who had not a fear of being followed would turn and look round on such a night as this."

Ulf was barefooted, for although he generally wore soft shoes which were almost as noiseless as the naked foot, he was dressed in rags, and a foot covering of any sort would have been out of place. Always keeping in the shade, having his eyes fixed on the man he was pursuing, and holding himself in readiness to leap into a doorway or throw himself down should he see him turn his head, he lessened the distance until he was within some fifty yards of the other. The man took several turns, and at last entered a long street leading down to the river. As soon as Ulf saw him enter it he darted off at full speed, turned down another lane, and then, when he got beyond the houses, and on to the broken ground that lay between them and the river, ran until he was nearly facing the end of the street which he had seen the man enter, and then threw himself down.

He had scarcely done so when he saw the figure issue from the street and strike across the open ground towards the water. Crawling along on his stomach Ulf followed him, until he halted on the bank. The man looked up and down the river, stamped his foot impatiently, and then began to walk to and fro. Presently he stopped and appeared to be listening; Ulf did the same, and soon heard the distant splash of oars. They came nearer and nearer. Ulf could not see the boat, for it was close under the bank, which was some twenty yards away from him, but presently when the boat seemed almost abreast of him the man on the bank said, "Where do you come from?"

"From fishing in deep water," a voice replied.

"That is right, come ashore."

The words were spoken by both in a language Ulf could not understand, and he muttered a Saxon oath. The thought that any conversation Fitz-Urse might have with a Norman would naturally be in that tongue had never once occurred to him. Three men mounted the bank. One shook hands with Fitz-Urse, the others had doffed their caps and stood listening bareheaded to the conversation between their superiors. It was long and animated. At first the stranger stamped his foot and seemed disappointed at the news Fitz-Urse gave him, then as the latter continued to speak he seemed more satisfied.

For fully half an hour they talked, then the men got into the boat and rowed away, and Fitz-Urse turned and walked back to the palace.

Ulf did not follow him. The meeting for which Fitz-Urse had come out had taken place, he would be sure to go straight back to the palace. Ulf lay there for some time fairly crying with vexation. He had done something, he had discovered that Fitz-Urse was indeed engaged in some undertaking that had to be conducted with the greatest secrecy; but this was little to what he would have learned had he understood the language. His only consolation was that both Wulf and Osgod had likewise forgotten the probability that the conversations he was charged to overhear might be in Norman.

Had Wulf still been in London he could have gone to him for fresh instructions, but he had started at daybreak, and the king's party would assuredly ride fast. There was no time to be lost. These men had a boat, and probably came from a ship in the port. Were there really a conspiracy against the king they might sail north and land in the Humber, though it seemed more probable that they would wait for his return, for on his journey he would be surrounded by his housecarls, and there would be far less chance of finding him alone and unguarded than in London. Had it been their intention to sail at once for the North, Walter Fitz-Urse would probably have rowed away with them without returning to the palace. At any rate it was too important a matter for him to trust to his own judgment, and he determined to take counsel with his master.

He had not been near the forge since he had begun the search, and was supposed to have gone down to stay with his family, who lived near Reading. He had hidden away his apprentice dress beneath some stones in a field half a mile from Westminster, and he presented himself in this at the forge in the morning.

"You are back sooner than I expected, Ulf," Ulred said as he entered. "I did not look for you for another week to come. Is all well at home?"

"All is well, master; but I have a message to deliver to you concerning some business."

The armourer saw that his apprentice wished to speak to him in private. He knew nothing of the reason for which Osgod had asked him to release the boy from his work at the forge for a time, but had quite understood that the wish to pay a visit to his family was but a cloak, and that the boy was to be employed in some service for Wulf. Guessing, therefore, that the message was one that should be delivered in private, he bade the boy follow him from the forge and took him into the room above.

"What is it you would say to me, Ulf? Mind, I wish to hear nothing about any private matter in which you may be engaged either by Wulf or Osgod. They are both away and may not return for a month or more. I judged the matter was a private one, as Osgod said nought of it to me."

"The matter is a private one, master, but as they are away I would fain take your counsel on it."

The armourer shook his head decidedly. "I can listen to nought about it, boy. It can be no business of mine, and unless he has given you license to speak I would not on any account meddle with the affairs of the young thane, who is a good lord to my son."

"That he has not done, sir; but I pray you to hear me," he added urgently as the armourer was turning to leave the room. "It is a matter that may touch the safety of our lord the king."

The armourer stopped. "Art well assured of what you say, Ulf?"

"For myself I can say nothing, master, but the young thane told me that he had fears that some attempt or other might be made from the other side of the sea against the king's life, and that although he had no strong grounds, he thought that Walter Fitz-Urse, who had just returned here, might be concerned in it, he having reasons for enmity against the king. Therefore he appointed me to watch him."

He then related the scene he had witnessed on the river bank the evening before.

"It is a strange story indeed, Ulf, and whatever it may mean, this meeting can have been for no good purpose. The secrecy with which it was conducted is enough to prove it. It is indeed unfortunate that you did not understand what was said, for much may depend upon it. Well, this is a grave affair, and I must think it over, Ulf. You have done well in telling me. Has any plan occurred to you?"

"I thought that you might accompany me, master."

"That would I willingly, but though I have picked up enough of their tongue to enable me to do business with the Normans at the king's court when they come in to buy a dagger or to have a piece of armour repaired, I could not follow their talk one with another. We must obtain someone who can speak their language well, and who can be trusted to be discreet and silent. Why, were it but whispered abroad that some Normans are plotting against the life of the king, there would be so angry a stir that every Norman in the land might be hunted down and slain. Do not go down to the forge, I will tell my wife to give you some food, and you had best then go up to the attic and sleep. You will have to be afoot again to-night, and it were well that you kept altogether away from the others, so as to avoid inconvenient questions. I will come up to you when I have thought the matter over."

"Is aught troubling you, Ulred?" the armourer's wife asked when breakfast was over and the men had gone downstairs again to their work. "Never have I seen you sit so silently at the board."

"I am worried about a matter which I have learned this morning. It matters not what it is now. Some time later you shall hear of it, but at present I am pledged to say no word about it. I want above all things to find one who speaks the Norman tongue well, and is yet a true Englishman. I have been puzzling my brains, but cannot bethink me of anyone. Canst thou help me?"

"Except about the court there are few such to be found, Ulred. If Wulf of Steyning had been here he could doubtless have assisted you had it been a matter you could have confided to him; for Osgod said that although he himself had learned but little Norman his master was able to talk freely with the Norman nobles."

"Ay, he learnt it partly when a page at court. But what you say reminds me that it was but yesterday afternoon his friend Beorn came into my shop. He had just arrived from his estate, and said how disappointed he was at finding that Wulf had left London. I will go to the palace and see him at once. I know but little of him save that I have heard from Osgod that he is Wulf's firmest friend, and they fought together across in Normandy and again against the Welsh. He has been here several times to have weapons repaired, and knows that Osgod is Wulf's man. I wonder I did not think of him, but my thoughts were running on people of our own condition."

Ulred at once put on his cap and proceeded to the palace, where he found Beorn without difficulty.

"You have not come to tell me that the blade I left with you yesterday cannot be fitted with a new hilt, Master Ulred? It is a favourite weapon of mine, and I would rather pay twice the price of a new one than lose it."

"I have come on another matter, my Lord Beorn. It is for your private ear. May I pray you to come with me to my house, where I can enter upon it without fear of being overheard?"

"Certainly I will come, Ulred, though I cannot think what this matter may be."

"It concerns in some way the Thane of Steyning, my lord, and others even higher in position."

"That is enough," Beorn said. "Anything that concerns Wulf concerns me, and as he is in the matter you can count on me without question."

Upon reaching his house Ulred left Beorn for a moment in the room upstairs, and fetched Ulf down from the attic.

"This is an apprentice lad of mine," he said, "and as it is he who has been employed by the Thane of Steyning in this affair, it were best that he himself informed you of it."

When Ulf had finished his story Beorn exclaimed, "I will go at once, and will put such an affront upon this Walter Fitz-Urse that he must needs meet me in mortal combat."

"But even if you slay him, my lord, that may not interfere with the carrying out of this enterprise, in which, as we know, another of equal rank with him is engaged."

"That is true, master armourer, and I spoke hastily. I thought perhaps it was for this that you had informed me of the matter."

"No, my lord; it seemed to me that the first thing was to assure ourselves for a certainty that the affair is really a plot against the king's life, of which we have as yet no manner of proof, but simply the suspicion entertained by my son's master. The first necessity is to find out for a truth that it is so, and secondly to learn how and when it is to be carried out; and this can only be by overhearing another conversation between the plotters. As you have heard, Ulf could have learnt all this if he had but understood the Norman tongue. Could I have spoken it well enough to follow the conversation I would not have troubled you, but it seemed to me that at their next meeting it needed that one should be present who could speak Norman well. After considering in vain how to find one who should at once know the Norman tongue and be a true and trustworthy Englishman, my thoughts fell upon you, of whom I have always heard my son speak as the companion and friend of his master, and I made bold to come and lay the matter before you, thinking that you might either take it in hand yourself or name one suitable for it."

"Certainly I will take it in hand myself," Beorn said, "and right glad am I that you came to me. A matter in which the king's life is concerned I would trust to no one but myself. And now, how think you shall we proceed? for it may well be that these plotters may not meet again for some time, seeing that the king is away."

"So it seems to me," the armourer said; "and, moreover, they may in their talk last night have appointed some other place of meeting."

"What think you, Ulf?" Beorn said, turning to the boy. "Wulf would not have chosen you for this business had he not had a good opinion of your shrewdness; and, indeed, you have shown yourself well worthy of his confidence."

"I should say, my lord, that I must go on the watch as before. It is most likely that the Norman will, sooner or later, go out in the same disguise and by the same way as before, and that the hour will be between seven and nine in the evening—most likely between seven and eight, in order that he may return from the meeting before the bishop's doors are closed for the night."

"I will keep watch with you, Ulf. Were I sure that the meeting would take place at the same spot as before you should show me where they landed, and I would lie down there in readiness, but as they may meet elsewhere, it seems to me that I must post myself by your side."

"It would be better, my lord, if you would take your place on the other side of the open space, for although I, being small, can escape notice, you might well be seen by those approaching the door. It will be necessary, too, that you should put on sandals of soft leather or cloth, so that your footfall should not be heard. Then, as I follow him, I would run to where you are posted, and you could follow me, so that you could keep me in sight and yet be beyond his view, for all our plans would be foiled should he suspect that he was being followed."

"I will do as you advise. Come with me now and we will fix upon a station to night, and afterwards you may be sure of finding me there between half-past six and ten. Should you wish to see me at any other time you will find me at the palace; I will not stir out between eight and nine in the morning. I must say I wish it were warmer weather, for a watch of three hours with the snow on the ground—and it is beginning to fall now—is not so pleasant a way of spending the evening as I had looked for when I came hither."

Beorn went out with Ulf, and they fixed upon a doorway some twenty yards from the street down which the Norman had before gone.

"We must hope he will go by the same way," Beorn said, "for should he turn to the right or left after issuing from the gate he will have gone so far before you can run across and fetch me that we may well fail to pick up his track again. It were well if we could arrange some signal by which you would let me know should he so turn off. It would not do for you to call or whistle."

"No, my lord; but I could howl like a dog. He would but think it some cur lying under the wall I might howl once if he turns to the right, twice if he turns to the left, and you could then cross the ground in that direction, and I could meet you on the way without losing sight of him for long."

"That would do well, Ulf, if you are sure you could imitate the howl of a dog so nearly that he would not suspect it."

"I can do that," Ulf said confidently. "I have used the signal before with my comrades, and to make sure will go out to the fields and practise daily."

A month passed. Harold was still away in the North, and complete success was attending his journey. The influence of Bishop Wulfstan, who was greatly respected throughout the kingdom, did much, but Harold himself did more. His noble presence, his courtesy to all, the assurances he gave of his desire that all men should be well and justly ruled, that evil-doers of whatever rank should be punished, that there should be no oppression and no exaction of taxes beyond those borne by the whole community, won the hearts of the people. They were, moreover, gratified by the confidence that he had shown in coming among them, and in seeing for the first time in the memory of man a monarch of England in Northumbria.

Ulf and Beorn had kept regular watch, but without success, and Ulf's comrades had as steadily watched the other entrances. Beorn had two or three conferences with Ulf. He was becoming impatient at the long delay, though he acknowledged that it was possible it had been arranged that no more meetings should take place until it was known that Harold was about to return. The armourer was perhaps the most impatient of the three. He was doing nothing, and his anxiety made him so irritable and captious at his work that his men wondered what had come over their master. After fretting for three weeks over his own inaction, he one morning told Ulf to go to Beorn and say that he begged to have speech with him. An hour later Beorn returned with Ulf.

"I bethought me last night, my lord," Ulred said, "while I lay awake wondering over the matter, whether these fellows are still on board ship or are in lodgings in London."

"It might be either, Ulred. I have frequently thought over the matter. Possibly they may have stayed on board their ship till she left, and then have come on shore in the guise of peaceful traders."

"If the ship did not return at once they may still be on board," the armourer said, "for the wind has blown steadily from the east for the last five weeks, and no ships have been able to leave the port. I blame myself sorely that I did not think of it before, but at least I will lose no time now if you think that good might come of it."

"It would certainly be good if you could find either the ship or the house where the men are in lodging, but seeing that you know nothing of their appearance or number, nor the name of the ship in which they came nor the port she sailed from, I see not how you could set about it."

"I will first go to the port-reeve's office and find out the names of the ships that arrived just before the time that the meeting by the river took place. She may have come in early that day, or on the day before. They would surely send word at once to him that they had arrived."

"You might learn something that way, Ulred, but we do not know that the meeting Ulf saw was their first."

"That is true. But as Ulf's friend declares that he certainly had not gone out that way during the evenings that he had been keeping watch, it is likely that it was their first meeting."

"That is so, Ulred; and at any rate it would be well that you should make the inquiries, and that, while we are keeping our watch as before, you should try to gather some tidings of the fellows in another way."

CHAPTER XVI. — A VOYAGE NORTH.

The armourer found without any difficulty that twenty-five vessels, exclusive of small coasters, had arrived in the port during the thirty-six hours previous to the time of the meeting on the bank. Of these, eighteen were from English ports, seven from Normandy, France, or Flanders. Three of the latter had sailed away, and of the four remaining in the port two were from Rouen, one from Calais, and one from Flanders. Having obtained the names of these, he took boat and rowed down the river and ascertained where each lay at anchor. He then, with the assistance of some citizens of standing of his acquaintance, obtained a view of the manifests of their cargoes. The Flemish vessel carried cloth, the other three miscellaneous cargoes—wine, dried fish, cloth, and other goods.

The Flemish vessel was the largest, those from Rouen and Calais were about the same size. All had discharged their cargoes, and were waiting for a change of wind to drop down the river. There was nothing unusual to be observed on any of the ships. The men were for the most part down in the forecastle, for the weather was too severe for them to lounge about on deck. He talked the matter over with Beorn, and they agreed that it was most probable that the men would embark from Calais rather than Rouen. It was a far shorter and less perilous voyage, and moreover, as Frenchmen they could move about without attracting attention, while as Normans they would be viewed with a certain amount of hostility and suspicion.

"I will make it my business to watch that vessel. I know not whether any good can come of it, but I would fain be doing something. If the wind changes she will doubtless proceed to sea, and if they are still on board of her they will come ashore, and I could see their numbers and where they put up."

"That will indeed be important," Beorn said, "for we should then have two places to watch, and should be almost certain to get to the root of the matter. But how will you watch her?"

"There are many houses near the water's edge, on the southern side of the river near which the ship is lying, she having moved away from the quays when she discharged her cargo. I will hire a room in one of these, and will there pass as much of my time as I can; and I will take with me my apprentice Ernulf, whom I shall bid keep his eye upon the ship whenever I myself am away. I need say nothing whatever of the reason of my desire that I should be acquainted with everything that passes on board."

Ulred succeeded in getting a room exactly opposite the French vessel, and sitting back from the window, was able, himself unseen, to notice everything that passed on board the ship, which lay scarce her own length from the shore. Upon the third day a boat containing a man wearing an ample cloak with a hood, which was pulled far over his face, rowed up to the side of the ship, and climbed up right nimbly into her waist.

"It is a Saxon cloak," the armourer said to himself, "but those are Norman leggings. The man is tall, and the quickness with which he climbed over shows that he is young. I doubt not that it is our man. I would give a year's profits of the forge to be hidden down below at present. However, it is much to have learnt that this is really the ship, and that the Norman's friends are still on board. I would that Wulf were in London. He has a keen wit, and would hit on some plan by which we might get to the bottom of the matter. Beorn is a brave young thane, and were Wulf here would second him valiantly, but he has none of the other's quickness of thought. As soon as this fellow leaves the ship I will hurry back to take counsel with him, and hear what the boy Ulf, who is a marvellously shrewd little knave, may think of the matter."

Half an hour later the boat put off again; a man came to the side with the visitor and retired below as soon as he left the ship. Ulred at once hurried off, hailed a boat a short distance higher up and was rowed to Westminster. As soon as he gained the house he despatched Ulf to Beorn. The latter listened to the discovery that had been made, and then asked the armourer what he advised should be done.

"That is just what I am at a loss about, my lord. Doubtless were we to go to the city and tell the port-reeve that there are men on that craft who have designs against the king's life, he would pounce upon them and throw them into jail. But we have no evidence to give in support of the charge."

Beorn nodded his head in agreement. "If I had half a dozen of my own men here," he said hotly, "I would go down in a boat after nightfall, seize the vessel, and put all on board to the sword."

"That would hardly do, my lord," the armourer said gravely. "On the high sea doubtless the thing might be done, but here in the port of London it would be a desperate undertaking, especially as we have nought that in the eyes of the law would in any way justify such action."

"Well, let us have your own advice, then," Beorn said impatiently. "You think they cannot be arrested and they may not be slain. What do you counsel shall be done!"

"I see nought to do but to continue to wait and to watch. We are better off than we were before, inasmuch as we know where these men are."

"Yes, but we do not know where they will be to-morrow, for we know nothing of what passed between Fitz-Urse and them; doubtless some settlement of their plans has been come to. They may land or may sail away, for methinks from the look of the sky there is like to be a change in the weather. You see, the Norman may have taken them news that Harold will soon be on his way back, for indeed a message arrived from him this morning with news that all things had been well-nigh settled, and that he will shortly make for York, where he is to wed the sister of the Northern earls. It may be that the ship may be bound thither also. You left your apprentice on the watch, I suppose?"

"Yes, I bade him keep his eye on the ship, and should any men leave her he is to follow on their track and mark their movements."

"At any rate there can be little need for me to watch this evening," Beorn said. "As Fitz-Urse has seen the others to-day he cannot want to meet them to-night."

"No, that is certain," the armourer agreed; "but with your permission I will call Ulf in. I told him before I sent him to you what I had observed. Are you going to watch again this evening, boy?" he asked when Ulf entered. "Methinks there can be little chance of his going out again to-night."

"I shall keep even a stricter watch than usual, master," Ulf said, "for it may be that the agreement at which they arrived to-day is that they sail north, and in that case Walter Fitz-Urse may go on board the ship, and hide there until the wind changes and they can get up sail."

"I think the boy is right, my lord. In a dark matter like this, where we know so little, it behoves us to provide for every chance. But I think not that there can be any need for you to be on watch, for it can hardly be that they will hold another consultation on the river bank."

Ulf returned soon after ten o'clock. "He has not gone out by my gate, master, but I find that my comrade is missing. When I went round as usual to the other entrance he was not there."

"Perhaps he was tired and went home."

"No, indeed," the boy replied indignantly; "he has sworn to do what I told him, and he knows that it would be bad for him if he broke his word; besides, we are sworn comrades. He has never before failed me, and I cannot but think that he must have seen the man go out and followed him. I instructed him that if at any time he saw a man like the one we are looking for he was to follow him wherever he went, and to bring me word whether he met anyone and whether he returned to the palace or went into any house. If he did so he was to make a small mark on the door-post with chalk, so that in the morning he would be able to point it out with surety. I will sit at my window and watch, and I warrant it will not be long before he is here."

Half an hour later Ulf heard steps rapidly approaching; then a low whistle. He put his head out of the window.

"What is the news, Edwyn?"

"A man came out in a cloak. He was tall. I followed him and heard a sword clink under the cloak, and so felt sure it was the man we have been looking for. I stole after him. He went straight down to the river and gave two short calls. A boat was rowed up. Only a word or two was spoken, and then he took his seat in it, and it was rowed away down the river."

"You have done well, comrade," Ulf said. "I warrant that some good will come to us through your discovery. Good-night."

Ulf went and knocked at his master's door, and on Ulred opening it he told him the news.

"I will go down right early," the armourer said.

"It is beginning to rain, master. The frost has broken, and the wind is soft and warm."

"So much the worse, boy. I will be up at daylight, and you shall go down the river with me. I may want to send you back with a message to Beorn."

Next morning they had rowed near to London Bridge when they saw a boat approaching. The day had broken, but the light was still uncertain. As the boat approached, however, Ulf said: "There is a boy in the boat, master, and he wears an apprentice's cap. Maybe that it is Ernulf." The other boat was keeping close inshore, for the tide had begun to run down. The armourer told the boatman to row closer in, and presently called the boy's name.

"Yes, master, it is I; I was just coming to you with news."

In a couple of minutes the boats were alongside of each other. "What is your news, Ernulf? But I can guess; the ship has sailed."

"Yes, master; I lay down by the open window, and an hour before day broke I was aroused by the creaking of ropes, and looking out could see that the ship was getting up sail. Tide was then just on the turn, and five minutes later her sails were spread and she went down the river. I came off to tell you, but was some time before I could get a boat."

"Come on board here, Ernulf," the armourer said, "your message has saved us further journey." He then paid off the lad's boatman, and with his two apprentices returned to Westminster. "Beorn will be up by this time, Ulf. You had best go and tell him the news. I will come with you to save time, though I see not that there is aught to be done."

The thane at once came out and chatted for some time with Ulred, while Ulf stood by, cap in hand. "It is certain that something should be done, and yet I see not what it can be. What think you, boy? I see by your eyes that you would fain speak."

"I should say, my lord, that it would be a good thing if we could discover whether the Norman is still at the bishop's palace. He may have returned early this morning."

"That can easily be done," Beorn said. "I will send my man to the bishop's and bid him ask one of the servants if Walter Fitz-Urse is in. He need not say that he comes from me, only that he has a message to deliver. If the servant says he is there I will bid my fellow slip away when the man goes to fetch him down. Supposing he has gone, as I should think he has done, what then?"

"Then, my lord, I think there is more danger than if the Norman remained here. It may be that the Normans have returned to France and abandoned any plans they may have entertained. But it seems to me far more likely that they have gone north to carry out the enterprise."

"Whither, think you, will they be bound, Ulf?"

"I should say to the Humber, my lord. They may on landing proceed to York, or, if they have really designs against the king's life, may take post somewhere on the road down from that city."

"By my faith the boy is right," Beorn said. "What say you, master armourer?"

"I say the same, my lord. The villains have slipped through our fingers, and we can do nought to stay them. It seems to me that not an hour should be lost in sending a warning to the Thane of Steyning."

"I will mount myself and ride north," Beorn said.

"And I, my lord, will at once go down to the port and inquire if there be a ship sailing to-day for the Humber. Scarce a day passes that one or more do not start for the northern ports. Yes, Ulf, I shall take you with me. You are charged with this business by the Thane of Steyning, and I am but aiding you in it. I will go straight away to the city, my lord, and if a ship be sailing—and after so long a bout of east wind it is like that many will be doing so—I will be back in an hour with the news. Maybe I can find a quick sailer, and shall be at one of the ports in the Humber before the craft that left this morning."

"By the time you return I shall have found out whether Fitz-Urse is at the bishop's palace, and shall have my horses ready to mount."

The armourer learnt in the city that several ships for the North had already dropped down the river, and that three others were hastily completing their lading, and would follow by the next tide. He learnt from a trader that one of them was considered especially fast, and being acquainted with the owner, he took the armourer with him, and arranged for a passage for him and the boy.

"You will have to be on board this afternoon," the owner said. "The shipmaster will not waste a tide, but as soon as it turns will up anchor and make his way down the river in the dark. He knows the channel well, and there will be light enough to enable him to hold on his course all night. The east wind may return again, and he might be caught; so he has decided to start as soon as the last bale is on board. He knows the sands well, and you may reckon on a speedy passage if the wind holds as it is, or even if it goes round to the east again, when he is once abreast of Harwich."

On returning to Westminster Ulred learnt from Beorn that Fitz-Urse was there no longer, having, as the servant said, left for Normandy.

"I am just starting, Ulred. Which will be at York first, you or I?"

"It depends upon the wind, my lord. A ship can sail night and day, but a horse and rider must take some rest. It may be that we shall lay to at night, but that must depend upon the shipmaster. If the breeze holds and the ship goes on without stopping, methinks we shall be there before you."

"At any rate," Beorn said, "we may feel sure that we shall both be in time. Whatever their designs they will have to lay their plans and wait their opportunity, and such may not come for some time. Farewell, then, Ulred, and a safe voyage to you. As for me, I have had enough of the sea, and never wish to set foot on board ship again; for what with the want of space and the tossing and the sickness, I would rather pass the time in bonds in a prison cell than be cooped up in a ship."

A few minutes later Beorn, attended by his servants, started for the North, and in the afternoon Ulred, after giving many orders to his head man as to the conduct of his business during his absence, took boat, and with Ulf went on board the ship. To the armourer it was a very serious undertaking upon which he was embarking. He had never before set foot on board of a ship, and a sea-voyage in those days was regarded as a very dangerous business. Nothing short of his loyalty to Harold would have induced him to have ventured on such an expedition. It was but a few months since that the Northumbrians had been burning and sacking the country round Northampton, and even putting aside the dangers of the sea, he regarded the visit to the North as full of peril.

Ulf on the other hand was delighted. To him the journey was full of interest and excitement, and on his return he would be regarded as a great traveller by his comrades. His face, therefore, as he climbed on board ship, was in strong contrast to the grave and serious visage of his master. Before the vessel had passed Greenwich he had made the acquaintance of the two ship's-boys, and soon felt perfectly at home on board. He watched with great interest other craft that they met or passed, and noted with great satisfaction that they overhauled several who had, when first seen, been two or three miles ahead. The wind was blowing briskly from the south-west, and with her great sail set the vessel ran quickly through the water. Even when the tide turned she held on her course, and keeping close inshore made good way against it. Many times during the night he went out from the close sleeping-place to assure himself that the vessel was still making way. When morning broke the tide had again turned, and Ulf found that the vessel was now holding her course near the middle of the river, which had widened to an extent that seemed wonderful to him.

"Where have we got to now?" he asked one of the boys. "Are we out at sea? There does not seem to be any land on the right hand."

"You would see it if it were clear. We are just opposite Foulness."

"The vessel rolls about a good deal."

"Do you feel ill?" the boy laughed. "This is nothing."

"No; I feel hungry, but that is all."

"If the wind holds as it is we shall not have it rougher than this, for we shall steer more and more north, and as we always keep inside the sands the land will shelter us. The shortest passage is straight ahead, but we generally go through a channel between two sands into the Wallet, which lies between the sands and the Essex shore. There are not many ship-masters who will come down the river below Sheerness at night, and even our master would not try it with a falling tide; but even if one does touch when the tide is rising, one soon gets off again. She won't roll about so much when we get inside the sands; and besides, I heard the master say that he thought the wind would fall lighter as the sun got up."

"I should like it to keep on just as it is," Ulf said. "I do not want it to blow so hard that we must go into port, and I don't want it to blow so light that we shall go slowly."

"What are you in such a hurry for?" the boy asked.

"There are some people my master knows who have gone up in a ship that started yesterday morning, and my master wants to be there before them."

"You need not be afraid, he is sure to be there first. Like enough we have passed them already. The wind was not so strong yesterday as it was in the night, and I expect they had to anchor when the tide turned. If they have a master who knows the sands well they may have gone on when the tide turned again, but it was likely they would anchor before they got down to Sheerness. If they did, we passed them three or four hours ago. But anyhow you are sure to be in first. We often beat vessels that started with us, by a week. Most of them go outside all the sands when it is fine weather, but we always keep inside; and it makes a great difference, for the tides do not run so strong, and even with a light wind we can make way against them, while those outside have to anchor."

"I can't make out how you can find your way in the dark."

"If it is a thick night and the weather is bad we anchor, but when it is clear enough to see the stars, or if the wind is steady so as to give us our direction, we go on. There is a man always standing at the side with a lead-line, and that tells us the depth of water, which is quite guide enough for the master. Of course we never sail in rough weather, for if we went on the sand then we should soon go to pieces; but if it is fine when we stick fast, which is very seldom, we put out the anchor and lower the sail, and go to sleep until the tide floats us again. Come up into the top; you can see a great deal farther from there than you can from the deck."

Ulf found no difficulty in mounting to the top, although he was much longer than his companion in getting up. There were several sail following them, and Ulf was surprised at the knowledge his companion showed of vessels that appeared to him almost precisely similar.

"The one nearest to us is the Alfred," he said. "I know her by that patch on her sail. She trades with Harwich. Those two smaller craft behind are bound, I should say, for Colchester or Maldon. That craft two miles ahead of us is a foreigner. You can see her sail has a longer yard than the others, and the sail is narrower at the bottom than it is at the top. Those two or three small craft you see more inshore have passed through the channel we shall follow into the Wallet. The farthest one is going on to Harwich, the others into the rivers. There is a craft about our own size hull down close by the land. She may be going to Harwich, or may be going on north. She looks to me like a foreigner. If so, she has come last from London. French and Flemish ships do not come within fifty miles of this. And now I must go down. We do the cooking, and breakfast must be ready in half an hour, or the master will be storming at us."

The wind held steadily from the south-west, and the vessel ran along near the shore in smooth water. The armourer had been ill the first night, but he came on deck soon after breakfast, and when once the vessel was past the mouth of Harwich Bay and was close inland, he soon recovered. On the morning of the fourth day after leaving port she entered the mouth of the Humber, and by nine o'clock arrived at Hull. Landing at once the armourer found a small vessel on the point of starting for York, and in half an hour from the time of weighing anchor the tide turned, and they ran rapidly along, helped by the flood.

"At what time will you reach York?" the armourer asked the master.

"By daylight to-morrow. We shall sail on until the flood is spent, and then anchor and go on again as soon as the ebb has done."

"How far will you be from York when you anchor?"

"We shall most likely get to Selby, some fourteen miles away by the road, though farther by the turns of the river."

"Could you put us ashore there, for we are anxious to reach the city as soon as possible?"

"Oh, yes. I will put you ashore in the boat either there or wherever else we may bring up."

They were three miles short of Selby when the ebb began to come down and the anchor was dropped. The armourer and Ulf were at once landed, and shouldering their bundles they set out at a brisk pace and passed through Selby at four o'clock. No questions were asked them. There was but small difference of dress between the people of the various parts of England, and it was no unusual sight to see traders and others passing along the road on their way to the Northern capital.

"I am right glad to be on firm land again," Ulred said; "for although, after the first night, matters have been better than I expected, there was always a movement that seemed to make my head swim."

"I liked it, master," Ulf said, "and if it were not that I am going to be an armourer I would gladly be a sailor."

"You might not have said so if you had seen bad weather; and moreover, it is one thing to be a passenger with nought to do but to amuse yourself, and another to be always hauling at ropes and washing down decks as a sailor. I am glad night is coming on, for I feel strange in this country I know nothing of, and in the dark one place is like another."

"I would much rather walk along this road in the dark," Ulf laughed, "than along some of the streets of London, where one may step any moment into a deep hole or stumble into a heap of refuse."

"At any rate, in the dark no one can see we are strangers, Ulf, and though I should not think there would be robbers on the road so near to York, these Danes are rough folk, and I want to meet none of them. One man, or even two, I in no ways fear, but when it comes to half a dozen even the best sword-player may wish himself out of it."

They met, however, but one or two men on the road, and beyond exchanging the usual salutation nothing was said; but Ulred was well pleased when about seven o'clock they entered the streets of York.

They had already learned that the royal marriage had taken place on the previous day, and that the king was expected to remain in York two days longer before journeying south. There was a banquet being held at the archbishop's palace, where the king was lodged, and on arriving there they found that it would at present be impossible to get at Wulf, as supper had just been served. A small bribe, however, was sufficient to induce one of the bishop's servants to take the message to Osgod, who would be stationed near his master's chair, that his father was at the entrance and prayed him to come out to him as soon as possible. A few minutes later the tall Saxon came out with an expression of utter bewilderment on his face.

"Is it really you, father, in flesh and blood?" he exclaimed as his eyes fell on Ulred.

"I have never been taken for a ghost, Osgod, and if I were to give thee a buffet methinks you would have no doubt upon the matter."

"But what brings you here, father? If they had told me that the great Abbey tower stood without I could not be more surprised."

"Do you not see that I have brought Ulf with me, Osgod? If your head were not so thick you would guess at once that I have come about the business with which he was charged."

Osgod looked relieved. That his father should be in York had seemed to him so strange and outrageous that he had first doubted his own eyes, and then his father's sanity. Now for the first time the object of his coming flashed upon him.

"Is there danger, father?"

"Methinks there is great danger. But the story is a long one."

"Then I cannot wait to hear it now, for I must needs return to Wulf. I whispered in his ear that I must leave for a moment, but that I should be back directly."

"Then just whisper to him again, Osgod, that I have urgent need for speech with him. I suppose Beorn has not arrived?"

"Beorn!" Osgod repeated vaguely.

"The Thane of Fareham," the armourer said sharply. "Are your wits wool-gathering altogether?"

"No, he is not here; nor has Wulf said a word of his coming, as he assuredly would have done had he expected him."

"Well, when I tell you that he is riding from London, while I have come thence by sea, you may suppose that we thought the matter urgent."

"I will tell Wulf at once, father, but I am sure that he cannot come out for an hour yet."

"The matter will keep that while. I will go and look for a lodging for us and get something to eat, for we have walked some seventeen miles, and my legs are not so accustomed to exercise as my arms. In an hour we will be here again."

Ulred and his apprentice had returned to the gate of the bishop's palace but a few minutes when Wulf came out, followed by Osgod. "Your message must be an important one, indeed, Ulred, to cause you to leave the forge and to undertake so long a voyage. And you say Beorn is riding hither on the same errand?"

"He is. It is a sort of race between us, and it seems that we have won."

"Let us step aside from here," Wulf said. "There are too many gathered about to stare at the guests as they come and go for us to talk unobserved. The cathedral yard is close by, and there will be no fear of eaves-droppers there."

"It is Ulf's story," the armourer said when they reached the shadow of the cathedral. "It is to him that the matter was committed, and though he was forced to take me into his confidence, the merit of following up the matter, if merit there be, is his."

Ulf accordingly related the story of his watching, the discovery he had made by the river, and how Walter Fitz-Urse had been afterwards seen to embark and had not returned. Ulred then stated how he had discovered the ship from which the boat had come, and had seen the Norman go on board, and how, when he learned that the ship had sailed, he had, after seeing Beorn, taken passage in another vessel. "We have come up fast," he said, "and the opinion of the master was that we have gained a full day on any craft that started that morning. Of course, we know not that the villains have come hither; they may have returned to France, they may have gone up some of the other rivers in order to take post on the road the king will follow on his way south. But at any rate we felt it right that you should know that Fitz-Urse, with those with whom he has been holding secret communication, have left London."

"You have done rightly indeed, Ulred, and in the king's name and for myself I thank you heartily. Of course, we are still without any proof that Fitz-Urse is conspiring against the king's life. It was unfortunate indeed that Ulf did not understand the first conversation he heard, but I ought to have foreseen that it was likely that any talk Fitz-Urse might have with others would be in Norman. I cannot think now how I could have overlooked such a probability. Of course, in the years that he has been over here he has learnt to speak our language, but it would be with Normans he would deal in the matter of which we suspect him. I will give myself the night to think over the matter before I decide what steps we had better take. Inside the bishop's palace, at any rate, the king is safe, and, as you say, it is not likely that the Normans can be here for a day at least. If their ship is a French one the master will be ignorant of the dangers of the coast, and instead of threading his way through the channels of the sands, as your master did, will have held his course far outside them. I would we knew how many men are engaged in the matter."

"As to that we have no clue," the armourer said. "There was the man of his own rank and the other two who met him on the bank, but whether these were all, or whether there were a score of others on board the ship, I know not. Certainly none showed themselves on the deck while I was watching them. But this proves nothing. They would naturally be kept in concealment, for had there been an unusual number of men on board, inquiries would have been made as to whom they were and their business."

"I will meet you here at seven to-morrow morning, Ulred, and we shall then have time to talk the matter over more fully."

CHAPTER XVII. — AN ATTEMPT AT ASSASSINATION.

When Wulf met the armourer next morning in the cathedral close he was accompanied by Beorn, who said, laughing, to the latter, "You have beaten me fairly, friend Ulred, and it is well that I had no wager with you on the race. But it was not by much, for I rode in here as the bells were chiming eleven. I was glad to hear from Wulf when I roused him up that he had learnt all the news from you, for indeed I was sore weary, and was right pleased to wrap myself in my cloak and go straight to sleep instead of having to sit up for an hour expounding my story."

"We have resolved in the first place, Ulred, to say nought of this matter to the king," began Wulf. "He will have enough to occupy all his thoughts in the affairs of the kingdom, and in the second place his nature is so open that he will refuse to believe in such villainy unless upon strong proof, and of actual proof we have none. Beorn's appearance here will excite no surprise. He will say that having nought in particular to occupy him he had ridden north to be at the wedding, and finding that he was too late, would at any rate ride back with the king. With him and me and Osgod ever on the watch, methinks there will be little fear of a surprise; and it is by surprise only that they can succeed, for Harold himself is a match for any four or five ordinary men if he has but time to draw his sword. I will, however, on some excuse have half a score of Harold's housecarls placed under my orders, and sleeping or waking the king shall never be a moment unguarded.

"I should not think it is likely that Fitz-Urse will have more than five or six men associated with him in such an enterprise. He would not take more into his confidence than he could help, and six would suffice as well as a score for a surprise; and that number could travel in disguise without exciting attention, while twenty would assuredly do so; therefore I feel sure that we shall not have to deal with more than six, including the two leaders. Ulf, do you station yourself at the river-bank and mark any vessels arriving. If the men come hither they will probably do as you did, leave their ship at Hull and come up by a local trader. They would thus avoid all questions they might be asked if passing through the country on foot."

"And what is there for me to do, my lord Wulf?" the armourer said. "Frankly, I have gone so far in this matter that I would fain see it through."

"Of course we reckon upon you, Ulred. I have been talking it over with Beorn, and it seemed to us that the best thing will be for you to ride with Osgod. You can either make some slight change in your clothes and ride as a man of mine, or you can ride as Osgod's father, who, having come up here on matters connected with your business, have obtained permission to ride in my train with him. I will see that you have that permission."

"I care not how I go so that I can be at hand if there is a blow to be struck for the king."

"Then in that case, Ulred, it were best you went as my man, for you would then have the entry of the houses where the king will stop and can aid us in keeping guard."

"That will do well for me," Ulred replied. "Ulf had best journey back as he came. He might go by ship after the king has left here."

"No, he shall travel with us. I will see the chamberlain who has charge of the arrangements of the journey, and will get leave for him to ride in the waggons with the servants."

During the three days before the king left York Ulf kept a vigilant watch over the boats that came up the river, but he could see nothing of the men he was searching for. Wulf had bought a horse for the armourer, and when they started the latter took his place by Osgod's side, while Ulf was seated in one of the waggons. The king rode with Bishop Wulfstan, next to them rode the four thanes who had accompanied them through their journey, and next to these Wulf and Beorn came on together. Behind came the queen's litter, with a guard of housecarls, the main body of whom rode just behind, while the waggons and servants brought up the rear.

"We need not trouble ourselves on the march, Beorn. It is not while the king rides with so strong a following that the blow will be struck."

"I see not when they can ever get a chance," Beorn said. "The king will stop always at religious houses, and they will scarcely storm a convent to get at him."

"They would not attempt to storm it, Beorn, but they might enter it secretly. But for my own part I think the most dangerous time is when he mounts or dismounts. There is always a crowd assembled to see him, and two or three reckless men might rush forward and stab him."

"It would be at the cost of their own lives," Beorn objected.

"It might be, but they would reckon much on the confusion that would follow, and might think so to get away. They would probably have horses somewhere close at hand, and might ride for the port where they had left their ship. It is a great stake they are playing for, and doubtless they are desperate men; though they would know the danger they might calculate that some at least would escape to claim the reward. Then again, they might manage to mingle with the servitors at one of the places where we stop. This would not be difficult, for many beside the usual establishment would be hired to aid in the preparations for the reception of the king. That might be their safest plan, for were he stabbed suddenly at a meal the assassins might very well escape in the confusion."

The first night they slept at a monastery at the village of Bautre. The establishment was but a small one, and could entertain only the king and queen, with the thanes and their personal attendants. The rest of the train were lodged in the village. Although they had little fear that an attack would be ventured in so quiet a village where the presence of strangers would at once attract attention, Wulf, Beorn, and Osgod kept watch in turns all night in the corridor. The night passed without cause of alarm, and the next day they rode to Nottingham, where they were lodged in the bishop's palace. Beorn and Wulf agreed that this was the place where there was the greatest likelihood of an attack being made on Harold's life. The ship might have sailed up the river and landed her passengers a few miles from the town, where, among the number of country people who would flock in to obtain sight of the king, no one would think of questioning strangers. The armourer and Ulf were charged to wander about the streets, and to closely scan every face. Wulf had with some difficulty obtained from Harold the command of twelve of the soldiers.

"I have my reasons, my lord king, though I would rather not state them. I would remind you that I have shown that it is not my habit to take alarm lightly. Your brother Gurth laughed at me when I begged to watch over his camp with my housecarls, and I saved him from a sudden attack by the Welsh thereby."

"Then you think that there is danger of an attack upon me, Wulf?"

"I said not so, my lord. I have only begged you to appoint twelve of your men to obey my orders solely, during your journey to London."

"You shall do as you like, Wulf," the king said at last. "You have proved yourself brave as well as prudent before now, and are not given to vain fears, therefore do as you please, but let me know nought about it. I shall have to receive the visits of all the thanes of the neighbourhood when I reach Nottingham, and the same in other towns. There will be many persons coming in with petitions for the redress of grievances, and I would not have my thoughts disturbed by other matters."

"You shall know nought about it, my lord," Wulf said. "It is like enough that nothing will come of the matter, and none will be more glad than myself to find that I am mistaken."

Orders accordingly had been given to the officer of the king's guard to hand over twelve of his men to Wulf, and the latter had begged him to choose twelve of his most intelligent men for this service. As soon as they reached Nottingham Wulf took his small command aside.

"You have been chosen," he said, "for a special duty. I have learned that there are disaffected men who may possibly make an attempt on the king's life. You are to say no word of what I tell you to anyone. Meet me over by that wall half an hour after sunset. Gather quietly one by one so as to attract no attention. You will be posted round the palace, to keep watch and ward during the night. As soon as it is daylight half of you will lie down and sleep till mid-day, and then be in readiness for fresh duty. The others I will instruct as to where to hold themselves. The king will remain here two days, and watch must be kept over his safety night and day."

As soon as their apartments were assigned to the different guests Wulf went outside and examined the windows of the rooms to be occupied by the king. They were on the first floor, and looked into a garden surrounded by a high wall.

"At any rate, there is little fear of a successful surprise from this side," Wulf said to Beorn, who was with him. "It would need a ladder to scale the wall; this would have to be pulled up for them to descend into the garden, and then carried across to mount to the window. If we post Ulred with two men here and let four others lie down near to change guard every two hours, it will be ample, for on an alarm being given, the Normans however numerous will see that their attempt must fail. We can therefore send the other six to bed after supper is over, for we cannot suppose that they would be so daring as to force their way into the palace at any other point."

As soon as it was dark Ulred and six of the soldiers were placed in the garden; the others were directed to hold themselves in readiness to take their post in the banqueting-hall. Just before the bell sounded for supper Wulf was told that a boy desired to speak to him at the gate. He hurried out, and, as he expected, saw Ulf waiting there.

"What news, Ulf,—hast seen Walter Fitz-Urse?"

"I have not seen him, my lord, but I am sure that I heard him speak. There was a great crowd in the square after the king had entered, and among those round me I heard one man speak to another in a foreign tongue, and the voice was assuredly that of Walter Fitz-Urse. It was but two or three words he said, but having listened to him for well-nigh half an hour that night by the river, I am certain I was not mistaken in the voice. Close beside me were two cowled monks, and I believe that it was one of them who spoke. I looked round at the faces of the other men standing near, but they all seemed honest countrymen or town folk. I should have followed the monks to see where they went, but at that moment there was a rush among the crowd to see some mummers who had just commenced their antics, and I was swept along by it; and though I have been searching ever since, and have so stared up into the cowls of monks, that I have been cursed as an insolent boy many times, I have not seen our man."

"Thanks, Ulf. It is something to have learned that he is here. As to his disguise, he may by this time have changed it. Still, I will be on my guard, and will take care that no cowled monk approaches too closely to the king. Take your place here at the gate and watch all who come in and out, and if you see aught suspicious send in a soldier, whom I will place by your side, to fetch me out."

One of the men was accordingly placed with the boy with orders to come to Wulf, whether at the table or in the king's room, the moment Ulf told him to do so. When the others went into the banquet Wulf posted two men just outside the door, and placed the other three back against the wall nearest to the king's chair. Here, standing against the arras, they were concealed from the sight of the guests by the crowd of servitors passing to and fro.

"Stand with your hands on your daggers," Wulf said to them, "and watch every man who approaches the king, no matter of what degree he may appear. Be ready to spring forward in an instant if you see his hand go to his dagger."

The bishop and king sat next to each other in the centre of the table on the dais; on either side were the king's thanes, abbots and other dignitaries of the church, and the nobles of the country. Wulf and Beorn had begged to be excused from supping, and permission had been readily granted by the king, as he knew that the bishop would be glad at having two extra seats at his disposal; and they also, standing back by the wall, closely scrutinized the movements of the attendants. It was a relief to them when supper was over and the bishop and his principal guests retired to a private room. The five soldiers were then told that they would not be required until morning.

Wulf went out to the gate, and learnt from Ulf that he had seen no one enter whom he took for Fitz-Urse.

"He may have gone in by some other entrance, my lord," he said, "for there are three or four ways into the palace."

"We shall be on watch inside, Ulf. You need stay no longer. Be here in the morning at seven."

After the king and queen had retired to bed and the palace was quiet Wulf, Beorn, and Osgod stole from their room, and noiselessly passed along the corridors until they came to the king's apartment, and then lay down across the door. They were to keep watch in turns, Osgod being told to keep the first watch and to rouse Wulf at midnight. This he did, and Wulf lay for some time listening intently. The corridor was faintly lit by two lamps, one at either end. Wulf had chosen the middle watch, because he thought that if any attempt was made it would be soon after midnight, as the assassins would wish to have many hours of darkness in which to make their escape. He knew that Beorn was a sound sleeper, and could scarcely be trusted to keep awake from midnight until four o'clock, and that it were best he himself watched during that time.

Half an hour passed, and then he heard a very slight noise. A moment later four figures appeared at the end of the corridor. He dared not wake his companions, for they might speak or move, but he grasped his sword-hilt, having drawn the blade in readiness when Osgod woke him. The men advanced stealthily, and as they approached he saw they had drawn swords in their hands. They paused a few paces away, and in a whisper one said:

"Here are three fellows asleep; what shall we do with them?"

"Draw your daggers and stab them to the heart," another replied. "Each take one, and do not bungle over it. As you strike I will open the door and rush in. Now!"

Wulf had gathered his legs under him in readiness to spring to his feet as soon as he saw the figures, and as they swiftly advanced he leapt up with a shout and crossed swords with the man nearest to him.

"Cut him down! Kill him! It is too late to draw back now!" one of the men cried. The others, who had recoiled a moment when Wulf sprang up, rushed at him just as he cut down the man he had first engaged.

"Cut them down and fly!" the one who had before given orders exclaimed, lunging furiously at Wulf.

"Easier said than done, Walter Fitz-Urse!" Wulf exclaimed, as he parried a blow and dealt one in return. It lighted on his opponent's shoulder, but the blade shivered in his hand, for it had fallen upon mail armour concealed under the Norman's garment.

"It is my turn now!" Fitz-Urse exclaimed, and raised his sword to strike a sweeping blow at Wulf's head, but before it could fall the latter leapt forward and caught the uplifted wrist, the impetus of the spring throwing his opponent backwards, while Wulf fell heavily upon him, and for a moment they rolled over and over. But Wulf was by far the most powerful, and speedily got the upper hand. He had not noticed that his opponent, while holding his sword in his right hand, had his dagger already drawn in his left. The sword had flown from Fitz-Urse's hand as he fell, and Wulf, believing him to be powerless, glanced round to see how the fray went with the others, when the Norman stabbed him deeply in the side. Before he could repeat the blow Wulf snatched his own dagger from his girdle and buried it in the assassin's throat Then he raised himself on his left hand. It was but a matter of seconds since the fight had commenced, but it was already over. Osgod had slain one man, Beorn was following a flying opponent down the corridor, and Harold, sword in hand, had just rushed from his chamber. Wulf saw no more, but fell over insensible by the side of his adversary.

"What is all this?" Harold shouted as he turned to Osgod, the only figure standing, raising his sword as he spoke, for in the dim light he did not recognize him.

"It means, my lord, that there has been an attempt on your life. I am Osgod, Wulf's man. I fear my brave young master is killed!" and he dropped on his knees by Wulf's side. By this time doors were opening all along the corridor, and the king's thanes and other guests, awakened by Wulf's shout and the clashing of swords, were pouring out, armed with the first weapon they could snatch up.

"Bring lights!" Harold shouted. "My life has been attempted, and I fear that the brave Thane of Steyning is killed."

The alarm spread fast, and the palace so lately hushed and silent was now in an uproar, while the bishop with many other ecclesiastics, with servants, retainers, and men-at-arms, mingled with the thanes.

"Keep all back!" Harold cried. "Let none approach these bodies until we have examined them."

Torches were soon brought. Harold seized one, and bent over Wulf's body.

"Is he dead?"

"His heart beats, but feebly, my lord," Osgod replied.

"Where is he hurt?"

"There is a great patch of blood here on his right side just over the hip. I see no other sign of a wound."

"We will carry him into my chamber," the king said. "But no; I forgot, the queen is there. We will take him into the room opposite; it matters not whose it is. Now, Osgod, aid me to lift him gently. Bishop, I pray you send for the leeches most skilled in the treatment of sword wounds in the city." Then he and Osgod carried Wulf into the chamber opposite his own, and laid him on a pallet.

"Now see to the staunching of the flow of blood till the leeches arrive. I must inquire into this matter. Who knows aught about it?" he asked as he went out into the corridor.

"I do, my lord king," Beorn replied as he pushed his way through the throng. "It was a plot to take your life. Wulf, his man Osgod, and myself had no certain knowledge of it, but we had cause for suspicion, and therefore lay outside your door. We were to take it in turns to watch. Wulf was on guard, and as I awoke at his shout I saw him cut down that villain who lies there with a cleft skull There were three others. I fell upon one, Osgod took another, while Wulf engaged the man who seemed to be the leader. Wulf's sword broke, but he closed with his opponent and they fell together. Osgod ran his man through, and my opponent fled. I could not catch him until he reached the door, but as that was closed he could fly no farther, and I slew him there."

"Who and what are these men, good Beorn?"

"They are, I believe, Normans; but I know naught for certain beyond the fact that the leader, he with whom Wulf was engaged, is Walter Fitz-Urse, who was a page of the Bishop William of London, and was well known at the court."

Exclamations of fury and indignation broke from those around, with the cries of "Death to the Normans!"

Harold raised his hand. "Silence, my friends. Let us be fair and just as it becomes Englishmen. There are villains of all nations, and it is not because four caitiffs have thought to do a good service to their duke by getting rid of me that we should blame men who will abhor this crime as much as we can do. First let us see if Beorn is right as to this man. Hold a torch to his face. It is Fitz-Urse truly. He was of knightly blood, but has died in a most unknightly business. Wulf's dagger is still in his throat. Let us see if we know anything of the others."

"I think that you will find them all strangers, my lord," Beorn said. "I believe they came from beyond the sea to do this deed."

The man whom Wulf had first slain was evidently by his dress a person of some rank; the other was of inferior station, as was also, as it was found, the man Beorn had killed.

"Now, my lord bishop," the king said calmly, "we have a right next to ask you how these men came to be in your palace. Know you aught of them?"

"I know nothing of them," the bishop replied. "So far as I am aware I have never seen any of their faces before, and assuredly they were not here with my cognizance. I will at once question all my people shrewdly, and woe be to him who has admitted strangers here unknown to me at the time when you were beneath my roof."

"And have this house searched from basement to roof, bishop. It may be that there are others in hiding."

"With your permission, my lord," said Beorn, "I will at once take your men, of whom we have posted six under your window, and will call up some more and search the town. It is likely that there are others without with horses held in readiness for these assassins to escape."

"Do so, Beorn. It will be well if we can catch some at least, so that we can get to the bottom of this matter."

The bishop at once ordered his armed retainers to accompany Beorn, and then proceeded to interrogate his officials and the domestics, and to see that the latter made a complete search of the palace. All denied any knowledge of strangers having entered, and the search revealed nothing but four monks' gowns and hoods found wrapped up in a bundle in a small room downstairs. Further questions had been then put. Some of the domestics remembered that four monks had entered the palace late in the evening, and one of the under chamberlains said that he had seen them, and they had told him that they had just arrived from Flanders, and craved permission to sleep in the palace for the night, as they were going on to Peterborough in the morning. He had told them that this was impossible, as he could give no permission without the leave of the bishop, who was at present with the king and could not be disturbed, and that, moreover, every room in the palace was occupied. He had given them the address of a citizen, who would he was sure take them in. They had thanked him, and said that they would go there, but doubtless instead of doing so they had slipped aside, and had hidden themselves in the room where their gowns were found. It was one used only for the storage of garments for poor travellers who came along, and no one was likely to enter it on such an evening.

This discovery was a great relief to the bishop and all within the palace, as it showed that they were not there with the connivance of any of the prelate's people. Before the matter was fully unravelled Beorn returned. They had in a quiet spot a short distance from the palace come upon two men with six horses. Before they could run up and seize them the two men had leapt up into the saddles and galloped furiously away. Unfortunately the other four horses had followed, and immediate pursuit was therefore impossible. The housecarls had run to the spot where their horses were stabled and had gone off in pursuit, but Beorn feared that the men would have far too great a start to be overtaken. One of the officers had ridden with the housecarls, and Beorn had told him to keep by the river-bank, as the men would assuredly make for a ship that was lying somewhere down the river, though whether at a distance of two miles or of twenty he knew not. Long before Beorn's return Wulf's wound had been examined. Unguents had been poured into it and bandages applied. The surgeons were of opinion that it was a very grave one, but that at present they could not say how the matter would terminate.

"Your story will keep till the morning, Beorn," the king said. "It is still five hours to daylight, and we may as well retire to rest, unless, indeed, you know that there are others engaged in the affair in London or elsewhere who should be arrested before the news of the night's business reaches them."

"I know of none such," Beorn said, "and believe that these four and the two who have escaped were alone concerned in it. I will bring with me in the morning a man and a boy who know more than I do of the matter; they and Osgod, with whom Wulf will assuredly have talked it over, will be able to tell you all that was known up to the moment when these men entered the palace."

The armourer and Ulf told their story in the morning, and Beorn took Osgod's place by Wulf's bedside, while he too was questioned by the king. The latter then went to Wulf's chamber.

"What say the leeches this morning, Beorn?

"They are somewhat more hopeful, my lord. They say that his heart beats more strongly than it did last night, Osgod says that he has not moved or opened his eyes, but they say that this is not a bad sign, and that it may be anxiety has brought on an exhaustion, for his breathing is more like that of one who sleeps than of a man wounded to death."

"His face has grieviously changed since yesterday," the king said sadly, looking down upon Wulf. "I would give my right hand rather than that he should die. You have of a surety saved my life among you, Beorn, you and his stout man-at-arms and the worthy armourer and that shrewd apprentice of his for had they entered my chamber and taken me unawares they would have slain me without doubt."

"I have done the best I could since I learnt from the armourer the suspicion that Wulf entertained, but the whole thing is Wulf's doing. Had I heard that Walter Fitz-Urse was back in London I should have given the matter no further thought than that it was one Norman the more. It was, as he told me, some words that Baron de Burg said when he saw him over in Normandy the other day that first set him thinking. Then, he could not understand why Fitz-Urse should return to London at this time, when Normans are not overwelcome there, and this caused him to have some sort of suspicion as to his reasons for undertaking such a journey, and determined him to set a watch on the fellow's movements. Had it been any other than Wulf who had so acted I should have laughed at his suspicions. But he is as a brother to me, and knowing how sharp are his wits I am always well content to follow him without question. I first heard of the matter after the discovery that the Norman was having secret meetings with some of his countrymen who were concealed on board a ship, and I at once felt sure that Wulf had not been running on a false trail, and so did the little I could to aid those who had the matter in hand."

"You have done well, Beorn, though as you say it is doubtless Wulf to whom the chief credit is due. I regretted at first that the other two men had escaped, but had they been taken they might, to save their own lives, have implicated others, and I might have been forced to lay a complaint against the Duke of Normandy. As it is now, the matter is at an end. Four men have tried to murder me, and have been killed. Their bodies have been buried this morning, and there is no more to be said about it.

"I was obliged to go down and show myself to the people an hour since, for they assembled in a great crowd, clamouring to see me so that they might know I was safe. I told them that while I thanked them for their loyal care, there was nought to be alarmed about. It was true that there had been an attempt on my life by four men, of whom the leader had a private grudge against me for a disservice I did him some years ago, but that all had been killed by my guards without even penetrating my chamber, and that I had run no sort of personal risk, nor had I any reason whatever to suppose that the malefactors had accomplices either within or without the palace."

Late in the evening, when the surgeons were applying pungent salts to his nostrils, Wulf opened his eyes. Osgod was standing beside him holding one of his hands.

"It is all well, master," he said. "We finished them all off, and no harm has happened to the king. You have been hurt, but I hope you will soon be better. The leeches say that you are not to talk, and you had best sleep as much as you can. They have got some stuff for you to drink here; do you lie still and I will pour it between your lips."

A look of intelligence came into Wulf's eyes as Osgod spoke; he smiled faintly, and murmured, "Thank God, the king is safe!" He swallowed a few spoonfuls of the potion Osgod held to his lips, and then closing his eyes his regular breathing soon showed that he was again asleep. On the following day the king proceeded on his way to London, Beorn remaining to nurse Wulf. The king would have loaded Ulred with presents, but the sturdy armourer refused to receive anything save a small gold cup in remembrance.

"I want no reward for doing my duty," he said. "I have my trade that keeps me, and should be no happier were I laden with money. All that I have done in the matter has been to watch for a few hours at a window, and to make a journey by ship to York, and I should be ashamed of myself indeed if I could not take that slight trouble for my king without looking for a reward."

As to Ulf he was thanked and praised, but the king decided to take no steps to alter his condition until Wulf should be well enough to be consulted in the matter. It was a fortnight before the doctors were able to state with any confidence that the young thane was on the road towards recovery, and still another month before he had gained sufficient strength to be carried in a litter to London.

CHAPTER XVIII. — THE NORTHERN INVASION.

The news of Harold's marriage to Ealdgyth put an end to the demands of William of Normandy that Harold should take one of his daughters to wife, and in the complaints that he addressed to all Christendom against Harold the breach of his promise in this respect was placed far more prominently than his failure to carry out his oath to be the duke's man. It must have been evident indeed to all that it was beyond the power of the English king to keep this oath, obtained from him by force and treachery. He had been elected by the voice of the English people, and had no more power than the meanest of his subjects to hand the crown they had bestowed to another.

The breach of this oath, however, served to obtain all the aid that the church could give to William. Harold was solemnly excommunicated, and the struggle for which the duke was preparing thereupon assumed the character of a sacred war. In England itself the Bull of excommunication had no effect whatever. The great bulk of bishops and clergy were Englishmen, and thought far more of their king than of any foreign prince or prelate. Even the bishops and abbots of Norman blood disregarded the commination, and remained staunch to Harold. He had been a generous patron to the church, had maintained them in all the privileges and dignities that Edward had bestowed upon them, and possessed the love of the whole English people; therefore, in spite of bann and interdict the churches remained open, services were held as usual, and people were married and buried as if the Papal Bull had never been issued.

But it was not so on the Continent. The Norman barons as a body had at first refused to support the duke in an invasion of England, but as individuals they had been brought round to join in William's project, and to give far more aid in ships and men than they were bound to do by their feudal engagements. Having accomplished this, William issued an invitation to all adventurous spirits in Europe to join him in his crusade against the excommunicated King of England, promising that all should share alike in the plunder of England and in the division of its land. The bait was a tempting one. Some joined the enterprise merely for the sake of gaining glory under the banner of one who was regarded as the greatest military leader in Europe, others were influenced by love of gain, while, as in the crusades, numbers joined to obtain absolution for past misdeeds by taking part in an enterprise blessed by the Pope. Thus the force which William was collecting greatly exceeded that which the resources of Normandy alone could have set on foot.

Among the first to hurry to the court of William, as soon as Harold's accession to the throne was known, was Tostig, in whose mind the refusal of Harold to embark in a civil war for his sake, and to force him upon the people of Northumbria in spite of their detestation of him, was an injury not to be forgiven. The fact that Tostig was ready thus to sacrifice England to his own private quarrel showed a baseness and recklessness that could hardly be expected from his early career. William naturally accepted the alliance, received Tostig's oath of allegiance, and aided him in fitting out a number of ships manned by Norman and Flemish adventurers. Evading the watch kept by the English fleet they crossed the sea, landed, and plundered and ravaged a considerable extent of country, and then retired, Tostig being enraged that William of Normandy was unwilling to send an expedition to act in concert with him until the whole of his plans were prepared and his great army ready for sea.

Normandy indeed had been converted into a vast camp. In every port great numbers of workmen laboured night and day building ships, for Normandy had ceased to be a naval power, and its shipping was utterly insufficient to carry the great army across. Tostig, impatient and hasty, thought no more of the oath of allegiance that he had sworn to William. Driven from Yorkshire by the forces of the northern earls he sailed to Scotland, where he was welcomed by King Malcolm, both as a sworn brother and as the enemy of England. From Scotland he entered into negotiations with Harold Hardrada of Norway. This warlike monarch was in a fit mood to listen to his advances; he had for years been engaged in a struggle with Denmark, which he had ineffectually attempted to conquer, and had at last been forced to conclude a treaty of peace with Sweyn, its king.

Tostig had already endeavoured by personal persuasions to induce Sweyn to revive his claim to the crown of England, and to undertake its conquest; but he altogether declined to undertake so dangerous and difficult an enterprise, and Tostig had then turned to Harold of Norway. Whether his interview with him was before he went to Scotland or whether he went thence to Norway is a point on which historians differ. Some deny that any interview took place, but the balance of probability lies strongly in favour of an early interview, at which Harold entered heartily into Tostig's plans, and began at once to make preparations for the enterprise.

It was certain that an invading force from Norway would land in Northumbria, and Harold, although he might not be able to rely greatly upon the assistance of the northern earls as against the Normans, knew that they would do their best to defeat an expedition landing on their own shores, especially when Tostig was a sharer in the invasion. His own thoughts were wholly bent upon repelling the mighty expedition gathering in Normandy, and for this purpose, by immense efforts, he collected the greatest army and fleet that had ever been got together in England. An incessant watch was kept up along the coast where the Normans might be expected to land, while the fleet cruised for months between the Thames and the Isle of Wight prepared to give battle to the invaders.

But the conditions of service in England were such that it was impossible to keep a great force on foot for an indefinite time. The housecarls were the only regular portion of the army The great bulk of the force, both land and sea, consisting of the levies or militia, whose term of service was very limited. It says much for the influence of Harold that he was able for four months to keep his army and navy together. Had the foe appeared, soldiers and sailors would have done their duty, but the long term of inaction, the weary waiting for a foe that never came, was too much, and when September arrived and the harvest was ready to be gathered it was impossible even for him to keep the men longer together. The army disbanded, the levies went to their homes, and the ships of the fleet sailed away to the ports to which they belonged. All the efforts and anxieties of Harold, all his lavish expenditure in feeding and providing for so great a number of men had been thrown away. England lay for a time absolutely defenceless against the coming storm.

It was not until August that Wulf had completely recovered his strength, and was able to join the army.

"This is not a time," Harold said to him on the day he arrived at the camp, "for the granting of dignities or the bestowal of grants. But if we are successful, and I remain King of England, the services you have rendered me at the risk of your life, Wulf, shall be worthily rewarded."

"I need no reward," Wulf replied. "My estates are sufficient for all my needs, and I desire neither land nor dignity, being more than content that I have been enabled to render a service to you and to England."

Wulf was, however, at once appointed as commander of the whole of the housecarls supplied by the thanes of the south coast of Sussex. None of these bodies were equal in strength to his own carefully prepared contingent, few of the thanes having kept up more than fifteen or twenty men constantly under arms, and these only for the past few months, in consequence of Harold's exhortations. Altogether the force amounted to about four hundred men. Each party had its own sub-officer, and Wulf did his best to weld them into one body. When the army broke up, he returned with the king to Westminster. The day after he arrived there a man met him as he issued from the palace, and handed him a letter. It contained but the words:

"I would fain see you. If you will follow the bearer he will bring you to me. Say naught to any one of this message. Edith."

"Is the distance far?" he asked the man.

"It is to Croydon, my lord. I have ridden here on horseback."

Wulf at once ordered his horse to be brought to him.

"Will you be back to-night, my lord," Osgod asked, as he mounted, "in case the king should wish to see you?"

"I shall not be back till late, possibly not until to-morrow I do not tell you where I am going, in order that if you are asked you may be able truly to reply that I said nothing before I mounted, as to my destination."

It was just mid-day when Wulf drew up his horse before a modest house standing in a secluded position a quarter of a mile from the village of Croydon. Edith met him at the doorway.

"I thank you, Wulf, for answering my request so speedily. There is much that I would ask you about my lord. I hear of him only by general report, for although from time to time I send him messages I give him no opportunity for writing to me, and I know that he has respected my wishes, and has caused no search to be made for me."

"Harold sometimes speaks to me of you, lady, and has in no way forgotten you. He did charge me to find out if I could the place of your abode; not that he would seek an interview with you, but, should there be need, he might be able to send a message." By this time they were seated in the room where Edith spent the greater part of her time.

"It is better that we should not meet," she said earnestly. "His mission is to work and to fight for England; mine to remain apart from all men and to spend my time in prayers for him. I know that he places great confidence in you, as indeed he well may, for I heard how you had saved his life, well nigh at the expense of your own. Is he happy with his new queen?"

"His thoughts at present, lady, are altogether turned to public affairs, and it is well perhaps that it should be so. I do not think that he receives much sympathy from the queen, who cares more, I should say, for her brothers, the northern earls, than for her husband."

"It is scarce a wonder that it should be so," Edith replied; "though it seems strange to me that any woman could live with Harold without loving him with all her heart. And yet she may well feel that she, like Harold, has been sacrificed. There was no shadow of love between them before their marriage, in fact she may even have hated him, for it was he who brought ruin and death upon her husband, the Welsh king. She must know that he only married her in order to gain the firm alliance of her brothers, and that her hand was given by them to Harold without any reference to her feelings. I would that the king were happy, even though it were with another. But it was not for his happiness that I left him, but that England might be one. Is it true that the army is broken up and the fleet scattered?"

"It is true, lady. Save for three or four thousand housecarls, there is not an armed man in readiness to defend England."

"It must be a terrible trial to him."

"It is, my lady. He returned to town yesterday dispirited and cast down at the failure of the work of months."

"Still they will reassemble rapidly," she said, "when the Normans really come?"

"Doubtless they will. But the loss of the fleet is greater than that of the army, for at sea we could have met and almost assuredly have conquered them, for the Normans are no match for our sailors; whereas to meet so great an army of trained soldiers, with hastily assembled levies, is to fight under every disadvantage."

"And is the rumour true which says that Tostig and Harold of Norway are also preparing for an invasion?"

"All reports that come to us through Denmark are to that effect."

"It is enough to make the stones cry out," Edith said indignantly, "that a son of Godwin should thus betray England. I never thought it of him. He was headstrong and passionate; yet as a young man he was loved almost as much as Harold himself, nay, some loved him more. But it was not on account of public affairs that I brought you here, but to talk of Harold. I know nought of his daily doings, of his thoughts, or his troubles. Tell me all you can of him, Wulf."

For a long time they talked of the king. She had from the first been drawn towards Wulf by seeing how he loved Harold, and as they talked her tears often fell.

"I am proud of him," she said at last; "more proud of him than when he was the light of my life. My sacrifice has not been in vain. He is what I would have him. One whose thoughts are all fixed upon his country; who gives all his energy, all his wisdom, all his time to her service. Humbler men can be happy, but a king has higher duties than others, and for him love and marriage, wife and children, the joys of the peasant, must be altogether secondary. The good of his country, the happiness and welfare of tens of thousands are in his hands; and if in these respects he acts worthily, if he gains the blessings of his people, he can afford to do without the home joys that are so much to lesser men. You are sure that he is not unhappy? If I did but know this, I would be content."

"I do not think he is unhappy," Wulf said confidently. "He has the applause and love of all men, and the knowledge that all his work is for the good of his country and his people. He may have regrets, but he has little time to spend upon them when he has in hand so vast a work, upon which night and day his every thought is directed."

"I suppose you wish to get back to-night, Wulf?"

"I should greatly prefer it," he said.

"And I would rather that you did not remain here. It may seem inhospitable, but I feel it would be better so. No one here knows who I am, and at first my servants were plied with questions whenever they went abroad; but the wonder has died away, and the villagers have come to believe that I am, as I gave out, the widow of a court official. Should it be known that a young thane stayed here the night, it would set them gossiping afresh. Stay and sup with me before you start."

"And am I to tell the king I have seen you?" he asked.

"What think you yourself, Wulf?"

"I am sure that he would be glad to know. I need not say where you are living. I will say that you have charged me to keep it secret, and he will forbear questioning me. But I am sure that it will give him deep pleasure to know that I have seen you, to learn how you look, how you are living, how you occupy yourself, and how you think of him. It cannot but be a trial to him to know nothing of one he so loves. More than once he has told me that he wondered whether you had entered a convent, whether you were in health, how you bore yourself, and other matters."

"Tell him then, Wulf. You can tell him that great as has been my grief over our separation, I can yet feel happy in my solitude in knowing how nobly he is doing his kingly work, and that I have never wavered in my assurance that I was right when I bade him go. Tell him that I have no thought of entering a cloister; that I have my old servants and my garden and needle-work; that I spend much of my time in ministering to my poorer neighbours, and that I am getting to be loved by them. Say that my health is good, and that I have every comfort I need save his presence. Tell him that if I fall ill, and the leeches say that I shall die, I shall send for him to see me once again, but that in such manner only will we meet in this life; and that it is my prayer that he will not seek to alter my resolution, for that the pain of parting again would be more than the joy of seeing him. He is another woman's now, and that by my act, therefore it would be a grievous sin for us, loving each other as we do, to meet again, unless he or I was on a death-bed."

The supper was served early, and when it was eaten Wulf's horse was brought round to the door.

"Am I to come again?" he asked.

She did not answer for a time. "Not unless I send for you, Wulf. Our meeting has given me much pleasure, and I shall be the happier for it, but for a time our talk of the past and present will unsettle me and stir up afresh regrets and longings. Therefore, it were best that you come not again until I send for you."

The darkness was just closing in when Wulf rode into Westminster.

"The king has twice asked for you, my lord," Osgod said, as he alighted. "The last time a quarter of an hour since."

Wulf at once went to the king's closet, where he was at work with two or three secretaries, to whom he was dictating.

"I want you, Wulf," the king said as he entered. "Where hast been?" Wulf glanced at the secretaries, and Harold bade them retire till he summoned them again. Wulf then related at length his interview with Edith. Harold listened in silence.

"I am right glad at your news," he said, when the latter had finished. "It is just what I thought she would do. Her words are lofty and wise; truly a king can little hope for happiness such as that which is in the reach of the humblest of his subjects. But we will talk of this again. For the present I must think of public business. News has been brought me by a sure hand from Denmark that the fleet of Norway has sailed. 'Tis said that Harold has called out a levy of half the fighting men of his kingdom, and that he has five hundred war-ships besides transports. His son, Magnus, has been left behind to rule Norway with the title of king. Harold intends to conquer England and reign here. I must lose no moment in sending the news to the northern earls. Doubtless it is on their coast he will first land. There is no one I would sooner trust than yourself, and you shall be my messenger.

"I have the letters already written to them, warning them that every man capable of bearing arms should be summoned to their standard, and every preparation made to repulse the foe. Of help at present I can give them none; my army is dispersed, my shores undefended, and at any moment William's fleet may appear off the coast. Let them meet the Norwegians, while I meet the Normans. It is for you to press upon them the counsels I give in my letters; and I would that you should remain with them, sending messages to me from time to time, giving me full tidings of what takes place at York and how they fare in their struggle with Harold of Norway, and, as I fear, with my brother Tostig. They met you at Northampton, and they know the confidence I place in you and the services you rendered in the Welsh campaign. However, although they may receive you well I fear that your counsel will go for nought. They are haughty and headstrong, and assuredly they will not be guided by one of my thanes. Do not, therefore, press the matter with them, or risk incurring their anger. I want you to stand well with them, for so only can you learn their views and keep me informed of what is doing. Being assured that you would undertake the duty I have highly commended you to them as my representative at York, and I doubt not that you will be well received. Brothers-in-law though they are I can count on but little aid from them in our struggle with the Normans, but there they will be fighting for their own earldoms and will do their best, though I fear the result, for they have been deaf to my entreaties to keep an army on foot, and the hurried levies of the North will scarce stand against the mighty army Harold Hardrada is bringing against them."

"I will start immediately, my lord."

"Here is a royal order upon all governors and thanes to give you changes of horses and to aid you in all ways. Take that giant of yours with you, he is a faithful fellow and is not wanting in sense; you will find him of great use there. You will, of course, accompany the earls to the field. Watch well how the levies fight, it is long since they have been called upon to meet a foe, and I would fain know how much they can be trusted on the day of battle. As your own horse has travelled to-day take two of my best, here is an order to the head of the stables to deliver them to you. Is there aught else that I can do for you?"

"Nothing, my lord. I understand your wishes, and will follow them as closely as I can."

"Do not expose yourself too much on the field of battle, Wulf. I cannot spare you, and therefore charge you not to be rash, and if matters go ill to provide for your safety as far as you may."

Wulf found Osgod awaiting him in the hall below.

"I thought you might require me, master, so I waited till you had seen the king."

"You did well, Osgod. I am starting on a journey to York and you are to accompany me. We ride armed, so get on your coat of mail and take your favourite axe, then carry this order to the stables and tell them to have the two horses ready at the gates in half an hour's time; then go to the kitchen and eat a hearty meal and put up some bread and cold meat in a wallet. We shall ride fast and with few stoppages, for I have the royal order for change of horses everywhere."

"That is good news, my lord. After dawdling away the last four months doing nothing I am glad to hear that there is a chance of striking a strong blow on someone, though who it is I know not."

"Now go, Osgod, I have also to change my clothes and drink a horn of ale and eat something, though I supped but three hours since. Put my gayest suit into the saddle-bag, for I may stay some time at York, and must make a fair show, going as I do as Harold's messenger."

The journey was accomplished at an extraordinary rate of speed, Harold's order procuring them a change of horses when ever they stopped; and they but once halted for a few hours' sleep. Wulf found that Edwin and Morcar were both at York, and alighted at the gate of their residence. Announcing himself as a messenger from the king, he was at once conducted into their presence.

"It is Wulf of Steyning, is it not?" Edwin said courteously. "The message must be urgent indeed since Harold has chosen you to carry it. When did you leave him?"

"I left Westminster at nine o'clock on the evening of Tuesday."

"And it is now but mid-day on Thursday," the earl said in a tone of astonishment. "You have ridden nigh two hundred miles in less than forty hours."

"The roads are good, my lord, and I had the king's order for changes of horses whenever needed. I slept six hours at Northampton, but have ridden without other stop save to take meals. I knew that the message I bore was of importance, as you will see by the king's letter."

Edwin opened the letter and laid it before Morcar, and the two read it together.

"This is serious news indeed," Edwin said when they had perused it. "So Harold of Norway is on his way hither with five hundred warships and half the males of Norway. Since the news has come from Denmark he must already have been nigh a fortnight at sea, and if he had sailed hitherwards we should have heard long ere this of his being within sight of our shores. As we have heard nought of him it may be that his object has been misreported, and that it is not against us that his fleet is bound."

"I fear that it can have no other destination," Wulf said; "though it may be that it has sailed first to Scotland to obtain assistance from Malcolm. There, too, he will find Tostig, whom the king fears is in alliance with him."

"Then assuredly it is against us that he comes," Morcar said, "and unless the winds shatter his fleet we shall hear of him before long. But he may land anywhere from the border of Scotland to the Humber, and it is useless our trying to hinder him along so great a line. He may delay his coming as William of Normandy has done, and our men, like those of Harold, will not remain under arms for months doing nothing. With so great an army he must move slowly and we shall have plenty of time to gather our forces to meet him. Harold urges us to call out the levies at once, but he does not know the Northumbrians as we do. They will fight, and stoutly, but they will scatter as soon as their term expires. It is but six weeks since we called them under arms to repulse Tostig, and unless they themselves see the danger presses they will not leave their homes again after so short an interval. I am glad to see by the king's letter that he has charged you to stay with us for a while. We shall be glad of your presence, both as the agent of our royal brother and as one who has already proved himself a valiant and skilful soldier."

Apartments were at once assigned to Wulf in the palace, and he was treated as an honoured guest. He had been furnished by the royal chamberlain with an ample sum of money, and every two or three days despatched messengers to London. He was greatly disturbed in mind, for the earls made no preparation whatever to meet the coming storm, but continued to hunt or to hawk, to give entertainments, and to pass their time as if the news of a mighty invasion had never reached them.

The first attempts he made to urge them to follow Harold's counsel were dismissed so curtly that he felt it useless to persevere.

A fortnight passed by, and then a messenger rode into York with the news that a vast fleet had entered the Tyne, and that the Norsemen were harrying and burning the country. Harold Hardrada had first sailed to the Isles of Shetland and Orkney, which, with the northern districts of the mainland, formed a powerful Scandinavian province. Paul and Erning, the two young earls of the state, and a large number of their subjects, joined the fleet, as did a Scotch contingent sent by Malcolm and commanded by Tostig, who also had with him the force he had brought from Flanders. Iceland, then a great Norwegian colony, sent ships and men, as did an Irish sovereign of Danish descent.

Roused to action at last the northern earls sent out summonses in all directions for the levies to assemble. The invaders were next heard of at Scarborough, which made a brave resistance, but the Norsemen took post on the steep hill overhanging the town, and gathering there a vast pile of wood set it on fire, and hurled blazing timbers down on the place. Many of the houses caught fire, and this spread rapidly. The inhabitants surrendered, but the greater portion was slaughtered and the town given up to plunder. Holderness, like Scarborough, bravely but unsuccessfully resisted the attack, and the great fleet sailing south entered the Humber. Hour by hour messengers rode into York bringing news of the progress of the invaders; hour by hour the Northumbrian levies poured into the capital.

Much as he had disapproved of their previous carelessness and delay, Wulf acknowledged that the two northern earls now bore themselves as men. They saw to the defences of the town, mustered all the inhabitants capable of bearing arms, arranged for the feeding and disposition of the levies, and did all that was possible at so short a notice to get them to take the field. But he saw, too, that this raw militia was but little calculated to stand before the assault of the Norsemen. There was no body of seasoned troops like the housecarls to serve as a nucleus, and to bear the chief brunt of the battle. All alike were raw, inexperienced, and badly armed, save for the axe, which was the favourite weapon of the English.

The great fleet made no stay but sailed up the Humber, packing closely in the river as it narrowed, till it seemed well-nigh covered from shore to shore with the crowded ships. It passed the little village of Selby, and cast anchor beside the left bank of the Ouse, near the village of Riccall, but nine miles' march from York. Olaf, the king's son, the two earls of Orkney, and the bishop of those islands remained on board to guard the ships, for the Northumbrian fleet, which was far too small to encounter so great an armament, had taken refuge up the Wharfe, and might descend and attack the Norse vessels were they left unguarded. The main body of the great army under the king and Tostig landed and prepared to march upon York. Sudden as the call had been there was no lack of spirit or patriotism in the English levies. Among their ranks were many priests and monks, who felt that it was their duty to aid in the defence of the land against the semi-heathen host that invaded it. The memory of the past invasion of the Norsemen, when the churches had been sacked and the priests slain on the altar, inspired them, and they and the monks responded as readily as did the laymen to the summons of the earls. These had not hesitated to consult Wulf as to the post where they had best station themselves to give battle, and the disposition of their forces. One who had distinguished himself under Duke William of Normandy, and under Harold in Wales, had, young though he was, more experience of war than any of the northern thanes, and as the representative of Harold all these were ready to listen with respect to his advice. He had already spent four or five days in surveying the ground in the direction from which the Norsemen were likely to advance, and had decided that a place known as Gate Fulford, two miles from the city, was best calculated for defence, it being situated on a narrow ridge, having the river and its swampy banks on one side, and a flat marshy country on the other. Thither the army of the earls marched to take up its position.

CHAPTER XIX. — STAMFORD BRIDGE.

Owing to the difficulty of getting the levies formed up and set in motion, the Norsemen had arrived on the ground and had taken up a defensive position before the English reached it. Had the force contained a strong body of housecarls, Wulf, who had talked the matter over with the earls, would have advised that they should fight on the defensive and allow the Norsemen to attack; but with freshly-raised troops, ready and eager for battle, but wanting the discipline that alone enables trained soldiers to endure patiently a long series of attacks, he thought that there was more chance of victory in attacking the enemy. Morcar commanded on the left, Edwin on the right. Wulf took up his position by the side of Morcar, and exchanged a few words with Osgod before advancing to the charge.

"This will be a right royal contest, master," the latter said as he fingered his heavy axe. "Never before have I seen a set battle like this."

"Do you keep close to me, Osgod."

"That I am sure to do, master," the latter broke in.

"Yes, I know that while we fight you will be by my side, but it may be that we shall have to fly. The Norsemen outnumber us greatly, and their king is a host in himself. This is a good position to defend, but a bad one to fly from. The king's last words were a charge to me not to throw away my life, and therefore while I shall fight as long as fighting can avail, I shall also do my best to save myself if we are defeated. As we came along I kept near to the edge of the swamp, and some hundred yards back I marked a spot where, as it seemed to me, there was a sort of path, worn either by broken men and outlaws, who may dwell somewhere in its recesses, or by men from a village beyond it. For this point, then, I shall make if we are defeated. It may be that it was not a path, but at least it offers a chance of escape. So when I give you the word, keep close to my side."

Osgod nodded. His confidence in Wulf was absolutely boundless, and though he revolted at the thought of retreat he knew well that so long as a chance of victory remained Wulf would not quit the field. When within two or three hundred yards of the enemy, Morcar advanced to the front of the line with his standard-bearer beside him.

"On men!" he shouted, and with a yell the English poured down to the attack The line of the Norsemen was on this side less strong than it was near the river where their king had posted himself, and the Norsemen gave way before the furious attack of the English. Morcar and many of his thanes fought in the front rank. Wulf was close beside him, and before their swords and the terrible axe of Osgod the invaders fell back foot by foot, and shouts of triumph rose from the English; but it was not for long. On the left Edwin could make no impression on the shield-wall of the enemy, and presently their king caused his horns to blow the signal for attack, and his line, hitherto immovable, flung itself on the English. The king, a head taller than any of his men, fought in their front rank, his terrible two-handed sword hewing down every man who opposed him. As the English gave way the assault became more and more impetuous, and in a few minutes the English broke and fled all along the line.

"All is lost, Osgod," Wulf said; as after fighting to the last he turned his back on the foe. The scene on the ridge was now terrible; the exulting Norsemen followed hard upon the flying English, uttering their shouts of victory and cutting down all they overtook. Hampered by the crowd in front of them great numbers of the English fell beneath the weapons of their pursuers, others turned to the right or left, and hundreds were smothered in the swamp by the river or in that on the other side. Once the flight began, Osgod placed himself in front of his master, his powerful figure and his weight enabling him to push his way through the crowd of fugitives. Wulf kept close behind him, and they followed the edge of the swamp until Wulf saw the faint indication of a path he had before noticed.

"Turn off here, Osgod; this is the place I spoke of. Let me go first, I am lightest."

The ground shook beneath their feet, the slime oozed up to their ankles, but, moderating their pace now, they sprang from tussock to tussock until two or three hundred yards from the edge of the swamp. Then they paused and looked round. The work of slaughter was still proceeding. Along the edge of the swamp numbers of English could be seen, some half immerged, some fast disappearing. In the din of the struggle none heard or heeded their cries, each man was occupied solely with the thought of flight or slaughter. Some half-dozen of the fugitives, seeing the two men were making their way across the swamp, had followed in their footsteps.

Slowly and cautiously Wulf moved forward again. Sometimes a treacherous tuft gave way and he slipped waist-deep into the mire, but Osgod was always close at hand, and his long arm enabled him to reach forward to his master from a firmer spot and to draw him from the bog. After an hour's painful work the ground began to be firmer, and before long they were safe in the forest beyond the swamp. Here for a while the party threw themselves down exhausted. After an hour's rest the others asked Wulf what they had best do.

"There is but one thing to be done," he replied; "make off to your homes. The remnant of the army will reach York, and the Norsemen will doubtless surround the city and lay siege to it. For the present our cause is lost, and there is nought for us to do but to try and save our lives, which have been spared well-nigh by a miracle."

Keeping south through the forest Wulf and his follower were several hours before they emerged from its shade. Another three miles' walking brought them to a village, where they learned they were six miles west of Selby. Here they obtained some food, and then bearing off so as to strike the south road arrived soon after nightfall at the house of the thane who had supplied them with their last change of horses on their way north. The news they brought excited the greatest consternation, but their host saw at once that the only hope now was that Harold might bring help, and at once placed the two horses which they had ridden to his house at their disposal. Wulf and Osgod mounted at once, and travelled southwards at a speed equal to that at which they had journeyed north.

When within a few miles of Peterborough they received news that seemed almost too good to be true. Harold at the head of a great army had already reached that town, and was pressing north at the top of his speed. From east and west he was being joined by the levies of the thanes. Riding forward to Peterborough they found the town crowded with troops, who, as they learned, were to march forward again in half an hour. Wulf at once made his way to the monastery, in which Harold was lodged.

"I need not ask your news, Wulf," Harold said, as, covered with dust and mire, and almost reeling with exhaustion, the young thane entered his private closet.

"The army of the northern earls has been well-nigh destroyed two miles from York. Whether the earls themselves escaped I know not, for I left the field while the slaughter was still going on. York will be at once besieged, and as most of its fighting men went out to the battle and a large proportion must have been slain, I fear that it can resist but a short time the attack of the Norsemen. It was good news indeed when I heard that you were advancing north."

"It is bad tidings that you bring, Wulf, but not unexpected. Directly I heard that the enemy's fleet were off our northern coast and were burning and pillaging unopposed, I speedily gathered what force I could in the South, and sending on messengers ahead to summon the levies of East Anglia to join me on the way, started north. Yesterday the news reached me that the great fleet of Norway had sailed up the Humber, and I saw that I should be too late to join Edwin and Morcar before they were forced to give battle before York. Now tell me of the fight, and how you managed to escape, for I see by your mail-coat and helmet, which are dinted and frayed and the steel rings shorn off in many places, that you were in the thick of it."

Wulf related the story of the battle, and the manner in which he had escaped.

"You did wisely, Wulf, to mark a way of retreat before the battle commenced. A good general should ever be prepared for defeat as well as for victory. So the levies fought well?"

"They did, my lord. They engaged the Norsemen gallantly and well—much better, indeed, than I had looked for them to do, and the day went favourably until the King of Norway with his picked men threw themselves upon them. Even after that they fought sturdily for a short time, and had there been but a body of housecarls to form a shield-wall, behind which they could have rallied, the day might still have been theirs. But you look ill, my lord."

"I was on a bed of sickness when the news came; but it was no time for lying abed. For the first two or three days' marches I was carried on a litter, but I am now well enough to sit my horse. It cost me a sore struggle to leave the South unguarded simply because my orders were not obeyed here in the North. But there was no help for it, and we have been marching well-nigh night and day in hopes that we might bring this matter to a close, and return south before the Norman fleet appears off the coast. We have already marched farther than would seem possible in the time, but the men are all in good heart and eager to meet the Norsemen, and I have addressed them and shown them the urgent necessity for speed. We shall set forward again in half an hour. They have had six hours for rest, so they can do another fifty miles before they halt again. You can tarry here for a day to rest yourself, and can then ride on and overtake us."

"I will go down and take a plunge in the river," Wulf said, "and shall be ready to mount again by the time that the rearguard is in motion. I could have kept on to London had it been needful, and shall be quite ready to proceed with the army."

They were within a day's march of York when the news came that the city had surrendered without waiting for an assault. The King of Norway had offered favourable terms; a local Gemot had been held, and it had been agreed to make peace with Harold of Norway, and not only to receive him as king but to join him in his warfare against the South. Hostages were given for their fidelity to their new lord, who in return gave hostages to York for the good conduct of his troops. It was the city only that had so treacherously behaved, and the surrender by no means included the whole province. It was arranged, however, by the earls, that hostages should be given for Northumbria at large, and they promised that a hundred and fifty of these should be handed over at Stamford Bridge, eight miles north-east of the city.

Here there was a palace of the old Northumbrian kings. The spot was favourable for the encampment of an army, for the country round was fertile and the bridge across the Derwent afforded facilities for the collection of provisions over a large area. The bridge was a wooden one, the country on either side of the river was flat, but considerably elevated above the stream, with a slope down to it on both sides of the bridge.

The news of the surrender of York made no change in Harold's plans. He had come to give battle to the Norsemen, whether he did so under the walls of the northern capital or elsewhere; accordingly he pressed rapidly forward.

In a few hours the army arrived in sight of York, which, had it resisted but a day longer, would have been saved the humiliation of the surrender and treaty. The invaders had all marched to Stamford Bridge, and the people opened its gates and received with rejoicing the king, whose authority they had the day before cast off. Beyond a short pause for food there was no delay. Harold's thoughts were on the South, and he grudged every hour that delayed his return to his post there. The men of the city and the survivors of the army defeated at Fulford joined the force, which kept on its way east to Stamford Bridge. The invaders, believing that Northumbria lay at their feet, and without a thought that Harold was advancing, were encamped in careless security on the low ground by the river. The greater portion of their host had crossed the bridge; their king, Tostig, and many of the great chiefs had taken up their abode in the royal palace at Aldby, and were preparing to return to York, where the king was to hold his court and formally to assume the government and to proclaim the laws for his new kingdom.

Already the cortege had set out, clad not in warlike armour but in court habiliments, when on the long road leading gently down to the river a cloud of dust and the sparkle of arms was seen. There was little room for doubt as to the nature of the arriving force. Northumbria could gather no array that would venture thus to approach the army that had but five days before crushed the levies of the North. It could only be Harold himself who, with the men of the South, had thus unexpectedly arrived. Tostig at once proposed a retreat to the ships at Riccall, so that the whole army might be gathered together, but Harold Hardrada strove to marshal his army for the battle, at the same time sending off mounted messengers to summons the party left at the ships. But while all was in confusion among the main body of the invaders on the eastern bank of the river, while men were buckling on their armour and gathering in their ranks, the cloud of war rolled rapidly down the descent, and with a mighty shout the English vanguard fell upon the Norsemen on the western bank.

Valiantly they fought, but there was no resisting the solid array of the English housecarls, or Thingmen as they were also called. Taken altogether unprepared, and for the most part without their defensive armour, the Norsemen could offer no successful resistance to the English host. Great numbers were killed; others were driven headlong across the bridge or were drowned in the stream, which is said to have been literally choked with dead. But for a time the advance of the English was stayed; for one Norseman, a man of great stature and prodigious strength, took post in the middle of the narrow bridge and barred the way to the English host. But one foe could attack him at a time, and so great was his strength and prowess that it is said forty Englishmen fell under the mighty blows of his two-handed sword, and at last he was only over-powered by one who made his way along beneath the timbers of the bridge and stabbed him with his spear from below.

His gallant stand, however, had sufficed to give his countrymen time to complete their preparations, and the shield-wall of the Norsemen stretched across the gentle ascent from the bridge. With his hands raised aloft, as a sign that his mission was a peaceful one, an English thane with twenty mounted horsemen rode across the bridge. He was met by the king, Tostig, and his chiefs. Raising his voice the thane addressed Tostig, "I bring to Tostig the greeting and message of his brother King Harold. Let him return to his allegiance and he shall again have the earldom of Northumberland; nay, he shall have a third of the kingdom to rule together with the king."

"What, then," Tostig asked, "shall be given to King Harold of Norway?"

"Seven feet of English ground!" the thane said sternly, "or more, perchance, seeing he is taller than other men."

"Return to King Harold of England," Tostig said, "and bid him make ready for the battle. Never shall men say in Norway that I brought their king hither to England and then went over to his foes."

Harold's ambassador returned with his men across the river with Tostig's message, and then in solid array the English Thingmen moved forward to the attack. Had the King of Norway advanced to the end of the bridge a battle would have been impossible, for the English could never have forced their way across. But the kings were equally anxious for a battle. Harold of Norway knew as well as the King of England that the host of Normandy was on the point of sailing, and it was as essential for him to crush the English army before the Normans landed as it was for Harold of England to dispose at once of the Norse invaders. There were three claimants for the English crown, and both kings felt the necessity of having their hands free to meet the Normans. Harold of Norway may well have believed that his host of tried warriors was capable of disposing of an army that, save for its small body of regular troops, was wholly unused to war; therefore, he held his array immovable while the English army crossed the bridge and formed up for battle.

Steadily and firmly the solid line of the housecarls moved up the ascent, and then as Harold's trumpet gave the signal of attack, flung themselves upon the shield-wall of the Norsemen. The conflict was a terrible one. The heavy two-handed axes of the English clashed against the long two-handed swords of the Norsemen. Against such terrible weapons wielded by such powerful arms, helmet and hauberk afforded but a poor defence. Casques and the heads beneath them were cleft like egg-shells under the terrible blows; but the gaps thus made in the ranks were at once filled from behind, and for hours the struggle continued with unabated vigour on both sides. Harold himself with a body of his thanes fought in the front line, his position marked to his followers by his standard kept flying close behind him. His great strength and height made him so formidable an assailant that his standard generally flew well in advance of his fighting line, while on the other side the still greater height and strength of the King of Norway rendered him equally conspicuous. At last the obstinate valour of the English housecarls prevailed over the resistance of the fierce Norsemen, and the invading host was driven backward step by step up the ascent until the level ground was reached.

Here the battle again raged as fiercely as ever. In vain did Harold of Norway, followed by his bravest warriors, hurl himself upon the ranks of the English, his terrible sword carrying death in its path. In vain did his followers again and again strive to take the offensive. The English line ever bore up against their attacks. The battle was still undecided when, as the sun was going down, an English arrow pierced the throat of the giant King of Norway. How Tostig, who had throughout the day fought by his side, fell, we know not, but he died, as did the Irish prince who had brought his followers to share in the plunder of England. There fell, too, most of the bravest warriors of Norway, the last of the sea-kings who had carried the banner, known as the land-waster, far and wide over Europe.

The slaughter was terrible, and at nightfall the Norsemen who survived broke and fled to the shelter of their ships. Never in the history of England was there a harder fought battle; never were English valour and endurance more splendidly shown. Terrible, too, had been the losses on their side. Many of the king's bravest thanes had fallen, and the ranks of the housecarls were fearfully thinned. Complete as had been the victory, absolute as had been the destruction of their foes, there was but little rejoicing in the English camp that night. So exhausted were the troops by their long march and the desperate struggle of the day that they threw themselves down to sleep on the ground they had won, thickly covered as it was with the bodies of friend and foe.

Wulf throughout the day had fought close to Harold. Osgod had kept close beside him, and had warded off many a sweeping blow and cut down many a pressing enemy. At the end of the day his left arm hung useless by his side, well-nigh cleft off by the blow of a Norseman's sword. Wulf himself had escaped without a scratch, thanks in a large measure to his follower's watchfulness. When the battle was over he was one of the few thanes who gathered round Harold. The latter felt no exultation at this victory. It had cost him the flower of his army and numbers of his most valued thanes. It had cost him, too, the life of a brother, to whom in spite of his faults he had been deeply attached. He knew that there was before him a struggle even more serious than that from which he had just emerged a victor, and there was no saying how that struggle might end.

"I thank God that you are spared to me, Wulf," he said as the young thane came up. "I marked you near me all through the battle, and none fought more bravely. It has been a terrible day, and our victory is dearly purchased indeed. I have sent a messenger to York, praying that every monk skilled in surgery will at once hasten hither, that all men and boys shall come and help to collect the wounded, and that such women as can aid will accompany them. I cannot ask the men who have marched well-nigh night and day since we left London, and borne the brunt of the day's battle, to do more. England has need of their strength. The messenger was to stop at Helmsley, and bid every soul left there to hurry to the field. It is but two miles away, and in half an hour they will be here. The first thing for them to do is to carry water to the wounded; there are no lack of vessels in the Norsemen's camp."

"I will go to the bridge, my lord, and take them in charge when they arrive, and set them at the work."

"You need rest as much as any, Wulf."

"I can rest to-morrow," Wulf said; "and at any rate could not sleep to-night, for I must see to Osgod, who will, I fear, lose an arm."

"I am sorry to hear it," Harold said, "for one could ill spare so brave a fellow. I saw the Norsemen going down under his axe, and assuredly no man did more than he to-day."

"I will tell him what you say, my lord; it will do him good. I left him sitting down on a bank bemoaning himself that he might not be cured in time to fight the Normans."

Harold shook his head. "I would give half my estates, Wulf, that he should be well enough to fight by your side in our first battle with the Normans. That would mean that they would not land before two months have passed, and by that time I would have all the force of England gathered to receive them. As you are willing that it should be so, I will leave you in charge of the camp to-night. It will be three hours before help can arrive from York. Till then there is nought to do but to carry water to the wounded. When they arrive the monks will dress the wounds, and the men and women carry such as can be moved down by the river, where they can be treated more easily than lying in the fields. Have a strict search made for the body of my brother, and place a guard over it. Sweyn is in charge of the Norse camp. There is great treasure there, which shall to-morrow be partly divided among the troops."

Wulf went at once down to the bridge, while Harold and his thanes lay down like the soldiers on the field of battle. In a short time men, women, and children came in from Helmsley. Having been told what they were required for, they had brought with them jugs and drinking cups, and also a supply of torches. The first search was made over the ground west of the river. Here few English had fallen, but the Norsemen lay thickly. Wulf ordered that water should be given to all, foe as well as friend. The number of living was small, for the heavy two handed axes had done their work thoroughly. When such as survived had been seen to, Wulf led the villagers over the bridge.

"Scatter right and left," he said, "and then move forward. You cannot go wrong." Having seen them all at work, he hurried away to the spot where he had left Osgod sitting. He had before leaving him staunched the flow of blood by winding a bow string round the arm above the wound and then twisting it tightly.

"How fares it with you, Osgod? Here is a ewer of water."

"That is good," Osgod said, after taking a mighty draught. "Truly I felt as if the moisture of my body had all dried up, and not only my mouth but my whole frame was parched."

"Why, Osgod," Wulf exclaimed, as he held the torch he carried close to him, "your arm has gone!"

"That is so, master, an arm after the bone has been cleft through is of no use to anyone, so I thought the sooner I got rid of it the better, and having my knife handy I just cut through the flesh that remained. That was the end of it. Would that we could get rid of all our evils as readily. To-morrow I will walk to York and get the wound seared."

"The king sent to York for aid directly the battle was over, and we shall have all the townsfolk here soon, among them monks and others skilled in the dressing of wounds. I told the king of your misfortune." And he then repeated what Harold had said.

"It does me good to hear that Harold is satisfied with me. I hope to strike many a good blow for him yet."

"How still it is here, Osgod! There is scarce a sound to be heard from all those lying round."

"There are but few with life in them, I reckon," Osgod said. "A Norse sword and an English axe let out the life quickly when they strike fair. This blow fell on my arm as my axe was raised to strike, and it were well it did so, or it would have taken me in the neck, and then neither monk nor leech could have brought me back to life. Had it been my right arm I would as lief have been killed at once, for what good is a man without his right arm?"

"You would have learned to use your left in time, Osgod. Now if you can walk, come down to the river, and I will see that you are among the first attended to."

"I will lie down here," Osgod said, "for in truth I feel as if I need sleep. For the last two days I have been scarce able to keep my eyes open, and now that I have had a drink I feel that a few hours' rest will do me more good than any monk."

Osgod's words came slowly and heavily, and as he ended he lay down on his back. Wulf saw that it was best that he should sleep, and so left him. In two hours a great number of lights were seen along the road, and soon a crowd of men and women from York appeared and scattered themselves over the battlefield, the monks pouring balm into wounds and bandaging them up, while the men and women carried the wounded, as fast as they were attended to, down to the river. The bodies of Tostig and of the King of Norway were both found, and a guard placed over them, and in the morning that of Tostig was carried to York for burial in the cathedral, while Harold Hardrada was buried where he fell.

Harold sent messengers to the Norsemen's fleet offering mercy to them if they would surrender, and their chiefs come to York and swear never again to raise their swords against England—an offer which was thankfully accepted, for the English fleet had entered the Humber, and their retreat was cut off.

The next day the Norse chiefs went to York and took the required oath, and were then escorted back to their ships. So terrible had been the slaughter, so complete the destruction of the invading army, that, even including the guard that remained at the fleet, twenty-four ships sufficed to carry away home the survivors of the mighty host. The task of burying the slain was too great to be undertaken, and for many years afterwards the field of battle was whitened with the bones of the invaders who had fallen there.

On the day after the battle Harold returned with his army to York. Here all who had fallen away from the cause of England were pardoned. Measures were taken for making the fighting strength of the North available for the general defence of the country. The wounded were cared for in the houses of the citizens, and for five days the troops rested after their prodigious exertions.

Early in the morning after the battle Osgod's wound had been seared with red-hot irons. He had borne the pain unflinchingly, saying that he had suffered as much from burns more than once while learning his trade as an armourer. Wulf was not present, as he had thrown himself down to sleep as soon as he had been relieved at daylight, but he saw him before he started with the king for York.

"Yes, it hurts a bit, master," Osgod replied in answer to his inquiries. "I could not expect otherwise. You will have to do without me for a few days. I have made friends with some peasants at Helmsley. I shall stay with them till the army marches south. If I were at York I should never keep quiet; and the monks tell me the quieter I am the sooner my wounds will heal. They are poor creatures, these monks; they wanted to make out that it might be two or three months before I was fit for service again. I told them it would be a shame to my manhood if in a fortnight I could not wield an axe again. It is not as if I had been brought up softly. I have burnt myself with hot irons many a time, and know that a few days suffices to heal a sore."

"It is not the sore, Osgod; it is the veins that might burst out bleeding again."

"That is what they said, master; but at present there is not much blood left in me, I think, and by the time it comes again my veins ought to have healed themselves. This plaguey bowstring hurts me well-nigh as much as the smart of the irons; but the monks say I must bear it for a couple of days, when they will put on some tight bandages in its place, but if I can bear the pain it were better that it should be kept there for a week or two."

Five days passed. The king laboured incessantly at making a settlement of the affairs of the North. The thanes came in from all Northumbria. They were full of thankfulness at the deliverance that had been wrought for them, and the victor of Stamford Bridge was far more to them than the King of England had ever been. All were received with kindness and courtesy, and Harold felt that at Stamford Bridge he had conquered not only the host of Norway but the Northern earldoms. On the evening of the fifth day after the battle they held a great banquet at York. The feasting was at its height when Harold was told that a messenger had arrived with urgent news, and the man was at once brought in. He had ridden in two days from the South, and brought the momentous news that on the third day after the victory of Stamford Bridge the Norman host had landed in Sussex.

CHAPTER XX. — THE LANDING OF THE FOE.

While Harold with his army had been anxiously and impatiently watching the sea on the southern coast of England, the mixed host of the Duke of Normandy had been no less anxiously awaiting a favourable breeze at the port where the whole of the expedition was gathered. William had, however, one great advantage. While Harold's army and navy were composed of levies, bound by feudal obligations to remain but a certain time under arms, and eager to return to their harvest operations, their wives and families, William's was made up to a great extent of seasoned troops and professional soldiers, gathered not only from his own dominions but from all parts of Europe.

These were far more amenable to orders than were the English militia. Tempted by the thought of the plunder of England, they had enlisted under the duke's banner for the expedition. They had no thought of returning home, and as long as they were well supplied with food, the delay in starting mattered comparatively little to them; and thus while at length the fleet and army of Harold scattered to their homes the Normans remained in their camp, ready to embark on board the ships as soon as a favourable wind blew. They were kept in good temper by receiving regular pay and provisions, and as all plundering was strictly forbidden the country people freely brought in supplies, and for a month the great army was fed without difficulty; but as the resources of the country became exhausted the duke grew more and more anxious to move to another port, and taking advantage of a change of wind to the west he embarked his army and sailed north along the coast of Normandy to the mouth of the Somme, and the troops disembarked and encamped round the town of St. Valery.

Here there was another long delay, and while Harold was marching north to meet the King of Norway the Normans were praying for a favourable wind at the holy shrine at the Abbey of St. Valery. Two days after the host of Harold Hardrada had been destroyed the wind suddenly shifted to the south. There had on the previous day been a great religious ceremony; the holy relics had been brought by the priests into the camp; the whole army had joined in a solemn service; precious gifts had been offered at the shrine, and as the change of wind was naturally ascribed to the influence of the saint, the army was filled with enthusiasm, and believed that heaven had declared in their favour.

From morning till night the scene of bustle and preparation went on, and when darkness fell the whole host had embarked. Every ship was ordered to bear a light, and a huge lantern was hoisted at the masthead of the Mora, the duke's own ship, and orders were issued that all vessels should follow the light. The Mora, however, was a quick sailer, and was not, like the other vessels, deeply laden down with horses and men. When daylight broke, therefore, she had so far outstripped the rest that no other sail was in sight, and she anchored until the fleet came up, when the voyage was continued, and at nine on the morning of Thursday the 28th of September the Normans landed on English soil, near the village of Pevensey.

The landing was unopposed; the housecarls were away north with their king, the levies were scattered to their homes. To the surprise of the Normans who landed in battle array no armed man was to be seen. Parties of mounted men at once examined the country for miles round, but without finding signs of the defending army they expected to meet. On the following morning a small force was left in the Roman fortifications near Pevensey to guard the ships, hauled up on the beach, from attack, and the duke with his army marched away along the Roman road to Hastings, where William established his headquarters and resolved to await the approach of the army of England. A wooden castle was raised on the height, and the country for miles round was harried by the Norman horse. Every house was given to the flames; men were slain, women and children taken as slaves, and the destruction was so complete that it seemed as if it had been done with the deliberate purpose of forcing Harold to come down and give battle.

No sooner did Harold hear the news that the Normans had landed and were harrying the land than he ordered the hall to be cleared and issued a summons for the assembly of a Gemot, and in an hour an assemblage of all the thanes gathered at York was held in the hall that had so shortly before been the scene of peaceful feasting. Harold proclaimed to them the news he had heard, and called upon them to arm and call together their levies for the defence of England. An enthusiastic reply was given. As the men of the South had crushed the invaders of the North, so would the men of the North assist to repel the invasion of the South. Morcar and Edwin promised solemnly to lead the forces of Northumbria and Mercia to London without a day's delay, and though Harold trusted his brothers-in-law but little, he hoped they would have to yield to the patriotic spirit of the thanes and to play their part as Englishmen.

An hour later messengers started on horseback for the South, bidding all men to assemble at London to fight for home and freedom against the foreign invader, and orders were issued that the troops who had fought at Stamford Bridge should march at daybreak. As soon as the council was over Wulf mounted his horse and rode at full speed to Helmsley. He had each day ridden over to see Osgod, who in his anxiety for a rapid cure was proving himself a most amenable patient, and was strictly carrying out the prescriptions of the monk who had taken charge of him and of other wounded who were lying in the village. He was asleep on a rough pallet when Wulf entered.

"A pest upon the Norman!" he exclaimed angrily when he heard Wulf's news. "He might have given me a week longer at any rate. I am feeling mightily better already, for to-day the monk has bandaged my arm, and that so tight as almost to numb it. But that I care little for, as he has now taken off that bow-string which was cutting its way into the flesh. He told me that everything depended upon my keeping absolutely quiet for another week, for the slightest exertion might make the wound break out afresh, and that if it burst there would be but a poor chance for me. Well, I must travel in a waggon instead of on horseback."

"You will do nothing of the sort, Osgod; I absolutely forbid it. It would be an act of sheer madness. Besides, you would be useless at present even if you went south, while if you rest here for three or four weeks you may be able to take part in some of the battles; and, moreover, it may be weeks before Harold moves against the Normans. At any rate, it is out of the question that you should move at present. I am not going to have you risk your life by such folly."

Osgod was silent for a minute or two and then said, "Well, master, I must obey your orders, but never before did I feel it so hard a thing to do."

"It is for your own good and mine, Osgod. I am not going to lose so faithful a follower, and would rather do without you for two months than for all my life. But now I must be going, for I shall ride on ahead so as to go down to Steyning and fetch our men. I was before sorry that, owing to my being here, they did not come down with the king; now I am glad, for I might have lost half of them, while as it is I shall have a hundred men as good as his own to help to fill up the ranks of Harold's housecarls, besides the general levy of my tenants."

On his march south Harold was joined by large numbers of men. The news of the destruction of the army of Harold Hardrada had excited the greatest enthusiasm, and the thanes presented themselves as a rule with more than the number of men they were bound to furnish. Wulf rode on fast to London. As soon as he arrived there he went to the armourer's shop. Ulred paused at his work as he entered. "Welcome back, my lord Wulf!" he said. "So you have come safe through the two great battles in the North. Has Osgod fared equally well, I see that you have come without him?"

"Not equally well, Ulred. He fought with me at Fulford and received no serious hurt, but at Stamford Bridge he was wounded so sorely that for a time we thought it would go hard with him; but he has rallied and is doing well, and save that he will come home without his left arm, he will, I trust, soon be recovered. No man fought more stoutly than he did at Stamford Bridge, and the king himself noticed his valour. Although his wound was but five days' old when we started, he would have come south at once if I would have suffered him, though he must assuredly have been carried the whole way in a litter. It troubled him greatly to hear that we should be face to face with the Normans, and he not there to strike a blow for England."

"I am glad to hear that the boy lives," the armourer said; "for indeed when I saw you alone my first thoughts were that he had fought his last battle. We have terrible news from the South. The

Normans are plundering and slaying from Beachy Head well-nigh to Dover, and the people are flying before them in crowds. However, matters will be changed as soon as the king returns to town. London will send her militia in full strength, and we hear that the thanes of the West are hurrying hither. 'Tis a pity indeed that Harold was drawn off north, for had he been here the Normans would have had to fight their best before they established themselves on our shores."

"They could have landed in any case, Ulred. It was not the King of Norway and Tostig, but the impatience of our sailors and troops, that left our shores unguarded. Harold tried his best to keep them together, but in vain. However, they rallied quickly when they heard of the landing in the North, and are coming in freely now."

"Will the troops of Northumbria be here?"

"I doubt it greatly, Ulred. They are not true men, Edwin and Morcar; they surrendered York before an arrow was shot against its walls, and received Harold Hardrada as their king. They would be equally willing to acknowledge William of Normandy so that they might but preserve their earldoms under him. They have promised to send their whole forces forward without delay, but I have no belief that they will be here. I am going to Steyning as soon as I have eaten a meal and rested for a few hours. I shall miss Osgod sorely. I trust that it will not be long before I have him by my side."

"When will the army be back here, master?"

"In three days at most, I imagine. There will be but short stay here before Harold marches south to meet the Normans. The news of the wanton destruction they are making has roused him to fury, and he will assuredly lose no time, even though he have but half the force of England behind him."

"It is as well to have something to fall back on," the armourer said. "It is not by one battle that England is to be conquered, and even if we lose the first we may gain the second. We can stand the loss better than the Normans, for doubtless William has brought all his strength with him, and if beaten must make his way back to his ships, while Harold would in a short time find himself at the head of a larger army than that with which he may first meet them. Was the slaughter as great as they say at Stamford Bridge?"

"It was terrible, Ulred; and though the Norsemen suffered vastly more than we did, the ranks of the housecarls, on whom the brunt of the fighting fell, have been sorely thinned. We shall feel their loss when we meet the Normans. Against their heavily-armed troops and their squadrons of knights and horsemen one of the Thingmen was worth three untried peasants. Had we but half the number of our foe, and that half all housecarls, I should not for a moment doubt the issue."

"London will put a strong body in the field, and though we have not the training of the Thingmen you may trust us to fight sternly, Master Wulf; and if we are beaten I will warrant that there will not be many of us to bring the tidings back."

"Of that I am sure, Ulred. The citizens have more to lose and better know what they are fighting for than the country levies, and as you say, I am sure they will do their part stoutly. Well, I must stay here no longer. I shall sleep for two or three hours, and then take a fresh horse from the king's stable and to-morrow shall be at Steyning. By nightfall I shall be on my way back with every man on the estate, a hundred and fifty besides the housecarls, and two days' march will bring us here again. Ulf is well, I hope? I do not see him."

"He has but carried home some arms I have been mending. We are working night and day; since the news that the Normans had landed came, there has been no thought of bed among the armourers and smiths of Westminster and London. Each man works until he can work no longer, then throws himself down for two or three hours' sleep, and then wakes up to work again; and so it will be till the army has moved south with most of us in its ranks."

Wulf reached Steyning soon after daybreak, and as soon as the news that he had arrived went round, the tenants flocked in. His coming had been anxiously expected, for the alarm caused by the incursions all over the country by the Norman horse was intense; and although, so far, none had come west of Beachy Head, there was a general feeling that at any moment they might make their appearance. The news, therefore, that Harold was marching south with his army, and that all were to share in a pitched battle with the invader instead of being slaughtered on their hearthstones, caused a deep feeling of satisfaction. Wulf gave orders that every man should assemble in fighting array at noon, and that if, later on, news came that the enemy were approaching, the houses were to be deserted, the stacks fired, and, driving the cattle before them, the women and children should cross the hills and take shelter in the great forest beyond. A few of the older men who were unfit to take part in a long day's fighting were to aid the women in their work.

The arms of all the men were carefully inspected, and the weapons remaining in the armoury served out to those worst provided. At one o'clock the force marched off, Wulf riding at the head of the hundred housecarls, while the tenants, a hundred and fifty strong, followed in good order. Each man carried six days' provisions. They camped that night in a forest twenty miles from Steyning, marched thirty miles the next day, and early the following morning joined the great array that was gathering on the hills south of London. To his great pleasure Wulf found that Beorn had arrived the day before with his levy. They had not met since they had returned from the North with Harold.

"So you have been up there again, Wulf, and fought at Fulford and Stamford Bridge. It was very unlucky I was not in London when the army marched north; but I received no summons, and heard nothing of it until the king was well on his march. None of the thanes along the south coast were summoned."

"So I heard, Beorn. I fancy the king thought that in case of a landing by the Normans the men near the coast would all be wanted to help take the women and cattle to places of security."

"No doubt that was the reason," Beorn said. "At any rate, I am sorry I missed the fight at Stamford Bridge. The other seems to have been a bad affair."

"Very bad; we suffered terribly. So much so, indeed, that the earls will have a good excuse for not getting their levies together in time for the battle with the Normans."

"They are false loons," Beorn said; "and brothers-in-law as they are of his, it would have been well had the king after Stamford Bridge had their heads smitten off for their traitorous surrender to the Norsemen."

"I have no doubt they will hold aloof now, Beorn, until they see how matters go in the South, and if we are worsted they will hasten to make their peace with William, and to swear to be his liegemen, just as they swore to be liegemen to Harold Hardrada. But they will find out their mistake in the end. William has promised to divide England among his needy adventurers if he wins, and Edwin and Morcar will very speedily find that they will not, in that case, be allowed to keep half the country as their share."

It was a great host that was gathered ready for the march south. Gurth had brought down the fighting men of East Anglia; the thanes of the West were there with their tenants; the Bishop of Winchester, Harold's uncle, not only brought the tenants of the church lands, but he himself with twelve of his monks had put on armour under their monkish robes. The Abbot of Peterborough headed a contingent from the Fen Country; the men of London under the sheriff of the Mid Saxons were there, and prepared to die in defence of the royal standard, which it was the special privilege of London to guard. In the Abbey of Westminster, where Harold had received his crown, and in every church of London, mass was celebrated day and night, and was attended by crowds of troops and citizens.

Harold himself snatched a day from the cares of preparation to visit Waltham, the abbey that he had founded, and in which he had taken so lively an interest, and there earnestly prayed for victory, with the vow that did he conquer in the strife he would regard himself as God's ransomed servant, and would throughout his life specially devote himself to His service. A day or two after Wulf's arrival in London a messenger came from William of Normandy calling upon Harold to come down from his throne, and to become, as he had sworn to be, the duke's man. Harold in reply sent back a full answer to William's claims. He admitted that Edward had promised the crown to William, but he said that according to the law of England a man might at any time revoke his will, and this Edward had done, and had named him as his successor. As to the oath he himself had sworn, he maintained that it was an extorted oath, and therefore of no binding force. Finally, he offered rich gifts to William if he would depart quietly, but added that if he was bent on war he would meet him in battle on the coming Saturday.

It is probable that William's insolent message was meant to have the effect of inducing Harold to march against him. The Norman position was a very strong one, and had been carefully fortified, and he hoped that Harold would attempt to storm it. Gurth urged his brother to remain in London, while he himself went with the army to battle. A large number of the levies had as yet not come in, and with these, should the first battle be unsuccessful, another army could be gathered to continue the struggle. Moreover, whether the oath Harold had sworn was binding or not, he had sworn, and it were better that another who was perfectly free in his conscience should lead the English to battle.

Then, too, Gurth urged, if he himself was slain, it would matter comparatively little, while Harold's death would jeopardize the whole kingdom. He prayed him therefore to stay in London, and to gather another and greater force, and to lay waste the whole land between London and the coast, so that the Normans, whether successful or not in their first battle, would be starved into a departure from the land. The counsel of Gurth was approved of by the thanes, but Harold rejected it. He declared that he would never let his brothers and friends go forth to danger on his behalf while he himself drew back from facing it, neither could he bring himself to harm the lands or the goods of any Englishman.

For six days Harold remained in London waiting, but in vain, for the forces from the North to join him, and on the Thursday morning set out with his army in order to meet the invaders on the day he had named. Accounts differ very widely as to the strength of that army. Norman writers, in order to glorify their own victory, speak of it as one of prodigious numbers. English writers, on the other hand, endeavour to explain the defeat by minimizing the number of those who followed Harold's standard. Doubtless the English king, knowing the proved valour of his housecarls, and fresh from the crushing defeat inflicted on the Norsemen, considered the numbers to be sufficient. His military genius was unquestionable, and next only to William the Norman he was regarded as the greatest general in Europe. As there was no occasion for haste so long as the Normans remained at Hastings he would not have moved forward with a force he deemed insufficient, when he knew that in another week its numbers would have been doubled.

On the day that the king made his last visit to Waltham, Wulf rode over to Croydon in compliance with an entreaty he received from Edith.

"When does the army march?" she asked anxiously as she entered.

"The day after to-morrow, lady."

"And my lord goes with it?"

"He does. I myself think that Gurth's counsel was good, and that it were best for England that he remained at Westminster; and yet I can understand well that he himself would feel it a shame did he remain behind."

"I feel sore misgivings," Edith said, bursting into tears. "When he marched north against the King of Norway and Tostig I felt no doubt he would return victorious; but night after night I have had evil dreams, and though I pray continually my spirit has no relief. I have never feared for him before. I have always felt sure that whoever died Harold would be spared for the sake of England, but I have no such feeling now. It seems to me that I sacrificed him and myself in vain when I bade him leave me and marry the sister of the Northern earls. No good has come of it. They are behaving now as traitors, and he has lost his life's happiness. And yet I did it for the best."

"It was a noble sacrifice, lady, and come what may you have no cause to regret it."

"The queen is not with him," Edith said bitterly.

"No, she is at Oxford. You must not think, lady, that the king has been unhappy since he came to the throne. He has been so incessantly occupied with work that he has had no time for domestic happiness, even if it had been within his reach. His thoughts are ever on England, and he has no thought of self. Labouring ever for the good of his subjects, he has his happiness alike in their love, and in the knowledge that he is doing all that man can for their welfare. If he dies, he will die the death not only of a soldier but of the noblest king that ever sat on the English throne, and at all times he will be enshrined in the hearts of the English people, whether Normans or Englishmen reign over the land."

"That is true, and I must take comfort from it, Wulf; but it was not for this that I sent for you, but to ask you where the battle is likely to be fought."

"Near Hastings, assuredly," Wulf replied.

"I shall travel south to-morrow. I have had a message from the king praying me to see him, but that would be too much for me. He is another woman's husband and I dare not meet him, it were sin for me to do so; but I would fain be nearer to the scene of battle, so that in a few hours I might journey there, in order that, if my lord dies, I might see him once again. I know the superior of a convent at Lewes, and there I will betake myself. Thence, as I believe, it is some sixteen miles to Hastings, and so far as I have heard the Norman plunderers have not gone so far west. Should aught happen to him, will you send a speedy messenger to me?"

"Should I live through the fight I will do so, lady, but even should I not return the news will travel swiftly; but God forfend that so great a loss should fall upon England."

"Amen," Edith murmured, "and yet I fear. Thanks, Wulf, for coming, perchance we may not meet again. I am thinking of entering a convent, probably that at Lewes. The struggle and pain here is wellnigh too great for me, but in the walls of a cloister I may find peace. If my fears are fulfilled I shall assuredly do this, and when I return to the convent I shall leave it no more. My life is over. I have a happy past to look back upon, in that am blest, and shall be happier than those who have no such consolation. Moreover, I can still be proud of Harold, and may love him as I might love the memory of a husband who is lost. God bless you, Wulf, and protect you through the coming battle!"

Wulf rode sadly back to the camp. Although he had denied it to Edith, he could not but admit to himself that the sacrifice that she and Harold had made had, so far, been unavailing. It had failed to draw the Northern earls closer to the king. The marriage had been productive of no happiness to Harold, and the only reward he had gained had been in the sympathy of the people, who knew well enough that he had sacrificed his love for the good of his country.

The army marched rapidly. Beorn and Wulf rode together, and talked over the chances of the coming battle.

"I cannot blame Harold for not remaining behind," Wulf said, "though it were certainly more politic for him to have stayed in London. As he could not do so, I think it would have been well had he bidden Gurth remain behind to gather another army with which to meet the Normans should we be defeated; or if he could not spare Gurth he might have left Leofric behind. It is assuredly a mistake for the three brothers all to come, for should all fall England would no longer have a head."

"Surely no such misfortune as that will befall us, Wulf."

"I know not. They will fight side by side, and should one fall all may perish together. One at least ought to remain behind. It matters not how many of us are killed, so that one of Godwin's sons is left to rally the kingdom. You may be sure that if we are conquered the victors will be in but poor condition to meet another foe; but if there is no one to gather an army and unite all England against the Normans they will eat us up piecemeal."

"We must not think of so terrible a thing, Wulf. It is not like you to look at the dark side. Why, when we were in Wales, and in as bad a plight as could well be, you always made light of danger, and managed affairs as if we were certain to succeed. Why should we be defeated? Why should the king be killed? He went through the terrible fight at Stamford Bridge without a scratch. We have seen the Normans at work, and know that they are not such terrible fellows; and as for their duke, I would assuredly rather meet him in battle, doughty as he may be, than have faced Harold Hardrada with his two-handed sword."

"I have every hope of winning the day, Beorn, but still I do regret much that Gurth and Leofric are both here. Do you remember that in Wales we agreed that it was always well to have a way of retreat in case of defeat? Well, I feel that defeat this time will mean not only the defeat of an army but the ruin of England."

On Friday afternoon the army reached rising ground near the village of Senlac, which Harold had beforehand fixed upon as the place where he would give battle to the invaders. Kent and Sussex he knew well. They had been the home of his family, and he owned vast estates there. Doubtless in the long weeks of waiting for the coming of the Norman fleet he had fixed upon this spot as one well suited for a battle. It was necessary that the English should fight on the defensive. The Normans were strong in cavalry, while the English were unaccustomed to fight on horseback, and would have been at a grievous disadvantage had they attacked the enemy.

The hill offered many advantages to a force standing on the defensive. The great eastern road passed close to its foot, and its possession barred the passage of the invaders in that direction. The ground between it and the sea was marshy and broken, and its occupation by an English force left the Normans no choice but to come out and attack them.

The sides were steep and the ground rose rapidly in the rear, so that the Norman cavalry could not attack from behind. It was, indeed, a sort of peninsula running southward from the main range of hills.

The moment the troops reached the ground the royal standard was planted, and the men set to work to fell trees and to form a triple palisade along the accessible sides of the hills. The force at Harold's command must have been far nearer to the estimate given of its strength by the English chroniclers than by the Normans, for the space occupied was insufficient for the standing room of such an army as that enumerated by the latter writers.

Harold relied almost entirely upon the housecarls. The levies might be brave, but they were undisciplined, and might easily be thrown into disorder; they would, too, be impatient under the trial of a long day's battle. It is even said that he sent away some of the ill-armed levies, who came flocking in from the country round, eager to revenge the injuries received at the hands of the Normans. It was upon the shield-wall, the favourite formation of the English, that he relied to win the battle. It was their national mode of fighting. It was that in which Alfred had led the Saxons to victory over the Danes. It was that in which they clashed against the shield-wall of Norway and shattered it, and he might well hope that the barons of Normandy and the adventurers from all parts of Europe who fought under William's banner might well try in vain to break it.

In the evening a messenger arrived from William, again bidding Harold resign the kingdom or meet the duke in single combat, the crown of England to be the prize of the victor. Harold refused the challenge. He had proved his personal courage too often for it to be supposed that he declined from any feeling of cowardice, but he knew well that the issue could not be thus decided. Were he to fall, the people would still refuse to accept William as their king; were William to fall, the host that had gathered for the plunder of England would still give battle. Nothing was therefore to be gained by the proposed combat.

CHAPTER XXI. — HASTINGS.

The fiction of the Norman historians, that while the Normans passed the night preceding the battle in prayer, the English spent it in feasting, is even more palpably absurd than the many other falsehoods invented for the purpose of damaging the character of Harold. The English army had marched nearly seventy miles in the course of two days, and had in addition laboured incessantly for many hours in erecting the palisades and in digging ditches. We may be sure that after two such days the great mass of the army lay down dog-tired directly their work was done, and slept till morning. Harold and his thanes had shared in their labours, and knowing the terrible work that awaited them in the morning, would most surely be disposed to get as long a sleep as possible to prepare for it.

But what is most opposed to the Norman story is the fact that Harold was a sincerely and deeply religious man, far more so than his rival. The life of the one man was in accordance with his professions — he was gentle and merciful, ever ready to forgive his enemies, averse to bloodshed, and so true a friend of the church that the whole of the prelates and clergy set the interdict of the pope at naught for his sake. The only exception in his clemency to the conquered was in the case of the Welsh, and in this instance the stern measures he adopted were in the end the most merciful. No oaths could bind these marauders, and the stern punishment he inflicted was the means of procuring for the West of England a respite from their incursions that lasted for three generations.

William of Normandy, on the contrary, was absolutely merciless in warfare. He was not cruel for the sake of cruelty, but where he deemed that the policy demanded it, he was ruthless, and spared neither age nor sex. He was lavish to the church, but it was rather because he needed and obtained its aid than from any feeling of real piety.

In point of ability, both civil and military, the Duke of Normandy and Harold of England were perhaps about equal; in point of nobility of character there was no comparison between them. We may be sure that the night before the battle Harold prayed as earnestly as he had prayed at Waltham for the aid of Heaven.

Wulf and Beorn lay down among the thanes, after Harold, sitting with them round a fire, had explained his plans for the battle. So calmly and confidently did he speak, and so strong was their position, that even those who had, like Wulf, doubted the wisdom of an advance until the whole force of England had assembled, now felt something like an assurance of victory, and all lay down to sleep with the belief that the victory at Stamford Bridge would be repeated.

On waking, Wulf visited his men. They were already astir, and he was astounded at seeing among them the towering figure of Osgod.

"Why, what means this, Osgod?" he exclaimed. "Did I not order you to rest quietly at York?"

"That did you, my lord," Osgod said, "and no man obeys your orders more readily than I, and anything that you bid me do I am willing to do if possible; but in this it was not possible, for I could not remain at York, either in rest or quiet. I should have had fever in my blood, and would by this time have been lying as deep in the earth as Harold of Norway himself. Therefore, in order to get the rest and quiet you had ordered, it was necessary for me to come south. As you had left me well supplied with money, I was able to do so in comfort, and though I could well enough walk I have had myself carried in a litter by easy stages. I reached London on Wednesday night, having been a fortnight on the way, and I arrived here an hour since. Each day I walked a little, so as to keep my health and exercise my limbs, and so well have I succeeded that my wound has well-nigh healed; and although I doubt whether I shall be able to use a heavy axe, I trust I shall be able to strike hard enough with the right hand to split a few Norman helms."

"But the exertion may set your wounds bleeding afresh, Osgod," Wulf said, unable to repress a smile at Osgod's argument.

"Methinks there is no fear of that. The most nights I have slept at monasteries, and have inquired from the monks, whom I told that I must needs stand by your side to-day, whether I should be fit. They said at first that there would be some risk in the matter, but that if I continued to take rest and quiet as I was doing, and the wound continued to heal favourably, it was possible, if I abstained from actual fighting, I might do so; but of late they have spoken more confidently. I told the monk who seared my arm to do it heartily, for a little pain more or less was of small account, so that he made a good job of it. And so, what with the rest and quiet and my mind being at ease, it went on so well that a monk who examined it at Westminster on Wednesday evening told me that save for the healing of the skin the wound was pretty nigh cured, and that he thought there was no chance whatever of its breaking out afresh. He bandaged it tightly to prevent any rush of blood into the veins, and though when I drove an axe just now into that stump yonder, I felt that I had not got back my strength fully, I expect when I warm to the work I shall strike as strongly as most."

"Well, at any rate you must take care of yourself, Osgod. You can aid me in keeping our men steady, but I charge you not to fight yourself unless you see the line waver. Then you can, of course, throw yourself into the fray."

"I will keep myself back for that, master; but I am sure we shall all have to do our best before sunset, and as all will be risking their lives there is no reason why I should not do so as well as the rest."

The troops made a hearty breakfast from the food they carried, and quenched their thirst at the little stream that ran down by the side of the slope, then they were told off to the ground they were to occupy.

At nine in the morning the vanguard of the Norman army appeared over the brow of a rise, and the English at once took up their positions. In the centre were the housecarls of the royal house and those of the thanes, together with the men of Kent, whose right it was ever to be in the front of a battle, and the London citizens under their sheriff. All these were armed and attired like the housecarls. In the centre of this array flew the royal standard, and around it were the three royal brothers, Aelfwig their uncle, with his monk's cowl over his helmet, and their nephew, Hakon, the son of Sweyn. The housecarls were in a triple line. To the left and right of them were the levies, as brave as their more heavily armed comrades, but altogether without discipline, and armed in the most primitive manner. A few only carried swords or axes, the majority had spears or javelins. Many had only forks or sharp stakes, while some carried stone hammers and axes, such as were used by their primitive ancestors.

As the Norman army wound down from the opposite hill and formed up in the order of battle, Harold rode along in front of his line exhorting all to stand firm.

"They were there," he said, "to defend their country, and to defend their country they had but to hold the hill. Were they steadfast and firm they could assuredly resist the attack of this host who came to capture and plunder England."

The order in which the Normans prepared for battle was similar to that of the English. Both commanders had been well informed by spies of the strength and position of their opponents, and the duke placed his tried Norman troops in the centre to match themselves against the English housecarls. His Breton contingent was on his left, while on the right were the French, the Flemings, and the other foreign adventurers who had come to fight under his banner. In the front line were the archers and slingers, who were to open the battle and shake the line of the defenders. Behind these came the infantry, who were to hew down the palisades and clear a way for the cavalry charge full into the centre of the English host.

A Norman trumpet gave the signal for the commencement of the battle, and the archers along the whole line poured a storm of arrows into the English. It was unanswered, for there were few bowmen among the defenders of the hill, and the distance was too great for the javelin-men to hurl their missiles. After the archers had shot several volleys of arrows they fell back, and the infantry advanced against the hill; but before they did so Taillifer, a Norman minstrel, dashed forward on horseback, and spurring up the ascent, tossing his sword in the air and catching it as it fell, rode up to the English line. One man he pierced with a lance, another he cut down with his sword, and then fell dead under the blow of a heavy axe. This mad exploit had scarce terminated when the Norman infantry advanced up the hill. They were greeted with a shower of stones and javelins, which slew many, but with unbroken front they pressed upwards until they reached the palisade. Here a desperate struggle began. The Norman sword and spear were met by the axes of the housecarls, and the clubs, spears, and forks of the levies. In vain Norman, Breton, Frenchmen, and Fleming strove to break the English line. The high position of the defenders gave them a great advantage over their assailants, among whose crowded ranks the javelin-men did great execution, while the Normans could receive little aid from their archers. Both sides fought with obstinate valour. The Norman battle-cry was "God help us!" the English "God Almighty and the Holy Cross!" The latter invocation being to the relic at Waltham, which was the king's special object of devotion.

With jeering cries too they greeted the efforts of their assailants to cross the palisade and break their line. At last the Norman infantry fell back broken and baffled, having suffered terrible loss, and now the knights and horsemen, who formed the backbone of William's army, rode up the hill. The duke himself, as well as his brother Odo, Bishop of Bayeau, who fought beside him, had laid aside their Norman swords, and were armed with heavy maces, weapons as formidable as the English axe. But the valour of the horsemen, the strength of their armour, the length of their lances, and the weight of their horses, availed no more against the shield-wall of the housecarls than the infantry had done. The superior height and strength of the English, and the sweep of their terrible battle-axes, counterbalanced the advantage the horses afforded to the Normans, and the hitherto irresistible chivalry of Normandy and France were, for the first time, dashed backwards by trained infantry.

In front of the English line the ground was thickly covered with fallen men and horses. There were but few wounded among them, for where the English axe fell, whether on horse or rider, it did its work thoroughly. But the English, too, had suffered. The action of swinging the axe with both arms above the head left the neck and upper part of the body exposed, and many had fallen pierced through and through by the Norman spears. A great shout of triumph rose from the English line as the Norman horsemen, unable to do more, fell sullenly back down the hill. As in the centre the king with his thanes and housecarls had repelled the attack of the Normans, so on the flanks the English levies had held their ground against the Bretons and French; but, carried away by their exultation, the levies on the right, forgetful of Harold's express orders that no man was to stir from his place until he himself gave the signal for pursuit, broke their line, and rushing down the hill fell on the retreating Bretons.

Unable to withstand the onslaught, and already disheartened by their failure, the Bretons fled in wild alarm, and rushing towards the centre for protection threw the Normans also into confusion. The panic spread rapidly, the host wavered, and had already begun to fly, when William, throwing off his helmet, rode among them, and exhorting some and striking others with a lance he had caught up, at last restored order, and the Breton infantry rallied and fell upon their pursuers, killing many and driving the rest back up the hill.

Again the Norman infantry and cavalry together advanced up the hill, and the terrible struggle recommenced. William and his brother the bishop performed prodigies of valour, but not less valiantly fought Harold of England and his brothers. The palisade was by this time destroyed in many places, and desperate hand-to-hand contests now took place. Cutting his way through meaner foes the duke strove to reach the royal standard and encounter Harold himself. He was nearing his goal, when Gurth sprang forward, eager above all things to protect Harold from harm. He hurled a javelin at William, but the dart struck the Norman's horse only, and it fell beneath him. William leapt to his feet, and springing upon Gurth smote with his heavy mace full on his helmet, and the noble Earl of East Anglia fell dead at his feet. Almost at the same moment his brother Leofwin, fighting sword in hand, was slain. But the fall of the two royal brothers in no way changed the fate of the battle. The men of Kent and Essex, furious at the fall of their beloved earls, fought even more fiercely than before to avenge their deaths.

William had remounted, but his second horse was also slain. Eustace of Boulogne offered him his horse, and himself mounting that of one of his followers they fell together upon the English line, but all the valour of the duke and his chivalry failed to break it. On the French left the Bretons had, indeed, succeeded in completely destroying the palisade, but the levies stood firm, and no impression was made upon their solid line. The attack had failed, and even William saw that it was hopeless any more to hurl his troops against the shield-wall, but the manner in which the English irregulars had been induced to break their array led him to try by a feigned retreat to induce them to repeat their error. While the fight yet raged around him he sent orders to the Bretons to turn and flee, and then if the defenders pursued them to turn upon them while he ordered a portion of his Norman force to make straight for the gap as soon as the English left their posts.

The stratagem was successful. Again with exulting shouts the levies poured out in pursuit of the Bretons. These fled for some distance, and then suddenly turning fell on their pursuers. Ill-armed and undisciplined as the levies were, and unable to withstand the attack of such overwhelming numbers, they bore themselves gallantly. One party took possession of a small outlying hill, and with showers of darts and stones they killed or drove off all who attacked them. The greater part, however, made their way to broken ground to the west of the hill, and made a stand on the steep bank of a small ravine. The French horsemen charging down upon them, unaware of the existence of the ravine, fell into it, and were slaughtered in such numbers by the knives and spears of the English that the ravine was well-nigh filled up with their dead bodies.

But gallantly as the levies had retrieved their error, it was a fatal one. As soon as they had left their line, the Normans told off for the duty pressed into the gap, and were followed by the whole of their main body, and thus the English lost the advantage of position, and the contending hosts faced each other on the hill, the ground now occupied by the Normans being somewhat higher than that on which the housecarls stood. It was now about three in the afternoon, and the fight had been raging for six hours, but though thus outflanked and the order of their battle destroyed, the veterans of Harold showed neither alarm nor discouragement. Their formation was changed, the shield-wall still faced the Normans, and for a time every effort to break it failed.

In vain the Norman cavalry charged down upon it, in vain their duke plied his terrible mace. Occasionally men worn out by the long defensive battle sprang from the English ranks and engaged knight or baron hand to hand. All along the line such single-handed conflicts were going on, and the roar of battle was as loud and fierce as at the beginning of the day. So for three more hours the fight went on; with diminishing numbers, but with undiminished bravery the English still held their ground, and as twilight was now closing in, it seemed as if they would maintain it till nightfall. Then William ordered up his archers again, bade them shoot their arrows high into the air, so that they should fall among the king and his thanes grouped round the standard.

The effect was terrible. Through helm and shoulder-guard the arrows made their way; the soldiers held their shields above their heads, but the thanes had no such protection. Harold glanced up for a moment, and as if directed by the hand of fate an arrow struck him full in the eye, and he fell prostrate as if struck by a thunderbolt. A cry of horror and dismay burst from the thanes around him, but there was no time for the indulgence of grief. The Normans too had seen the king fall, and with shouts of triumph a body of knights tried to force their way in to take possession of his body. But so long as an Englishman could swing axe this was not to be, and the assault was repulsed as others had been before. Nor, when the news of Harold's fall spread, did the brave housecarls lose heart, but sternly and obstinately as ever held together.

At last the Normans burst in at the centre, each baron and knight striving to be the first to pluck down the standards, the one the king's own cognizance, the other the national banner, that waved side by side. One after another the thanes were smitten down. Not one asked for quarter, not one turned his back upon the foe.

Beorn and Wulf had, through the long fight, stood side by side, and the watchfulness with which they guarded each other had carried them so far unharmed through it.

"It is all over now, Beorn," Wulf said. "But it is not hard to die, for with Harold the cause of England is lost."

"At any rate we will sell our lives dearly," Beorn said, as he struck a Norman knight from his horse. But they were the last defenders of the standards, and the end was at hand. Blows rained down upon them. Beorn was beaten on to one knee; Wulf was so exhausted by his exertions that he could scarce swing his axe, when a Norman baron pressed his horse through the throng, and springing to the ground held his sword aloft and shouted: "Stand back! stand back! these two men hold the duke's solemn pledge for their lives!" Some of the others still pressed on, but he shouted again: "Whoever strikes at them strikes at me!"

There was still hesitation, so furious were the Normans at the resistance they had met with and the tremendous losses they had suffered. But another baron exclaimed, "De Burg is right! I heard the pledge given, and so did many of you. This is the young Saxon who saved the duke's camp from the attack by the Bretons, and bore the brunt of their assault till we had time to arm. The other brought with him the news that Harold was wrecked." The words were decisive, and the Normans turned aside their horses to attack other foes.

"Thank God I arrived in time, Wulf," Baron de Burg said. "I knew you would be near the standard, but I was fighting elsewhere when the news reached me that the line was broken and the standard on the point of capture. Are you badly hurt, Beorn?"

"I am dizzy and faint," Beorn, who had risen to his feet, replied unsteadily, "but I think not badly wounded."

"Walk by me one on each side holding my stirrup-leathers. I would place you on my horse, but it were best that I myself should be seen."

He removed his helmet, and bareheaded moved off with the young thanes walking beside him. Many Normans stopped as he made his way down the hill, but to their questions he replied, "The duke has himself guaranteed the safety of these thanes," and as he was well known to stand high in the duke's favour his word was at once accepted.

In the meantime Harold's standard, whose emblem was a fighting man, and the golden dragon, the national banner, had been carried off in triumph. Four of the Normans whose names were long held in infamy by the English discovered the body of the dying king, for it is said that he still breathed. One of these was Eustace of Boulogne, the only man in the two armies who had during the engagement shown signs of craven fear. Another was the son of that Count of Ponthieu, who had once held Harold prisoner. The others were Gifford and Montfort. One ran his spear through Harold's breast, another struck off his head with his sword, a third pierced the dead body, while the fourth further insulted the dead hero by cutting off one of his legs — an action, however, which William when he heard of it pronounced to be shameful, and expelled its perpetrator from the army.

But though the king was dead and the standard lost, the survivors of the housecarls still fought on until darkness fell. The levies had fled just before, hotly pursued by the Norman horse. Knowing the ground well the light-armed footmen fled across a bog, and in the fast-gathering darkness their pursuers did not notice the nature of the ground, but galloping on plunged into the morass, where great numbers of them perished miserably, either suffocated in the mud or slain by the English, who turned and fell upon them with axe and spear as soon as they saw their plight. So great was the slaughter, that those who had reined up their horses in time were stricken with horror even after all the carnage they had witnessed on the field of battle.

With darkness the battle came to an end. Few indeed of the housecarls drew off under cover of the darkness; their force being almost annihilated. With them had perished almost the whole of the thanes of the South of England and East Anglia. The Sheriff of London had been carried off desperately wounded by a few of his friends, but with this exception none of Harold's companions and thanes left the field alive while daylight lasted. A few only the next morning were found breathing among the mass of dead, and some of these survived and returned at last to their homes: for William, satisfied with the complete victory he had gained, issued orders that all found alive on the field were to be well treated. He felt that he was now King of England, and that clemency was his best policy. Permission was given to the women who flocked in from the country round, to search for the bodies of their friends and to remove them for burial. He also commanded a search to be made for the body of Harold, but during the night, while the exhausted soldiers slept heavily after their labours, the camp-followers had been busy with the work of plunder, busiest round the spot where the standards had stood, for here were stores of gold bracelets and rings, the emblems of authority of the thanes, to be collected, and rich garments to be carried off. Thus then, the heaps of corpses that marked the spot where the fighting had all day been heaviest, were unrecognizable, so terrible had been the wounds dealt by sword, battle-axe, and mace.

De Burg had kept Wulf and Beorn with him all night, and they had lain down and slept together. In the morning he committed them to the charge of some of his personal followers, while he went to the duke to inform him of what he had done.

"Thank you, De Burg," William said; "they are two brave young fellows. I marked them in the fight more than once when I was near the standard, and I should have grieved if ill had befallen them, for they did me loyal service. I had given my word that they should retain their estates in case I ever came to the throne here. I know not what to do with them. Were I to let them go now, they would assuredly take part in any further resistance that the English may offer to me. I will not ask them now to swear allegiance to me, for fresh from the battle where they have lost so many friends and the earl they loved so loyally, they would assuredly refuse."

"If you will grant me a short leave I will take ship back to Normandy and place them in the care of my wife, where they can remain until matters have settled down here."

"It is a good idea, De Burg; do so without delay. Methinks that after yesterday there will be no real resistance offered to me. Harold and his brothers and all the leading thanes lie dead. There is no one left to lead the people or organize a resistance, therefore I can spare you for a time."

Thanking the duke, De Burg returned to his captives and told them what had been arranged.

"We owe you our heartiest thanks, Lord de Burg, for your kindness," Beorn said. "Assuredly so long as England resists we will not acknowledge William of Normandy as king, but when resistance ceases, we will of course take the oath to him if only for the sake of our people; partial risings could but bring down his vengeance and cause suffering and ruin to all concerned. Therefore, we gratefully accept your offer, but first of all we beg you to let us go to the spot where our housecarls fought. You remember Wulf's man, Osgod?"

"That do I indeed," De Burg replied. "The great fellow who fought by his side that night against the Bretons, and saved my son's life. Was he there?"

"He was," Wulf said, "though greatly against my wishes; for he had lost an arm in the fight at Stamford Bridge, and though it is little more than a fortnight since, he had himself carried down here, contrary to my orders, and insisted upon joining in the battle. I would fain search for his body and give him burial."

"I will come with you at once," the Norman said, "I too owe him a debt of gratitude."

The housecarls of Steyning had fallen to a man where they stood, and among them after some searching they came upon the body of Osgod, distinguished alike by its bulk and the loss of an arm. His axe lay with a broken shaft by his side. His helmet was cleft asunder, and his face covered with blood.

"His body is yet warm," Wulf said, as he lifted his arm. "I believe he still lives."

De Burg called upon two Norman soldiers near to aid, and with their assistance Wulf and Beorn carried Osgod down to the stream, where they washed the blood from his face and bathed the wound in his head.

"He is certainly alive," Beorn said. "Doubtless he was stunned by the blow, and has remained unconscious from the loss of blood."

De Burg sent for a flask of wine, and a little of this was poured through Osgod's lips. Presently there was a deep sigh and a slight motion of the figure, and then Osgod opened his eyes.

At first he seemed bewildered, but as his eyes fell on Wulf a look of pleasure came into them, and he smiled faintly.

"I am alive, Osgod, and glad indeed to find that you are also. Beorn has also escaped. Take a draught of wine; you have lost a lot of blood and had none to spare."

They lifted him into a sitting position, and held the cup to his lips while he drank a long draught.

"That is better," he murmured. "I can feel it going through my veins. I shall be able to wield an axe yet again. This comes of fighting with a weapon you don't know. The shaft broke as I was guarding my head, and I don't remember anything after."

"It saved your life though, Osgod, for it broke the force of the blow which would otherwise have cleft your skull. As it is, it has not gone very deep, and the blood you have lost has run chiefly from a wound on your left shoulder."

"How is it that you are here?" Osgod asked, looking round at the Normans.

"We are prisoners, though we have not surrendered," Wulf replied. "We were saved by our good friend Lord de Burg, who has joined us in our search for you. We are to be taken to Normandy as prisoners, and to remain in charge of Lady de Burg."

"You shall go too, Osgod," De Burg said. "You will find it hard to be nursed here, and my wife will see that your wounds are well cared for. Your master will stay with you for the present, for I have matters to see about before we start for the coast."

In half an hour he returned. "I have to ask you to perform a last service to your dead king," he said. "The bodies of Gurth and Leofwin have been found and borne away by your people for burial, but none can find the body of Harold. All the dead that were near the standard were removed last night by the soldiers, and among the great pile of dead none can recognize that of your king."

Well as they knew him, Wulf and Beorn were unable to recognize the body of Harold among the ghastly heap of mutilated corpses. After a time Wulf said:

"There is one who might recognize it when all others failed. It is Edith, whom he so long loved as his wife. She may recognize it by some mark or sign unknown to others. If you will give me leave I will ride to Lewes, where she is staying, and bring her hither."

"Certainly, Wulf; I will obtain a safe conduct for you from the duke."

Wulf had ridden, however, but a mile along the western road when he saw a litter approaching borne by four men. He reined in his horse by its side. An order was given from within, and as the bearers lowered it to the ground Edith stepped out. She was deadly pale. Her eyes were red with weeping, and she seemed to Wulf to have aged years since he saw her a week before.

"My presentiments have come true, Wulf," she said. "It was no surprise to me when last night the news came that the battle was lost and Harold slain. I had looked and waited for it. You were coming to fetch me?"

"Yes, lady; Harold's body has not been found. Early this morning two monks of Waltham, who had followed the army and seen the fight afar off, came into camp, and with them Gytha, Harold's mother. She saw the duke, and begged for Harold's body, offering its weight in gold if she might carry it for burial to the Abbey of Waltham. The duke refused, saying that an excommunicated man could not be buried in a holy place; she might remove the bodies of her other two sons, but Harold's, when found, should be buried by the seacoast. The monks searched in vain for the body. Beorn and I have done the same, but have failed to recognize it in so vast a heap of slain."

"I shall know it," Edith said. "Among a thousand dead I should know Harold."

"It is a terrible sight, lady, for a woman to look upon," Wulf said gently.

"I shall see nothing but him," she replied firmly.

He accompanied her back to the battle-ground, where the two monks joined her. Wulf, who was greatly shaken by the sight of her set and white face, left her with them.

What the eye of friendship had failed to accomplish, that of love detected unerringly. There were marks on Harold's body by which Edith recognized it. One of the monks bore the news to the duke, who charged Sir William Malet to superintend the burial, and to do it with all honour. The remains were collected and reverently placed together. They were wrapped in a purple robe, and laid on a litter. Beorn and Wulf and the two monks lifted it; Edith walked behind, followed by Lord de Burg and several other Norman knights and barons who had known Harold in Normandy, and could admire and appreciate the valour of the dead hero. The little procession went down to the shore, where Norman soldiers had already dug a grave, and there by the coast he had defended so well Harold was laid to rest, and over his body a great cairn of stones was raised by order of the duke.

CHAPTER XXII. — THE LORD OF BRAMBER.

Edith stood by while the Norman soldiers piled the stones over the grave. No tear had fallen from her eyes from the time that she had reached the field of battle. Her face was as pale as marble, and looked almost as rigid. When the last stone was placed on the top of the cairn she turned to Wulf and Beorn:

"Farewell, Wulf! farewell, Beorn! I am glad you were here. I am glad that beside me stood two of his most trusted thanes, and two of the monks from the abbey he founded, and whose welfare was so dear to him. I go to Lewes, and when the doors of the convent close on me I shall be dead to the world. Would that I were lying beneath that cairn by the side of my dear lord. I cannot weep for him now, the springs of my heart seem frozen, but I have time for that. Farewell, thanes! I shall remember you in my prayers." So saying she turned away, and walked back to the litter.

"Poor lady!" Beorn exclaimed as he watched the litter, escorted by the two monks, carried along the road.

"Poor lady indeed!" Wulf repeated; "and yet there are thousands in England and Normandy who were widowed yesterday, and maybe she is better off than many. She lost Harold the day she resigned him to another, and it was harder perhaps to be parted from him in that fashion than to know that he is dead now. She can think of him as his true widow, for assuredly the queen who never cared aught for him is a widow but in name. Before, Edith was tortured by the desire to see him and to comfort him, and yet his marriage stood as a gulf between them, a gulf that she would never have passed. Now she can think of him as her very own, as the man who had loved her even as she had loved him. It is a grief, a terrible grief, but one without bitterness. But see, Lord de Burg is coming this way, and as there is a litter behind him I suppose all is ready for our departure."

"I am ready, young thanes," De Burg said as he came up. "We ride at once for Pevensey, whither an order was sent some hours ago for a ship to be in readiness to sail for Normandy."

Three horses were led up and mounted. They rode away, followed by an armed party and the litter on which Osgod was laid.

"You have done your last duty to your king," the Norman said. "It is a fit grave for a hero, and assuredly Harold was one. Maybe that it is not his last resting-place. The duke at present doubtless felt constrained at first to refuse him Christian burial, for had he granted Gytha's request, it would have been an acknowledgment that the charges brought against him were unfounded, and the excommunication of no avail; but I doubt not that in time he will allow his body to be taken to his abbey at Waltham. Now," he said less gravely, in order to turn their thoughts from the sad scenes they had witnessed, "what think you of the future, will the Northern earls head a national movement against us?"

"They are foul traitors!" Beorn exclaimed passionately; "and I would that Wulf and I could meet them in fair lists and fight them."

"They will do nothing," Wulf said more quietly. "They will hasten to make the best terms they can for themselves, and will ask to be permitted to hold their earldoms as his vassals. But they will not long enjoy their treachery; they are ever intriguers, and as soon as they see their opportunity will conspire against William as they conspired against Harold. Thank heaven they will receive scantier mercy at his hands than they received at the king's. As for the South and East, who is to lead them? There is no one left to whom they can look for guidance; doubtless in some places they will resist, but such resistance can only bring ruin upon those who attempt it. Maybe some will take to the forests or the great eastern marshes, and may perhaps hold out for months, or even years. But what can it avail in the end? Had Harold escaped alive there would have been many a battle as obstinate as that of yesterday to fight before England was conquered. Had any of the greater thanes escaped men would have flocked to them, but they are all gone, save the few that were found well-nigh lifeless this morning. Perhaps it is better as it is; for now that William is victorious he will soon receive large bodies of reinforcements, and as resistance would be vain, it were best that no resistance were made. Duke William has shown himself a wise and just ruler in Normandy, and will doubtless prove himself the same in England if he be not angered by revolts and risings. It is hard that Englishmen should be ruled by a foreigner, but it is no new thing for us. We Saxons conquered the Britons, and in turn Danish kings have ruled over us; but Saxon and Dane have become almost one, and the old grudges have died out. Maybe in time you Normans also may become English."

"You would take the oath of allegiance to William then, Wulf?"

"Not now, my lord, but when England accepts him as her king I should be willing to hold my lands from him as I have held them before from our kings, that is, if the lands remain mine."

"They will remain yours," Lord de Burg said confidently. "The duke's promise was publicly made, and he will certainly adhere to it; even if he wished it, he could not, after charging Harold with perjury, break his own promise."

The sun was sinking when they reached Pevensey, for the search for Harold's body and the building of his cairn had occupied many hours. They went at once on board one of the ships De Burg had himself furnished for the expedition, and two days later landed at Rouen. They had brought horses with them, and the two young thanes at once rode with the baron to his chateau, leaving Osgod to be brought after them in his litter. Lord de Burg was received with the greatest joy by his wife, Guy, and Agnes. They had been in a state of terrible anxiety for the last twenty-four hours, for a swift ship had been despatched by the duke with the news of the victory, at daybreak after the battle, and it was known that the fight had been long and desperately contested, and that a great number of barons and knights had fallen. As soon as the first outburst of delight was over the baron called in Wulf and Beorn, who had not followed him into the room, feeling that he would prefer to greet his family alone. Guy gave an exclamation of surprise and pleasure as they came forward.

"These are my prisoners," the baron said with a smile, "if I can call prisoners those who have never surrendered. The duke has intrusted them to my keeping, and has ordered that you shall hold them in safe custody."

"Lord de Burg does not tell you, lady, that he saved our lives, which but for him were assuredly lost. We were well-nigh spent, and were surrounded by a ring of foes when he broke in and stood beside us proclaiming that the duke himself had given a pledge for our safety."

"I have paid part of the debt we owe," the baron said, "though I saved them at no cost to myself, while Wulf defended Guy at the risk of his life."

"How long do you stay with us, my lord?"

"As long as I can, wife. I went, as you know, unwillingly to the war, but when all the Norman barons followed the duke I could not hold back. But I trust to have no more of it; so terrible a field no man living has seen, and in truth until twilight fell it seemed that we should be beaten, with such obstinacy and endurance did the English fight. We won, but it was a victory over the dead rather than the living. Of Harold's regular troops no man turned, no man asked for quarter, they fell where they stood; and even the irregulars, who had fought with equal bravery, when, as night fell and all was lost, they fled, inflicted well-nigh as heavy a blow upon us as had been dealt during the day. I have no animosity against them, they are valiant men, and were in their right in defending their country, and I would that I could stay peacefully here until the last blow has been struck. I am well content with my estates, and need no foot of English land, no share in English spoil I must fight for my liege lord as long as fighting goes on, but that over I hope to return here and live in peace. At any rate I can tarry quietly here for a week. Certainly no force can be raised in time to oppose the duke's advance on London, and my sword therefore may well rest in its scabbard. I suppose, thanes, you will not object to give me your parole to attempt no escape?"

"Willingly, my lord," Beorn said. "If, contrary to our opinion, England should rise and fight one more battle for freedom, we will give you due notice that we shall if possible escape and cross the sea to join our countrymen."

"That is fair enough," De Burg said with a smile, "and the moment you give me notice I will clap you into so firm a cage that

I warrant you will not escape from it; but I trust the necessity will not arise. Now, Guy, take your friends to their chambers and see to their comfort. I will not tell the story of the battle until you return, for doubtless you are burning to hear it, and in truth it will be famous in all times, both as one of the sturdiest fights ever heard of, and because such great issues depended on its results."

When Guy returned with his friends and a meal had been eaten, De Burg told the story of the battle of Senlac.

"Such is the story as far as I know it," he added in conclusion, "but in truth beyond the beginning and the end, and the fact that we twice fell back and at one time were flying in headlong rout to our ships, I know nothing. All day I was striving to break through a living wall, and striving in vain. I can see now the close line of shields, the helmet covered faces above them, and the terrible axes rising and falling, cleaving through helmet and hauberk as if they had been pasteboard. It may well-nigh be said that we have no wounded, for each man struck fell in his track as if smitten by lightning. Can you add more, thanes?"

Beorn shook his head.

"It is like a dream," Wulf said. "We never moved through the long day. At times there was a short lull, and then each man was fighting as best he could. I know that my arms grew tired and that my axe seemed to grow heavier, that horse and foot swept up to us, and there was occasionally breathing time; that the royal brothers' voices rose ever cheeringly and encouragingly until Gurth and Leofwin fell, and after that Harold's alone was heard, though I think it came to my ears as from a distance, so great was the tumult, so great our exertions. When Harold died I knew that all was lost, but even that did not seem to affect me. I had become a sort of machine, and fought almost mechanically, with a dim consciousness that the end was close at hand. It was only at the last, when Beorn and I stood back to back, that I seemed myself again, and was animated with new strength that came, I suppose, from despair."

"It was an awful day," De Burg said. "I have fought in many battles under the duke's banner, but the sternest of them were but paltry skirmishes in comparison to this. Half of the nobles of Normandy lie dead, half the army that filled the mighty fleet that sailed from St.

Valery have fallen. William is King of England, but whether that will in the end repay Normandy for the loss she has suffered seems to me very doubtful. And now let us to bed. I sleep not well on shipboard, and in truth I had such dreams of death and slaughter that I ever awoke bathed with sweat, and in such fear that I dared not go to sleep again."

At the end of a week the baron sailed again for England. To the two young Englishmen the following weeks passed pleasantly. Ships came frequently from England with news of what was doing there. William had tarried for some time at his camp at Hastings, expecting to receive the submission of all England. But not an Englishman came to bow before him. The Northern earls had hurried to London as soon as they heard of the defeat at Senlac and the death of the king and his brothers, and a Witan was instantly summoned to choose his successor to the throne.

Edwin and Morcar thought that the choice of the nation would surely fall upon one or other of them, as in rank and position they were now the first men in the realm. They exerted themselves to the utmost to bring this about, but no true-hearted Englishman could forgive either their acceptance of Harold Hardrada as their king, or the long and treacherous delay that had left Southern England to stand alone on the day of battle. The choice of the Witan fell on the young Edgar, the grandson of Edmund Ironside, the last male survivor of the royal blood. Edgar, however, was never crowned, as that ceremony could only take place at one of the festivals of the church, and it was therefore postponed until Christmas. London was eager for resistance. Alfred had fought battle after battle against the Danes, and though without their natural leaders, the people throughout Southern England looked forward to a long and determined struggle. With the army of the North as a rallying centre a force more numerous than that which Harold had led might soon be gathered. But these hopes were dashed to the ground by the treacherous Northern earls. Had one of them been chosen to sit on the vacant throne they would doubtless have done their best to maintain that throne, but they had been passed over, and oblivious of the fact that it was to the South they owed the rescue of their earldoms from the sway of the King of Norway and Tostig, they sullenly marched away with their army and left the South to its fate.

While the cause of England was thus being betrayed and ruined, William was advancing eastward along the coast ravaging and destroying. Romney was levelled to the ground and its inhabitants slain. Dover opened its gates. It is probable that most of the male population had joined Harold, and had fallen at Senlac; and that the terrible fate of Romney had struck such terror into the hearts of the inhabitants, who knew there was no army that could advance to their assistance, that they surrendered at the Conqueror's approach. To them William behaved with lenity and kindness. His severity at Romney and his lenity at Dover had their effect. There being no central authority, no army in the field, each town and district was left to shift for itself; and assuredly none of them unaided could hope to offer prolonged resistance to the Normans. As, after eight days' stay at Dover, William advanced towards Canterbury, he was met by a deputation of the citizens offering their submission, and soon from all parts of Kent similar messages came in.

Kent had done its full share in the national defence on the hill near Hastings, and was not to be blamed if, when all England remained supine and inactive, its villagers refused to throw away their lives uselessly. The duke was detained by sickness for a month near Canterbury, and there received the submission of Kent and Sussex, and also that of the great ecclesiastical city of Winchester; but the spirit of resistance in London still burned brightly, and William was indisposed to risk the loss that would be incurred by an assault upon its walls. He, therefore, moved round in a wide circle, wasting the land, plundering and destroying, till the citizens, convinced that resistance could only bring destruction upon themselves and their city, and in spite of the efforts of their wounded sheriff, sent an embassy to the duke at Berkhampstead to submit and do homage to him.

Not London alone was represented by this embassy. The young king, elected but uncrowned, was with it; two archbishops, two bishops, and many of the chief men in England accompanied it, and although they were not the spokesmen of any Witan, they might be said fairly to represent London and Southern England.

Deserted by the North, without a leader, and seeing their land exposed to wholesale ravages, the South and West Saxons were scarcely to be blamed for preferring submission to destruction. They doubtless thought that William, the wise ruler of Normandy, would make a far better king than the boy they had chosen, who was himself almost as much a foreigner as William, save that there was a strain of English royal blood in his veins. So had England accepted Canute the Dane as her king, and he had ruled as an English monarch wisely and well.

The embassy offered William the crown. The Norman prelates and priests, who held so many of the dignities in the English Church, had worked hard to incline men's minds to this end. Silent while England stood united under its king to oppose the invader, their tongues were loosed as soon as the strength of England was broken and its king dead, and they pointed out that God had clearly designated William as their king by giving him victory and by destroying alike Harold and his brothers.

William went through the farce of hesitating to accept the offer of the crown, and held a consultation with his officers as to the answer he should give. They of course replied that he should accept the offer. William, therefore, marched with his army to London, where on Christmas-day the same prelate who had anointed Harold King of England crowned William as his successor.

A few days later Beorn and Wulf with Osgod, who had now completely recovered from his wounds, set sail for England. There was no longer any reason why they should not take their oaths to serve William. He was the crowned king of England, the accepted of the people, as Harold had been, and when all Southern England had submitted it was not for them, who had received special favours at William's hand, to hold back. With them went Lady de Burg, Guy, and Agnes, with many other Norman ladies on their way to rejoin their lords in London. Baron de Burg, on the day after their arrival at Westminster, led the two young thanes to the private apartment of the king. He received them graciously.

"There are none of your nation," he said, "whose homage I more gladly accept. You fought valiantly before under my banner, and will, I am sure, be ready to do so again should occasion arise. I am thankful to my Lord de Burg that he interposed in my name and saved your lives. I have not forgotten the other part of my promise, and have this morning ordered my justiciar to add to your estates forfeited lands adjoining."

Beorn and Wulf had previously talked the matter over. Their own inclinations would have led them to refuse the offer, but as it was certain that all the land forfeited to the crown by the death of its holders in battle would be apportioned among William's Norman followers, they thought that it would be wholly for the benefit both of the families of the late thanes and for their tenants and people that they should accept any estate William might bestow on them. They, therefore, thanked the duke in suitable terms, and at once took the oaths for the lands he might be pleased to bestow on them. A week later they received the formal deeds, which in both cases more than doubled the estates they before possessed.

The same evening Lord de Burg said to Wulf, who had tarried in London, while Beorn had at once set out for Fareham: "I think the time has come, Wulf, when I can speak of a subject that has been in my thoughts for a long time, and which, although you have not spoken, has, as my wife and I have both seen, been dear to you. Normandy and England are now one, and we are vassals of the same king. As long as there was a probability that Englishmen and Normans might again be ranged in battle against each other, it was not expedient that aught should be done in the matter, but, now this obstacle is removed, I can offer you the alliance on which I am sure your heart is set, and give you the hand of my daughter in marriage."

"It is the greatest wish of my life," Wulf replied gratefully. "I should have asked you for her hand before had it not been for the position of public affairs. I love her dearly, though I have until now abstained from speaking; and yet I would not wed her unless her heart went freely with her hand."

"I think not that she will be disobedient to my wishes," De Burg said smiling. "She has proved deaf to all her Norman suitors, and although among them were some whom few maidens would have said no to, her mother and I had no wish to force her inclinations, especially as we both shrewdly suspected where her heart had been bestowed. This alliance, too, has long been the dearest wish of Guy. On the bed of sickness where he lay so long, and from which it seemed at one time that he would never rise, he often spoke to me of it. He was fondly attached to his sister, and again and again said that he wished of all things that you should some day become her husband, as he was sure her happiness would be safe with you, and that you would worthily fill his place to us, and would, when the time came, rule nobly over the lands of De Burg."

"God forbid that that should ever be the case," Wulf said earnestly. "I trust that Guy will live long, and that he will marry and leave descendants to follow him."

The baron shook his head sadly. "Guy is better," he said, "but he is still weak and fragile, and the leeches tell me that a rough winter or an illness that would be nought to others might carry him off. I have small hopes that he will ever marry. I am sure that no such thought is in his mind. He is as eager now as he was four years ago that you should be a son to us, and a husband to Agnes. He has also earnestly expressed the wish, in which I also join, that you should take our name. You English have no family names, but that will come with other Norman customs, and marrying a De Burg it would seem natural that you should yourself become Wulf de Burg."

"I should feel it a high honour. There is no more noble name in Normandy, and I trust I may prove worthy of bearing it."

"That I have no fear of, Wulf, else I should not have offered you the hand of my daughter. I will bring my wife and Guy in. I have offered you the hand of Agnes, but it is right that you should ask her mother's consent, although beforehand assured of it."

He left the room, and soon returned with Lady de Burg and Guy.

"My lord has told me," she said, before Wulf could speak, "that you would ask my consent to your marriage with Agnes. I give it you unasked, freely and gladly. I have but one regret—that the seas will divide us."

"Not so," the baron said; "William's court will be held in London, and for years he will reside here far more than in Normandy, and will expect his nobles to be frequently with him. I certainly shall not come alone, and you will therefore have as many opportunities of seeing Agnes as if she were married to a Norman whose estates did not lie near our own."

"I thank you most deeply, Lady de Burg, for the confidence which you show in intrusting your daughter's happiness to me. I swear that with all my might and power I will strive to make her happy, and will spare her to visit you in Normandy whensoever you may wish it."

Guy came forward now and grasped Wulf's hand.

"How I have longed for this time, my brother," he said. "How I have hoped that I might at least live long enough to know that the dearest wish of my heart would be gratified. I can go hence now right willingly when God calls me, knowing that my father and mother have another son to fill my place, and that the happiness of my sister is secured."

"And now, wife, will you fetch Agnes from her chamber," the baron said.

In two or three minutes the baroness returned, leading Agnes, to whom she had told the reason of her summons. The baron stepped forward and took her hand.

"My daughter," he said, "the Thane of Steyning has asked for your hand in marriage, and your mother and I have given our free and full consent, but he would fain know from your own lips that you will come to him willingly."

"I have loved you, Agnes, since while still but a boy I first saw you, and my love has grown ever since. The happiness of my life depends upon your answer, but unless your heart goes with your hand I would rather remain unmarried to my dying day."

The girl had stood with downcast eyes and with flushed face until now. When Wulf ceased speaking she looked up into his face:

"I love you, Wulf; I have always loved you. It is for your sake that I have said no to the suitors of my own race who have sought my hand. I will be a true wife and loving to you."

"Then take her, Wulf," the baron said, placing her hand in his. "You are now her betrothed husband and our adopted son."

Wulf stooped and kissed the girl's lips, and the betrothal was completed. After some talk it was arranged that Wulf should at once journey down to Steyning, assume possession of his new estates, set the house in order, and prepare for their coming. Guy was to accompany him, and as soon as all was in readiness Wulf would come up to London and return with Lord and Lady de Burg and Agnes, who would pay a short visit and all would then cross to Normandy, for the marriage was to take place at their chateau there.

"I was sure how it would be," Osgod said when Wulf told him the news that night. "I should have been blind indeed if I had not seen it long ago. I love not the Normans, but I make exception in the case of Lord de Burg and his family. And truly it will in all respects be a good thing for your tenants. Although the duke, or I suppose I ought to say the king, promises greatly at present, there is no saying what he may do later on; and he has all these locusts to provide for. 'Tis well indeed, then, that there should be a Norman lady as well as an English thane at Steyning."

Wulf's return home gave rise to demonstrations of the greatest joy among his tenants. They had heard nothing of him since the battle, and had deemed him to have fallen with the rest of the defenders of the standard, and had been living in fear of the arrival of some Norman baron to be their lord. Wulf was greatly pleased to find that, although not one of his housecarls had returned from Hastings, the greater portion of his irregular levies had escaped at nightfall with the party who had inflicted so heavy a blow upon their pursuers. For the next few days Wulf was thoroughly occupied. The tenants of his new estates received him almost as joyfully as his own had done, for, like them, they had expected the advent of a Norman master. In one of the two estates that had fallen to him the thane he had succeeded had left no heirs; while the other thane had left a widow and a young family. Wulf arranged that these should remain in their home, receiving for their maintenance half the rents of the estate.

Guy was greatly pleased with the fair country in which his sister's lot was to be cast, but he owned frankly that the house seemed unworthy now of the large estate, and was indeed but a poor place in comparison with the noble chateau in which she had been brought up.

"That shall be remedied, Guy, as soon as matters settle down. I have laid by none of my revenues, for the keeping up of a hundred housecarls has taxed them to the utmost, but now that my income is more than doubled, and this expense has altogether ceased, I shall have funds with which I can soon begin to build. When I was young, Steyning seemed to me a fine house, but after your Norman castles it is indeed but a poor place."

When, a fortnight later, the De Burgs arrived with Wulf, while Agnes expressed herself delighted with the quaintness of the old Saxon home, her father and mother were decidedly of Guy's opinion.

"The house is a good house in its way," the Baron said, "but there will be great changes in the land. Much of it will be transferred to

Norman hands, and ere long castles and chateaux like ours at home will rise everywhere, and as an English noble with broad lands it is but fit that your residence should vie with others. But this shall be my care, and shall be my daughter's special dowry. I foresee that it will be long ere matters wholly settle down. Moreover, though William's hand is strong that of his successor may be weak, and in time there will be the same troubles here among the barons that there were in Normandy before William put them down with a strong hand. Therefore, I should say we will build a castle rather than a chateau, for such I am sure will be the style of all the Norman buildings here, until England settles down to peace and quiet. I would not disturb this house, Wulf; it is doubtless dear to you, and will, moreover, serve as a dowager-house or as an abode for a younger son. We will fix on a new site altogether, and there we will rear a castle worthy of the estate. By the way, I have spoken to the king of your betrothal to my daughter, and he is highly pleased. He says that it is his earnest wish that his Norman nobles shall marry English heiresses, both because they will thus come into possession of lands without disturbing the owners, and because such mixture of blood will the more speedily weld the two peoples into one; and that, similarly, he is glad to see a Norman maiden united to an English noble of whom he has so high an opinion."

Fond as Wulf was of his old home he saw that it would be best to abandon it for a new residence more suited to the times and more in accordance with his own increased possessions and the home from which he was taking his wife. After riding round the estates Lord de Burg and he fixed upon a knoll of rising ground near the village of Bramber, and not far from the religious house where Wulf had spent so many evenings, and whose prior had been one of the first to welcome his return.

"I will charter a ship at Rouen," Lord de Burg said, "and send over a master craftsman, skilful in designing and building castles, and a large number of quarrymen, masons, and carpenters. Labour here is scarce, and the men are unskilled at this kind of work. Rough labour can doubtless be obtained, and your tenants can transport the stones from the quarry and dig the fosse. I will send over a goodly number of men. It will cost no more to employ three hundred for six months than fifty for three years."

A week later Wulf sailed for Rouen with the De Burgs. Beorn accompanied him, as well as Osgod, to be present at the wedding, which took place at Rouen Cathedral. A month later Wulf returned with his wife to Steyning. Already an army of men were at work at Bramber. The tenants all gave their assistance readily, and far beyond the amount their feudal tenure required, for they saw the advantage it would be to them to have a strong castle in their midst to which they could retire in case of danger. Labourers had been engaged in large numbers from the country round by the master craftsmen. The outlines of the castle had been traced, and the ground dug for its foundations, while already the broad deep fosse which was to surround it had been dug to a depth of several feet. The stones had to be brought from a considerable distance, but as at this time of year there was little work for the carts, those belonging not only to the tenants of the estate, but to the cultivators for miles round were engaged in the service.

In six months a stately pile had risen in the midst of the tranquil glade. When it was ready for occupation Lord and Lady de Burg and their son came over, and great festivities were held when Wulf de Burg (now Lord of Bramber) moved into the castle.

Soon after the birth of their first son Wulf and his wife received a hasty summons to cross the sea, and arrived in time to stand by the death-bed of Guy. Wulf had been greatly moved by the storm of war that had swept over the North of England, and the terrible vengeance taken by William there. He had no pity for the traitor earls, but he grieved for the men who, but for their treachery, would have fought at Hastings. He regretted deeply the isolated risings in various parts of the country, whose only effect was to bring ruin upon whole districts and to increase the sternness and rigour of William's rule.

Wulf's after-life was divided between England and Normandy, as he became a baron of the latter country at the death of Lord de Burg. He fought no more in England, but more than once followed William's banner in his struggles with his rebellious sons and turbulent nobles. He lived to see the animosities between Englishmen and Normans beginning to die out, and to find our kings relying upon sturdy English men-at-arms and bow-men in their struggles with French kings and with the Norman barons who held so large a portion of English soil. Osgod became the seneschal of the castle, and held it for his lord during his absences in Normandy. Wulf took an interest in the fortunes of Ulf, who in the course of time succeeded to the business of Ulred, and became one of the most skilled and famous armourers in London. Beorn married the former heiress of one of the estates William had granted him, and his firm friendship with the Lord of Bramber remained unbroken to the end of their lives.